VAT Enforcement and Appeals Manual

Alan Buckett
12/9/86

VAT Enforcement and Appeals Manual

Alan Buckett BA
Partner, Binder Hamlyn/BDO, London

London
Butterworths
1986

United Kingdom	Butterworth & Co (Publishers) Ltd, 88 Kingsway, LONDON WC2B and 61A North Castle Street, EDINBURGH EH2 3LT
Australia	Butterworths Pty Ltd, SYDNEY, MELBOURNE, BRISBANE, ADELAIDE, PERTH, CANBERRA and HOBART
Canada	Butterworths. A division of Reed Inc., TORONTO and VANCOUVER
New Zealand	Butterworths of New Zealand Ltd, WELLINGTON and AUCKLAND
Singapore	Butterworth & Co (Asia) Pty Ltd, SINGAPORE
South Africa	Butterworth Publishers (Pty) Ltd, DURBAN and PRETORIA
USA	Butterworth Legal Publishers, ST PAUL, Minnesota, SEATTLE, Washington, BOSTON, Massachusetts, AUSTIN, Texas and D & S Publishers, CLEARWATER, Florida

© Alan Buckett 1986

All rights reserved. No part of this publication may be reproduced or transmitted in any form or by any means, including photocopying and recording, without the written permission of the copyright holder, application for which should be addressed to the publisher. Such written permission must also be obtained before any part of this publication is stored in a retrieval system of any nature.

This book is sold subject to the Standard Conditions of Sale of Net Books and may not be re-sold in the UK below the net price fixed by Butterworths for the book in our current catalogue.

British Library Cataloguing in Publication Data

Buckett, Alan
  VAT enforcement and appeals manual.
  1. Value added tax—Law and legislation
  —Great Britain
  I. Title   II. Hamlyn, Binder/BDO
  344.1035′5   KD5586

ISBN 0 406 50420 2

Typeset by Phoenix Photosetting, Chatham
Printed and bound in Great Britain by Mackays of Chatham, Ltd

For Pauline, Christopher, Gillian and David

Preface

Value Added Tax was introduced into the United Kingdom by the Finance Act 1972 at the time of accession to the European Community. Since that date a mass of legislation, orders, regulations, case law decisions, explanatory notices and leaflets support a system which has become increasingly complex.

The results of the survey carried out for the Government's White Paper entitled 'Burdens on Business' reveal that VAT was seen as by far the heaviest burden on businesses. One of the main reasons for this was that although the tax provides an increasing proportion of tax revenue for the Government (£18,535.3 million in the financial year 1984/1985) the charging and collection of the tax, together with the detailed record requirements, has frequently led many of those businesses registered for the tax to complain that they are in effect 'unpaid tax collectors'.

Despite these claims it became clear in the early 1980s that many registered businesses were in fact receiving a considerable cash flow benefit from the VAT system by collecting VAT from their customers and retaining it for many months after the dates by which such VAT was legally payable to Customs and Excise.

Unfortunately for Customs and Excise the original VAT legislation had prescribed that such offences were criminal offences and to exact penalties Customs and Excise had to prosecute offenders through the courts. With a VAT registered community in excess of one million it was not possible to prosecute more than the worst offenders through the courts.

This factor was one of many considered by the independent Keith Committee which was set up by the Government in July 1980 to review the enforcement powers of the Inland Revenue and Customs and Excise. Following its recommendations and various consultation stages the Finance Act 1985 saw the introduction of a range of new civil penalties into the UK's VAT legislation.

Although the new penalty regime is to a large extent deterrent in nature there is no doubt that the 1985 legislation represented a major milestone in the development of VAT in the United Kingdom and many have expressed fears over the potential severity of some of the new powers and penalties which have been given to Customs and Excise. I have therefore sought to allay some of the fears of the unknown by considering the new powers and penalties and commenting on how they are likely to be applied by Customs and Excise.

With the potential financial consequences for those who fall foul of the new provisions being severe and in many cases automatic it is likely that many more VAT registered organisations will dispute Customs and Excise contentions both in negotiations and at the VAT tribunals.

This book not only provides practical guidance on how to avoid disputes occurring in the first place, but also includes a detailed commentary on the

Preface

Customs and Excise organisation and VAT control methods, dispute situations and the VAT appeal machinery.

I am indebted to many for the knowledge and experience gained over the years and for the co-operation given by the VAT Administration Directorate of Customs and Excise and the Registrar of the VAT tribunals which has enabled me to complete this work. I am also grateful to my colleagues at Binder Hamlyn for their administrative support, in particular my secretaries Barbara Drogman and Janet Dryer, whose patience and determination helped to make it possible. All forms in Appendices 1–17 are reproduced by kind permission of the Controller of Her Majesty's Stationery Office.

ADB
May 1986

Contents

Preface v
Table of statutes xiii
Table of cases xvii
Abbreviations xix

1 Civil penalties, interest and surcharges 1
  Introduction 1
    Revenue 1
    Administrative burdens 1
    Compliance 3
    The Keith Committee 3
    The collection of VAT 5
    Reasons for change 5
  The 1985 legislation 7
    Timetable for implementation 8
    Tax evasion: conduct involving dishonesty (FA 1985, s 13) 9
    Serious misdeclaration (FA 1985, s 14) 11
    Failure to notify liability for registration (FA 1985, s 15(1)(a)) 16
    The default surcharge (FA 1985, s 19) 19
    Repayment supplement (FA 1985, s 20) 21
    Interest (FA 1985, s 18) 22
    Breaches of regulations (FA 1985, s 17) 24
    Unauthorised issue of invoices (FA 1985, s 15(1)(b)) 26
    The interaction of the penalties 26
    A survival checklist 27

2 Criminal offences and penalties 29
  The position from 25 July 1985 29
    a) Offences under VAT legislation 29
    b) Offences under Customs and Excise legislation 37
    c) Offences arising under criminal law 38
  The position prior to 25 July 1985 38
  Compounding 42
  Procedural matters 46
    Time limit 46
    Service of summons 47
    Institution of proceedings 47
    Onus and standard of proof 47
    Evidence 47

Contents

3 VAT control methods 49
  Introduction 49
  Organisation and structure of Customs and Excise 50
    Board of Commissioners 50
    VAT Administration Directorate 51
    VAT Control Directorate 51
    Other Directorates 51
    Local VAT offices 52
    VAT sub-offices (VSOs) 53
  Control techniques 53
    VAT registrations 53
    VAT control objectives 53
    The role of the VAT Central Unit 54
    Types of local visit 54
    VAT staff 56
    VAT staff training 56
    Control visits 57
    Control of large payers 62
    Investigation techniques 64
    'Mark-up' exercises 66

4 Disputes and appeals 71
    How disputes arise in practice 71
    Dealing with dispute situations 72
    Misdirection 75
    Waiver of tax 76
    Extra-statutory concessions 76
    Appealable decisions 77
    Prevention of disputes 78
    Survival checklist 78
    Notification of errors 78
    Acquiring knowledge of VAT offences and errors 79
    Time to pay 79
    Decision making and checklists 79
    Interaction of VAT and direct taxes 80
    Customs and Excise Public Notices and leaflets 80
    Entering into transactions 80
    'Equity' or 'letter of the law' 81
    Appeals 81
    Further appeals 91
    The impact of the FA 1985 legislation on VAT tribunal appeals 91

5 Powers 93
  Introduction 93
  Powers under VAT legislation 95
  Commentary 106
    What to do if Customs and Excise appear to have exceeded their powers 107
    The right of appeal against discretionary powers 107
    Judicial review 108
    Professional privilege 109
  Conclusion 110

Contents

Appendix 1 Foreword to the Government paper entitled 'The Collection of VAT' (November 1984) 111
Appendix 2 Introduction by Customs and Excise to the Government paper entitled 'The Collection of VAT' (November 1984) 113
Appendix 3 Specimen VAT return form (VAT 100) 114
Appendix 4 Extract from leaflet regarding the default surcharge system 116
Appendix 5 Extract from leaflet regarding the repayment supplement scheme 118
Appendix 6 List of regulations and examples of Treasury orders 119
Appendix 7 Application for registration (VAT 1) 121
Appendix 8 Compound settlement offer 125
Appendix 9 Extra-statutory VAT concessions 127
Appendix 10 List of public notices and leaflets 145
Appendix 11 VAT tribunal forms 153
Appendix 12 The Value Added Tax Tribunals Rules 1986 165
Appendix 13 Letter and Notes regarding further appeals 180
Appendix 14 Centrally issued VAT assessment 182
Appendix 15 Assessment issued on or following control visit 185
Appendix 16 VAT leaflet: serious misdeclaration 187
Appendix 17 VAT leaflet: default interest 190

Index 193

Table of statutes

	PARA
Perjury Act 1911	
ss 1, 5	2.38
Theft Act 1968	2.09, 2.15
s 17	2.38
32(1)(a)	2.38, 2.66
Taxes Management Act 1970	
s 88	1.93
European Communities Act 1972:	1.28, 1.103
Finance Act 1972	1.01, 5.01
s 38	1.19, 2.46
(3)	2.23
(4)	2.25
127	3.38, 5.50
Sch 3 para 3	4.14, 5.28, 5.58
Criminal Law Act 1977	
s 1(1)	2.66
Finance Act 1977	
s 11	5.49, 5.51, 5.52
Theft Act 1978	2.09
s 2	2.38
Customs and Excise Management Act 1979	
s 1(1)	2.35
15(2)	2.36
(3)	2.37
16	2.36
93	5.57
141	5.64
146	2.67
147(1)	2.66
150(1)	2.68
151(1)	5.53
152	2.47, 5.64
(1)	2.50
167	2.36, 2.37
171(4)	2.68
Finance Act 1980	
s 17	5.49, 5.51
Magistrates' Courts Act 1980	
s 32(2), (9)	2.03
Finance Act 1981	
s 15	5.60
Supreme Court Act 1981	
s 31	5.62

	PARA
Criminal Justice Act 1982	
s 37(2)	2.03
Value Added Tax Act 1983	1.31, 1.83, 1.103, 2.45, 4.59, 5.40
s 2(5)	5.06
5	5.07
14	5.08
(5)	2.09
15	1.108, 5.09
16	5.10
18	5.11
19	5.12
20	5.13
21	2.09, 5.14
22	2.09, 5.15
23	2.09, 5.16
26	5.17
27	5.18
29	1.106, 2.42, 5.19
(4)	5.19, 5.59
(5)–(7)	5.19
31(1)	5.20
(2)–(5)	5.21
32(1)	5.22
(4)	5.23
33	5.24
35	5.25
37	5.26
38	5.29
39	2.33, 2.39, 2.50
(1)	2.03, 2.04, 2.05, 2.19, 2.39
(1A)	2.04, 2.09, 2.10
(2)	2.04, 2.19
(a)	2.03, 2.12, 2.39
(b)	2.03, 2.16, 2.39
(2C)	2.15
(3)	2.03, 2.19, 2.23, 2.39
(a)	5.48
(4)	2.03, 2.24, 2.25, 2.39
(5)	2.03, 2.08, 2.26, 2.41
(a)	1.28, 2.39, 2.41
(b)	2.39
(6)	1.28, 2.39, 2.42
(7)	1.28, 2.34, 2.39, 2.43 2.44

xiii

Table of statutes

	PARA
Value Added Tax Act 1983—*contd.*	
s 39(8) . . . 1.28, 2.03, 2.32, 2.33, 2.39	
(9) 2.03, 2.50, 2.66, 5.53	
40(1) 4.41, 5.61	
(n)	2.28
(o)	1.39
(2)	4.43
(3)(a)	1.41
(b)	4.43
(4)	4.65
(6)	5.61
44	5.27
Sch 1	5.06
para 1 . . . . 1.64, 5.06	
2	5.06
3 . . . . 1.62, 1.64, 5.06	
4 . . . . 1.62, 1.65, 5.06	
5	5.06
8–10	5.06
11(1)(a)	5.06
(b) 5.06, 5.61	
(2)	1.69
Sch 2	
para 5	3.57
Sch 4	5.28
para 3 . . . . 4.14, 5.28, 5.58	
Sch 7 . . . . 3.16, 5.29	
para 1(1) 2.35, 3.06	
4	5.41
(1) . . . 4.43, 5.39, 5.41, 5.42	
(2) 4.43, 5.41	
(b)	5.39
(5) 5.43, 5.47	
(6) 3.55, 4.43, 5.42	
5	5.38
(2) 2.26, 2.27	
6	5.41
(1)	5.49
(2)	1.104
(4) 5.39, 5.49	
7	5.30
(1)	5.30
(2)	5.31
(3)	2.71
8	5.68
(2)	5.32
(b)	3.26
(4) 3.37, 5.32	
(4A)–(4C)	5.33
9	5.35
9A	5.36
10 . . . . 5.37, 5.68	
(1)	3.23
(3)	5.37
(b)	5.33

	PARA
Value Added Tax Act 1983—*contd.*	
Sch 7	
para 10B	3.30
11(2)	2.71
Sch 8	4.34
para 10	4.48
Finance Act 1985 . . . . . 1.30, 1.31, 1.67,	
1.108, 2.01, 3.17, 3.45,	
4.25, 4.67, 5.03, 5.04,	
5.31, 5.32, 5.55	
s 10 . . . . 5.04, 5.34	
(4) 2.03, 5.34	
12 . . . . 2.15, 2.50	
(2) 2.04, 2.15, 5.04	
(3) 2.09, 2.10	
(5)	2.15
(6) 2.15, 5.04, 5.48	
(8) 1.99, 2.33, 2.34	
13 . . . . 1.28, 1.107, 4.44, 4.53,	
5.04, 5.44, 5.54	
(1)	1.33
(b)	1.35
(2)(a)–(c)	1.34
(4)	1.36
(5) 1.37, 2.70	
(6)	2.70
(7)	1.35
14 . . . . 1.28, 1.44, 1.107, 5.04,	
5.44, 5.54	
(1)	1.45
(a), (b)	1.44
(2)	1.44
(b)	1.46
(4)	1.48
(6)(a), (b)	1.49
(7) 1.40, 1.50	
15 . . . . 1.107, 5.04, 5.44, 5.54	
(1)(a) 1.28, 1.69	
(b) 1.28, 1.104	
(2)	1.106
(4) 1.68, 1.72, 1.105	
(5) 1.66, 1.105	
(b)	1.40
16 . . . . 1.28, 1.107, 5.04, 5.44,	
5.54	
(1)	1.100
(4)	1.101
(5)	1.100
17 . . . . 1.80, 1.107, 5.04, 5.44,	
5.54	
(1)(a)–(c) 1.28, 1.98	
(2) 1.97, 1.98	
(3)	1.97
(a)	1.97
(5) 1.28, 1.97, 1.98	

Table of statutes

Finance Act 1985—*contd.*	PARA
s 17(6)	1.97
(9)	1.101
(10)	1.40, 1.99
(b)	1.50
18	1.29, 1.107, 5.04
(1)	1.94
(a), (b), (c)	1.93
(2)–(9)	1.93, 1.94
19	1.29, 1.107, 2.32, 5.04, 5.44
(1)	1.74
(a)	1.82
(2)	1.75
(3)	1.77
(4)(a), (b)	1.79
(6)(a)	1.84
(10)	2.32
20	1.29, 5.04
(2)(a)–(d)	1.88
(5)	1.89
21	5.04, 5.41, 5.44
(1)	1.70
(a)–(d)	1.87
(3)	5.45
(4)	1.95
(5)	5.45
(7)	1.41
22	5.04, 5.46
(2)	5.04

Finance Act 1985—*contd.*	PARA
s 22(4)	1.38, 5.04
(7)	5.04, 5.47
24	4.41, 4.67
(1)	5.04
(2)	1.41, 4.41, 5.04
(3)	1.61
(5)	4.67, 5.04
25	4.21, 4.68, 5.04
26	4.67, 5.04
27	4.67
(1)	1.39
28	4.48, 4.67
29	4.67
33(2)	1.58, 1.79
Sch 7 para 1(3)	5.04
2	5.04
3	5.65
(3)	5.66
4	5.04, 5.36
5, 6	5.04
Insolvency Act 1985	
Sch 4 para 2	5.49
Finance Act 1986	
s 10	5.06
14	5.54
15	1.28, 1.103, 5.54
53(1)	1.107
(b)	1.94
(2)	1.90

Table of cases

	PARA
Aikman v White [1986] STC 1	1.83
Arora v C & E Comrs [1976] VATTR 53	3.53
Benton v C & E Comrs [1975] VATTR 138	3.55
Boots Company plc, The, v C & E Comrs LON/85/600	4.17
Brookes (T) & Co Ltd v C & E Comrs MAN/77/236, 101 Taxation 184	3.69
Brown v C & E Comrs LON/80/109, (unreported)	3.56
Brutus v Cozens [1972] 2 All ER 1297	4.59
Calmforce Ltd v C & E Comrs LON/83/254	2.30
C & E Comrs v A E Hamlin & Co [1983] STC 780, [1983] 3 All ER 654	5.68
C & E Comrs v J H Corbitt (Numismatists) Ltd [1980] STC 231	5.60
Cole Bros of Malden Ltd v C & E Comrs LON/82/136, (unreported)	3.55
Direct Cosmetics Ltd v C & E Comrs LON/85/377, [1985] STC 479	4.14, 5.28, 5.58
Eccles (ACS) & Co v C & E Comrs EDN/85/71	4.59
Evans v C & E Comrs [1979] VATTR 194	2.31
Faith Construction Ltd v C & E Comrs LON/85/522	1.42
Furby v C & E Comrs MAN/77/316, 102 Taxation 104	3.55
Furniss v Dawson [1984] 1 All ER 530, [1984] STC 153, HL	1.42
Gaumont British Distributors Ltd v Henry [1939] 2 KB 711, [1939] 2 All ER 808	2.06
Gloucester Old Boys Rugby Football Social Club v C & E Comrs CAR/77/133, 100 Taxation 148	3.47
Goode v C & E Comrs LON/77/118, 100 Taxation 148	3.55
Green v C & E Comrs LON/76/207, 99 Taxation 380	3.68
Grice v Needs and Hale [1979] 3 All ER 501	2.34
Hedges and Butler Ltd v C & E Comrs (unreported)	5.57
International Warranty Co (UK) Ltd v C & E Comrs EDN/85/28	4.32
Kazemi v C & E Comrs EDN/77/40, 101 Taxation 497	3.55
Lam v C & E Comrs LON/82/183, (unreported)	3.57
Laughtons Photographs v C & E Comrs LON/85/428	5.28
Lees Chinese Food Centre v C & E Comrs MAN/82/134	3.66
London and Globe Finance Corporation Ltd, Re [1903] 1 Ch 728, [1900–1903] All ER Rep 891	2.13
Lovat Road Hotel v C & E Comrs MAN/75/26, 95 Taxation 359	3.55
Mareva Compania Naviera SA v International Bulk Carriers SA [1980] 1 All ER 213, (1975) 2 Lloyd's Rep 509	5.49
National Pari-Mutuel Association Ltd v R (1930) 47 TLR 110	4.13
Nolan v C & E Comrs [1977] VATTR 219	3.64
Parson's Nose v C & E Comrs LON/77/263, 101 Taxation 61	3.60
Patel v Spencer [1976] 1 WLR 1268	2.55
Pinetree Housing Association Ltd v C & E Comrs [1983] VATTR 227	5.61
R v C & E Comrs ex p Howarth QBD 17 July 1985	5.64
R v Grunwald [1960] 3 All ER 380	2.17
R v McCarthy [1981] STC 298, CA	2.11
R v Tyson (1867) LR I CCR 107, 37 LJMC 7	2.14
Ramsay v IRC [1981] 1 All ER 673, [1981] STC 174, HL	1.42
Rawcliffe v C & E Comrs MAN/78/258, 103 Taxation 306	3.66

Table of cases

	PARA
Rhodes (LM) v C & E Comrs LON/86/25	1.60, 1.68
Richardson v C & E Comrs CAR/79/133, (unreported)	3.60
Robinson v C & E Comrs MAN/76/48, 102 Taxation 152	3.69
Roocroft v C & E Comrs MAN/76/110, 98 Taxation 266	3.56
Ross v C & E Comrs MAN/76/98, 102 Taxation 333	3.57
Scanlon v C & E Comrs LON/76/59, 99 Taxation 22	3.55
Serendipity v C & E Comrs MAN/77/284, 101 Taxation 374	3.60
Shaw's Bar v C & E Comrs EDN/76/28, 100 Taxation 363	3.67
Stockman v C & E Comrs LON/79/347, 106 Taxation 458	3.67
Streamline Taxis (Southampton) Ltd v C & E Comrs LON/85/499	4.64
UFD Ltd v C & E Comrs [1981] VATTR 199	4.60
Van Boeckel v C & E Comrs [1981] STC 290, [1981] 2 All ER 505	3.66, 5.42
Wynn (JD) v C & E Comrs LON/85/467	4.31
Yoga for Health Foundation v C & E Comrs LON/82/228, [1983] VATTR 297, [1984] STC 630	4.60

Abbreviations

AAO	Advanced Accountancy Officers
CEMA 1979	Customs and Excise Management Act 1979
CIU	Collection Investigation Unit
CJA 1982	Criminal Justice Act 1982
CLA 1977	Criminal Law Act 1977
Customs and Excise	HM Commissioners of Customs and Excise
EC	European Communities
ECA 1972	European Communities Act 1972
ECJ	European Court of Justice
EEC	European Economic Community
FA 1972	Finance Act 1972
FA 1985	Finance Act 1985
IA 1985	Insolvency Act 1985
ID	Investigation Division
IT	Input Tax
LA	Local authority
LVO	Local VAT Office
MCA 1980	Magistrates' Courts Act 1980
NIC	National Insurance Contributions
NT	Net Tax
OT	Output Tax
PA 1911	Perjury Act 1911
QBD	Queen's Bench Division
RSC	Rules of the Supreme Court
TA 1968	Theft Act 1968
TA 1978	Theft Act 1978
TMA 1970	Taxes Management Act 1970
UK	United Kingdom
VAD	VAT Administration Directorate
VAT	Value Added Tax
VATA 1983	Value Added Tax Act 1983
VCU	VAT Central Unit
VSO	VAT sub-office

1 Civil penalties, interest and surcharges

Enforcement powers are necessary not only to coerce the dishonest and neglectful, but to encourage the honest and conscientious.

Keith Committee 1983

INTRODUCTION

1.01 Value Added Tax (VAT) was introduced into the United Kingdom (UK) on 1 April 1973 by the Finance Act 1972 as part of the process by which the UK became a member of what is commonly known as the European Economic Community (EEC). Since its introduction as a conceptually simple form of taxation a mass of legislation, orders, regulations, case law and explanatory leaflets and notices have led to a system which has become increasingly complex. Practitioners and businesses who had become accustomed to dealing with the Inland Revenue on the direct taxation of income, profits and capital gains had to accept and adapt to the often very different system of VAT under the administration of Customs and Excise.

Revenue

1.02 In terms of revenue collected the annual report of the Commissioners of HM Customs and Excise (referred to in this work as 'Customs and Excise') for the year ended 31 March 1985 indicated that net revenue collected by the department during the year, which includes not only VAT, but also receipts from hydrocarbon oils, tobacco products, Customs duties, car tax, betting and gaming and alcoholic drinks, was £35,536.8 million. This represented more than 40% of the total Government revenue in the year. Of this total VAT receipts at £18,535.3 million represented 52% of Customs and Excise receipts. One has only to compare this with the figure of net VAT receipts of only £4,234 million for the year ended 31 March 1978, when the standard rate of VAT was admittedly only 8%, to realise how the importance of VAT revenue to the Government has increased.

Administrative burdens

1.03 Despite the increasing yields for the Government from VAT the tax has not been short of critics attacking not only the seeming illogicality of the system, but also the burdens which the system places on those subjected to registration for VAT. In the early years of the tax it attracted descriptions such as 'the tax we love to hate' and the popular cry from the registered trader was that not only was he faced with having to run his business, but that he was also burdened with acting as an 'unpaid tax collector' for the Government. Indeed, the claims of the Customs and Excise Department that its costs of administering VAT have consistently been less than 2p for every pound of net revenue collected serves to illustrate that the real burdens of what is basically a self-assessment tax system fall on those who are obliged to register for VAT.

1.04 Civil penalties, interest and surcharges

1.04 Although it may be argued that the detailed record keeping requirements under the VAT system benefit a business by providing a detailed and regular analysis of the profitability or otherwise of the business, and that the method of collecting and paying over VAT provides real cash flow benefits for certain categories of traders, the fact that businesses registered for VAT are obliged to charge VAT and collect it from their customers, off-set any VAT credit allowed on their expenditure and declare and pay over or reclaim their net VAT liability to or from Customs and Excise must place a degree of administrative burden on those businesses.

1.05 An extensive analysis of the costs and benefits of the workings of the VAT system is beyond the scope of this book and was in fact the subject of a detailed research project undertaken by Professor C Sandford and others in 1981. Since that project, however, the Government itself has examined the burdens imposed on the business community, especially on small businesses, by administrative and legislative requirements of central and local government. Its report entitled 'Burdens on Business', published in 1985, contained an interesting analysis which revealed VAT as the most frequent burden facing the small business. The following graph illustrates how far out in front the burden of VAT was seen in relation to other Government requirements.

Burdens on businesses

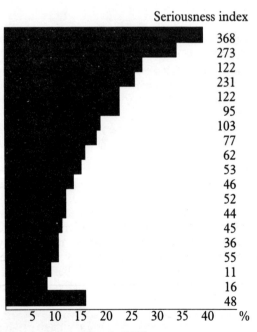

	Seriousness index
VAT	368
Employment protection	273
Statistics	122
LA planning	231
Emp/self emp tx treat	122
Sick pay	95
PAYE	103
Health and safety	77
LA building	62
Environment	53
Fire regulations	46
Consumer law	52
Company law	44
NIC	45
Minimum wages	36
Restrict trade pract	55
Anti-discrimination	11
Data protection	16
Others	48

Source: Page 31 Burdens on Business Report March 1985

1.06 Somewhat unfortunately for the Government, the report was published in the same month as the Chancellor announced formally in his Budget that the 1985 Finance Bill would include a range of new and revised powers and penalties in relation to VAT. A Press Notice issued by the Customs and Excise

Department on Budget day 1985 indicated that the Government's proposals were designed to achieve a careful balance between the interests of the individual taxpayer and the Exchequer and to improve both the fairness and the efficiency of the arrangements for collecting VAT.

Compliance

1.07 Before analysing the legislation which was enacted as a result of such a statement of intention it is worth considering briefly the background and reasons which led the Government to the view that after twelve years of VAT major new legislative compliance provisions were required.

The Keith Committee

1.08 It is necessary to go back as far as 17 July 1980 when the Government announced in Parliament the setting up of an independent inquiry to consider and make recommendations upon the tax enforcement powers of the Board of Inland Revenue and the Board of Customs and Excise. The committee set up to conduct the Inquiry was chaired by the Rt Hon Lord Keith of Kinkel PC and the subsequent report produced by the Committee is commonly referred to as the 'Keith Report'.

1.09 The Committee's terms of reference were broadly as follows:

a) To enquire into the tax enforcement powers of the Board of Inland Revenue and the Board of Customs and Excise, including:
i) powers of investigation into the accuracy of returns including powers to call for information and documents;
ii) powers of entry and of search of premises and persons;
iii) powers relating to cases of fraud, wilful default or neglect and to cases of reckless action: but not including the ordinary processes of collecting outstanding tax and the charge of interest thereon.
b) To consider whether these powers are suited to their purposes having regard both to the need to ensure compliance with the law and to avoid excessive burdens upon taxpayers and to make recommendations.

1.10 At the time of the Committee's appointment there was both widespread interest in the phenomenon known as the 'black economy' and evidence that the VAT system was vulnerable to attack by those deliberately aiming to defraud it of large sums of money. In considering its terms of reference the Committee realised that the task before it was not without difficulty. On the one hand it had to consider the effectiveness of the enforcement powers and penalties to ensure compliance and suppress fraud and yet, on the other hand, it recognised the need to avoid excessive burdens on taxpayers.

1.11 In formulating its conclusions and recommendations the Committee indicated in its Report that it had endeavoured to keep in mind the following principles:

a) Enforcement powers should be precise, and logically formulated, and should so far as practicable be harmonized over the whole direct and indirect tax field.

1.11 Civil penalties, interest and surcharges

b) The scope for administrative discretion should be reduced to a minimum, so that it is available only where required for strictly practical reasons. As a general rule particular consequences should follow particular acts or omissions in every case. In this way, everyone knows where they stand, and compliance is likely to be improved. If everyone is treated alike, grounds for complaint are minimised, provided always that the sanction is regarded as broadly fair.

c) Routine regulatory mechanisms should not, in the tax field, be fenced with criminal sanctions. Automatic civil surcharges and penalties are more appropriate, and more reliable in their application. Criminal prosecution, which turns on administrative discretion and is necessarily selective, is unsuited to the situation.

d) All enforcement procedures should be subject to ultimate judicial control both broadly and in matters of detail, and such control should be capable of being applied in a summary and expeditious way. This is the only reliable and satisfactory means of securing that the taxpayer is adequately safeguarded.

e) Opportunities for successful concealment of facts relevant to tax liability should be reduced.

f) Effective criminal sanctions should be available to check the incidence of deliberate and serious frauds.

1.12 In considering VAT the Committee considered written and oral submissions not only from Customs and Excise, but also from many other organisations who had been invited to contribute their views. To ensure that no views could be overlooked an advertisement issued by the Committee requesting evidence on the topics under consideration was included in various national and local newspapers.

1.13 The Keith Committee considered that although VAT is a modern tax and the associated enforcement powers were thought out as a coherent whole when the tax was introduced, experience since 1972 had nevertheless revealed a number of deficiencies and anomalies. In view of the increasing attraction of VAT fraud amongst professional criminals (see for example paras **2.48** and **2.49** in ch 2) the Committee proposed various modifications to the VAT criminal offence code. Beyond this the Committee proposed the introduction of a new civil code for the punishment of certain VAT defaults. Such a civil code, it was proposed, would not only replace the use of criminal sanctions for regulatory matters, but would also introduce a range of defaulting conduct punishable by civil penalties to run in parallel with the regime of criminal prosecution and compounding for fraud alone.

1.14 The publication of the Committee's proposals and recommendations resulted in much debate amongst various organisations as to the advantages and disadvantages which might follow the adoption of such measures. A formal consultation exercise between Customs and Excise and trade and professional bodies was also carried out and the results reported to Treasury ministers in March 1984. In reply to a parliamentary question on 18 May 1984 the Chancellor indicated that the Government hoped to announce its conclusions on VAT towards the end of 1984 in time for any necessary legislation to be included in the 1985 Finance Bill.

The collection of VAT

1.15 On 21 November 1984 the Chancellor announced in Parliament the publication of a paper entitled 'The Collection of VAT' setting out detailed proposals and draft clauses for the implementation of the VAT recommendations in volumes 1 and 2 of the Keith Report. Even though the paper, which ran to 64 pages including 30 pages of draft legislative clauses and schedules, was not released until 21 November 1984, detailed comments on the draft legislative proposals were required by Customs and Excise by 7 January 1985, in order to allow the parliamentary draftsman sufficient time to prepare the final legislative proposals for the 1985 Finance Bill.

1.16 As widely predicted the publication of the draft VAT clauses was met with a storm of protest from many VAT commentators, evoking such headlines as 'A National Disgrace', 'An Affront to Civil Liberties' and 'A Sledgehammer to Crack a Nut'. Although the Chancellor was at pains to emphasise that none of the proposals on VAT in any way pre-judged the Government's decisions on direct tax recommendations many practitioners feared that the Government would be monitoring the level of opposition or acceptance to the VAT clauses and that the reactions would probably influence the timing and extent of any changes on the direct tax front. Although the aim in November 1984 as regards direct taxes was to publish a Consultation Paper in 1985, with any necessary legislation being included in the 1986 Finance Bill, this proposed timetable has currently been postponed.

1.17 Between the publication of the paper in November 1984 and publication of the 1985 Finance Bill on 16 April 1985, representations regarding the technical content and severity of many of the draft clauses were taken into account and a number of important changes were incorporated. There were still many, however, who feared that if such legislation were implemented the risk of the honest businessman being subjected to the severity of some of the penalties through innocent error was still too great. Throughout the progress of the Bill during the committee stage debates the VAT clauses of the Bill were the subject of many further representations, which were duly considered, and in some cases led to further changes being incorporated into the draft clauses at that stage.

Reasons for change

1.18 Before analysing the detailed provisions which reached the Statute Book the fundamental reasons for decriminalising many of the previous criminal VAT sanctions for regulatory offences and substituting them with the new civil sanctions should be realised.

1.19 It is necessary to consider the information presented by Customs and Excise to the Keith Committee on prosecutions for failure to render VAT returns or pay VAT due in order to realise the extent of one of the major problems which faced Customs and Excise in its previous administration of the tax. Under the VAT legislation existing at the time both failure to furnish VAT returns and failure to pay tax by the due dates (normally one month after the end of a quarterly or monthly VAT period) were classified as criminal offences (FA 1972, s 38).

1.20 Civil penalties, interest and surcharges

1.20 The Keith Committee heard evidence that some 4,500 cases were prosecuted via the courts each year under the 'failure to render returns' and 'failure to pay' provisions and appropriate fines were imposed by the courts. It must be remembered, however, that with a VAT registered population of approximately 1.4 million in the UK and with Customs and Excise claiming that over 80% of such population submitted their VAT returns and payments late, faced with this scale of non-compliance, both Customs and Excise and the courts could only deal with the most persistent offenders.

1.21 The civil penalty provisions are therefore designed to secure a marked improvement in the reported large scale non-compliance in this area, in particular by the introduction of a default surcharge, to be imposed automatically by Customs and Excise on persistent late payers (see para **1.73**).

1.22 The Government was also concerned about the number and frequency of underdeclarations of VAT found on control visits by VAT officers and the introduction of a new 'serious misdeclaration' penalty is expected to improve the accuracy of the figures declared on VAT returns, thus improving the overall collection of VAT revenue (see para **1.44**).

1.23 A Press Notice (No 988) issued by Customs and Excise on Budget Day 1985 indicated that the proposals would, in their view, have the following revenue effects:

a) improved revenue flow of £50 million in 1985/1986 through more accurate and increased assessments on taxpayers who persistently failed to furnish VAT returns;
b) a once and for all increase in revenue flow amounting to £600 million by 1988/1989 through a reduction of outstanding VAT arrears;
c) annual revenue from default surcharge, interest and penalties building up to £150 million over time.

1.24 Although many organisations accepted the broad thrust of the proposed changes in the paper entitled 'The Collection of VAT' there was no shortage of commentators ready to criticise the detail within the proposed clauses. Such criticism was concerned mainly with the fact that the new penalties appeared too harsh, that they would be exigible for levels of non-compliance which were too low and that there was a great danger of the honest businessman being penalised by the proposed penalties, even though the errors which gave rise to the penalties may have been caused by innocent error, ignorance of the complex areas of the legislation or sheer inability to cope with regulatory burdens placed on a business, particularly the small, but fast expanding business. There were also those who vociferously attacked the whole philosophy of the proposals arguing that the balance between the interests of taxpayers at large and the interests of the Customs and Excise would be tipped too far in favour of the latter at the expense of the former.

1.25 For the Government's part the proposals contained in the paper published in November 1984 were prefaced by a forward by the Chancellor of the Exchequer in which the package as a whole was commended to taxpayers and their professional advisers. The full text of the forward is set out in Appendix 1.

The 1985 legislation 1.28

1.26 The case for supporting the new proposals was also expressed by Customs and Excise in an introduction to the paper, extracts from which are set out in Appendix 2.

THE 1985 LEGISLATION

1.27 As already mentioned certain of the details and limits which gave most cause for concern were either removed or modified slightly by the time of publication of the 1985 Finance Bill and further changes were made during the Committee Stage and Report Stage debates of the Bill, although most of the proposals, albeit in modified form, reached the Statute Book on 25 July 1985 on Royal Assent of the Bill. As will be seen in the analysis of the new offence and penalty provisions certain of the provisions enacted in the Finance Act 1985 were enabling legislation only at that stage and required the Treasury to make orders appointing the dates on which the individual provisions would become effective. The main reason for this appears to have been not to provide the business community with a transitional period in which to become accustomed to the new penalty provisions as they are introduced, but merely because the Customs and Excise, in order to be able to implement many of the new provisions, recognised that it would have to purchase and program new computer systems which would take between one and three years.

1.28 The following table sets out the defaults, breaches and failures which give rise to civil, as opposed to criminal, penalties. Also shown for comparative purposes are the criminal penalties (if any) which they replaced. The timetable for implementation of the new rules is set out and explained in subsequent paragraphs.

FA 1985 civil penalty provisions

Default/Failure/Breach	Finance Act 1985 Provision	Previous Value Added Tax Act 1983 Provision
1. Tax evasion: conduct involving dishonesty	s 13	—
2. Serious misdeclaration or neglect resulting in understatements or overclaims	s 14	—
3. Failure to notify liability to registration and failure to notify changes in circumstances	s 15(1)(a)	s 39(5)(a)
4. Unauthorised issue of invoices	s 15(1)(b)	s 39(6)
5. Breaches of walking possession agreements	s 16	—
6. Failure to notify cessation of taxable supplies	s 17(1)(a)	s 39(5)(a)
7. Failure to keep records	s 17(1)(b)	s 39(7)
8. Failure to furnish information or produce documents	s 17(1)(b)	s 39(7)
9. Failure to comply with regulations or rules made under VATA 1983[1]	s 17(1)(c)	s 39(7)
10. Failure to furnish returns or pay tax by due dates[2]	s 17(1)(c) & s 17(5)	s 39(8)
11. Failure to preserve records	s 17(2)	s 39(7)

1.28 Civil penalties, interest and surcharges

Notes

[1]FA 1986, s 15 extended this provision to include breaches of Treasury orders made under VATA 1983 or ECA 1972 relating to VAT.
[2]This provision comes into operation only on a date to be appointed by Treasury order. Until such time these defaults continue to be subject to the VATA 1983 criminal provisions. The appointed date is 1 October 1986.

1.29 In addition to the introduction of the civil penalties listed in the above table, FA 1985 also introduced into the VAT legislation for the first time the provision for interest to be charged on tax, etc, recovered or recoverable by assessment (FA 1985, s 18), a default surcharge for those persistently late in furnishing returns and/or tax (FA 1985, s 19) and a repayment supplement to be paid by Customs and Excise in respect of certain delayed repayments (FA 1985, s 20).

1.30 FA 1985 also extended and modified Customs and Excise powers and certain rules relating to VAT tribunal appeals. These are considered in the chapters on appeals (ch 4) and Customs and Excise powers (ch 5) although certain comments, where appropriate, are included in this chapter also.

Timetable for implementation

1.31 As regards the implementation of the FA 1985 provisions the following table sets out those provisions which were effective from 25 July 1985 and the proposed timetable for implementation of the remaining provisions described above. Certain sections of the FA 1985 legislation remain enabling legislation only and require the Treasury to make orders by statutory instruments to give effect to the provisions.

Provisions effective from 25 July 1985:

1. Tax evasion: conduct involving dishonesty
2. Failure to notify liability to registration and failure to notify changes in circumstances
3. Unauthorised issue of tax invoices
4. Breaches of walking possession agreements
5. Failure to notify cessation of taxable supplies
6. Failure to keep records
7. Failure to furnish information or produce documents
8. Failure to comply with regulations or rules under VATA 1983[1]
9. Failure to preserve records.

Note

[1]Except for the failure to render VAT returns and tax by the due dates which temporarily remain criminal offences until 1 October 1986.

The 1985 legislation 1.36

Expected date of implementation – 1 October 1986:

1. Failure to furnish returns or pay tax due
2. Default surcharge
3. Repayment supplement

Expected date of implementation – 1 July 1988:

1. Interest
2. Serious misdeclaration

1.32 In the following paragraphs the new provisions are analysed and comments on the implications which will need to be borne in mind are also included. Following the detailed analysis a checklist is included of ways of ensuring that the legislation is complied with and that the incidence of incurring potential penalties, interest or surcharges is kept to a minimum (see para **1.108**).

Tax evasion: conduct involving dishonesty (FA 1985, s 13/FA 1986, s 14)

1.33 This is a new offence of 'civil fraud' with a penalty of up to 100% of the tax evaded (s 13(1)). It arises where a person acts dishonestly in seeking to evade tax. See FA 1986, s 14, relating to personal liability of directors and/or managing officers for a penalty imposed under this provision.

i) Evading tax

1.34 The term 'evading tax' includes obtaining any of the following when not entitled:

a) payment of net input tax (s 13(2)(a))
b) refund of tax under the Do-It-Yourself Housebuilders Scheme (s 13(2)(b))
c) a refund of tax under the bad debt relief provisions (s 13(2)(b))
d) a repayment of tax under the EEC Eighth Directive Refund Scheme (79/1072/EEC), whereby UK VAT is repaid to persons carrying on business in an EEC member state other than the UK (s 13(2)(c))

ii) Interaction with criminal code

1.35 An important aspect of this provision is that conduct involves dishonesty whether or not it is such as to give rise to criminal liability (s 13(1)(b)). This means that Customs and Excise may, as an alternative to prosecution for criminal offences, use this provision to exact civil penalties. It is, however, made clear in s 13(7) that a person who is convicted of a criminal offence cannot also be liable to a 'civil fraud' penalty under this provision.

iii) Mitigation

1.36 The penalty of 100% of the tax may be mitigated down to not less than 50% of the tax, but only to reflect the extent of a person's co-operation in the Customs and Excise investigation (s 13(4)). Both Customs and Excise, or on appeal, a VAT tribunal, are given such powers of mitigation, but it should be

1.36 Civil penalties, interest and surcharges

noted that the penalty, if found to be due, can never be reduced to less than 50% of the tax, either by Customs and Excise or the VAT tribunal (s 13(4)). The aim behind this provision was to provide a civil penalty which could be imposed without recourse to the courts and which would be broadly in line with the average level of compounded settlements for alleged criminal offences (see para **2.61**).

iv) Induced evidence

1.37 A further important aspect of this provision is that under s 13(5) statements made or documents produced by a person are not inadmissible in criminal proceedings even if the person's attention has been drawn to the fact that Customs and Excise may impose a civil penalty instead of instituting criminal proceedings, or that their practice is to be influenced by a full confession and full facilities for investigation, or that a civil penalty for dishonest conduct may be reduced based on the degree of co-operation given.

v) Time limit for assessment

1.38 By virtue of FA 1985, s 22(4), Customs and Excise are empowered to make an assessment for tax lost as a result of civil fraud, or fraud for which a person has been convicted, for a 20 year period instead of the normal six year period.

vi) Right of appeal and burden of proof

1.39 A right of appeal to a VAT tribunal is given under VATA 1983, s 40(1)(o), against liability to a penalty under this provision and by virtue of FA 1985, s 27(1), the burden of proof is expressly on Customs and Excise and not the appellant. It should be remembered that in a VAT tribunal hearing Customs and Excise have only to satisfy the Tribunal on a 'balance of probabilities' test rather than to the higher criminal standard of 'beyond reasonable doubt'.

vii) Interaction with other civil penalties

1.40 An assessment to a penalty under the civil fraud provision precludes liability to a penalty for the following by virtue of the provisions of FA 1985 indicated:

a) serious misdeclaration (s 14(7))
b) failure to notify liability to be registered (s 15(5)(b))
c) the issue of invoices by unauthorised persons (s 15(5)(b))
d) failure to keep, produce or preserve VAT records (s 17(10))
e) breach of other regulatory requirements (s 17(10)).

viii) Commentary

1.41 It should be noted that once a VAT tribunal has decided that civil fraud has 'on the balance of probabilities' occurred, it has no power to reduce a penalty to below 50% of the tax involved (FA 1985, s 24(2)). Furthermore, unless a prospective appellant can establish hardship, it would appear, by virtue of VATA 1983, s 40(3)(a), in conjunction with FA 1985, s 21(7), that he may have to lodge both the tax and the penalty before the appeal can be entertained.

1.42 Whether the offence and penalty could apply if a scheme which was genuinely thought to involve legal tax avoidance is challenged by Customs and Excise as being invalid and representing conduct involving dishonesty for the purpose of evading tax, is open to doubt. Clearly the only sound basis on which to proceed is to seek written clearance from Customs and Excise by giving them all relevant facts. For a case in which Customs and Excise unsuccessfully argued that a scheme was artificial and in which they sought to rely on the principles laid down by the House of Lords in the cases of *Ramsay v IRC* [1981] 1 All ER 673, [1981] STC 174, HL, and *Furniss v Dawson* [1984] 1 All ER 530, [1984] STC 153, HL, see *Faith Construction Ltd v Comrs C & E* (LON/85/522). The decision is likely to be appealed to the High Court.

1.43 Although it is difficult to gauge how the Customs and Excise policy on fraud may develop initial discussions with Customs and Excise have indicated that serious VAT fraud on a parallel to the 'gold fraud' cases in recent years (see paras **2.48** and **2.49**) will tend to continue to be prosecuted through the courts, but that most other cases of VAT fraud may tend to be settled by use of the civil rather than criminal fraud provisions.

Serious misdeclaration (FA 1985, s 14)

1.44 This is a new civil offence which will be committed by a person from a date to be appointed by the Treasury (expected to be 1 July 1988) if he:

a) makes a return which understates his liability (s 14(1)(a));
b) claims a repayment on a return to which he is not entitled (s 14(1)(a)); or
c) receives an assessment from Customs and Excise which understates his liability, and, within a period of 30 days from the date on which the assessment was issued, fails to take all reasonable steps to advise them accordingly (s 14(1)(b)).

However, the offence is not committed unless the understatement or overclaim for the period in question equals or exceeds either:

d) 30% of the true amount of tax payable or repayable or charged by assessment; or
e) the greater of £10,000 and 5% of the true amount of tax (s 14(2)).

i) Penalty

1.45 The penalty is 30% of the tax which would have been lost if the inaccuracy had not been discovered, or in other words the amount by which the tax shown on the return was understated or overclaimed, or the assessment understated (s 14(1)).

ii) Persistent misdeclarations

1.46 The 30% limit referred to at para **1.44** d), above, is reduced to only 15% where in any period of four years beginning within six years before the end of the VAT accounting period in question there were at least two VAT accounting periods, beginning after the effective date appointed by the Treasury, in which serious misdeclarations occurred. For this purpose only, the 15% limit refers to all the misdeclarations (s 14(2)(b)). Thus, although an

1.46 Civil penalties, interest and surcharges

error exceeding 15% will not, on the first two occasions, give rise to a penalty, unless the higher limits are also exceeded, it will count towards the two misdeclarations in four years which will then trigger the lower 15% limit. This is designed to penalise not only those persons who make an occasional serious error in calculating their VAT liabilities, but also those who persistently miscalculate their correct liability by more than an insignificant amount.

iii) Limits

1.47 The following tables illustrate the margins of errors which will not result in a penalty under this provision.

True amount of tax payable/repayable	Minimum level of understated/overclaimed tax which will trigger a penalty
£	
0 – 33,333	30%
33,334 – 200,000	£10,000
Over 200,000	5%

If the 15% limit applies due to previous serious misdeclarations the position will be as follows:

£	
0 – 66,667	15%
66,668 – 200,000	£10,000
Over 200,000	5%

iv) Underdeclarations and overdeclarations

1.48 If a person has understated his output tax, but also understated his input tax (ie he has not reclaimed tax to which he is legally entitled), or overstated his input tax but overstated his output tax also, or a mixture of the two circumstances, allowance will be made in calculating the net underdeclarations (s 14(4)).

Example 1

VAT return for the period

	£
Output tax declared	5,000
Input tax declared	3,000
Net amount declared	2,000

If the true amount of tax should have been:

	£
Output tax	8,000
Input tax	3,000
Net amount	5,000

It can be seen that the underdeclaration of £3,000 is greater than 30% of the true net tax. The potential penalty applicable would be 30% of £3,000, ie £900 in addition to the £3,000 tax arrears payable.

Example 2

VAT return for period

	£
Output tax declared	5,000
Input tax declared	3,000
Net tax declared	2,000

If output tax has been underdeclared by £1,000, but the person has also omitted to claim £500 of input tax to which he is entitled the true position is;

	£
Output tax	6,000
Input tax	3,500
Net tax	2,500

As the net underdeclaration of £500 is less than 30% of the correct net tax and is also less than £10,000 (notwithstanding that it is greater than 5% of the true tax) the penalty will not apply, even though considered in isolation the £1,000 underdeclared output tax exceeds 30% of the true net tax position.

v) Exceptions

1.49 Serious misdeclaration, as defined above, will not give rise to a penalty, nor count towards the two misdeclarations in a four year period if:

a) there is a 'reasonable excuse' (see paras **1.58 – 1.61**) to the satisfaction of Customs and Excise or, on appeal, a VAT tribunal (s 14(6)(a)); or
b) full information with regard to the inaccuracy was provided to Customs and Excise at a time when the taxpayer had no reason to believe that his VAT affairs were under inquiry (s 14(6)(b)).

vi) Interaction with other penalties

1.50 Assessment to a serious misdeclaration penalty precludes liability to a penalty for breaches of other regulatory requirements (FA 1985, s 17(10)(b)).

Additionally, by virtue of FA 1985, s 14(7), if a person is convicted of a criminal offence, or assessed to a penalty for 'civil fraud', he will neither incur a penalty for serious misdeclaration nor will his conduct count towards the two misdeclarations in a four year period.

vii) Commentary

1.51 This provision has probably raised more concern amongst practitioners, trade organisations and the business community generally than any of the other provisions which have been or are being introduced. Although the provision is not expected to come into effect until 1 July 1988 there are a number of causes for concern over its potential application, which are discussed in the following paragraphs. Even though the provision will not be effective until July 1988 Customs and Excise issued an information sheet on 1 June 1986 and this is included in Appendix 16.

1.52 It will have been seen above that the criteria for establishing whether a penalty is to apply are based on purely arithmetic objective tests. Customs and Excise for their part have indicated that if the mental state of intent to deceive

1.52 Civil penalties, interest and surcharges

had to be proved before a penalty applies, this would tie up investigation resources which could be used on alternative civil or criminal fraud matters. This view, coupled with the fact that the provision is not to be effective until 1988, suggest that the VAT computer systems are to be programmed to calculate automatically whether an assessment to be issued by a local VAT office for understatements or overclaims exceeds the de minimis limits and constitutes a 'serious misdeclaration'.

1.53 A further consideration which should be noted is that the trigger limits, by their arithmetic and percentage nature, are likely to result in smaller businesses, whose input tax and output tax levels are consistently close in amount, being more likely to be subjected to serious misdeclaration penalties. This will arise because the net tax position for such persons will be fairly small and hence it will require relatively small inaccuracies to trigger the serious misdeclaration penalties.

1.54 No provision appears to have been made for the situation which may arise where a genuinely honest taxpayer understates his liability by more than the de minimis limits through innocent error, honest mistake or ignorance of one of the many rules or regulations within the VAT legislation. If Customs and Excise have publicised the correct treatment in their public notices, leaflets, pamphlets, press releases and other official literature, it is doubtful whether they will accept that the taxpayer has a reasonable excuse if it is discovered by Customs and Excise on a control visit. In this respect Customs and Excise would do well to consider the instructions to its own VAT staff, which was reproduced in Note 12 of the Keith Committee Report and reads:

'Most traders will be conscientiously trying to meet their obligations and any irregularities will often be the result of their honest and unintended misinterpretation of our requirements.'

1.55 On the same point reference should also be made to the statement made in 1983 by the small business section of the Conservative Central Office and quoted by Lord Bruce in the House of Lords debate on the Keith Committee Report, 1983 HL Official Report (5th series) col 1211:

'What the tax inspectors and their colleagues in Customs and Excise need to learn is a different attitude. Instead of being superior in their understanding of taxation and accounting systems and sure that those who make mistakes are doing so deliberately, they might remember that every penny that is available to tax gatherers, is earned by people with different skills from their own and that it would certainly be much better to assume an honest mistake and make it easy for the taxpayer to discuss it with them, than to elaborate the sanctions and penalties hanging over the businessman.'

1.56 Whilst there can be no doubt that public opinion is totally supportive of provisions which are designed to prevent evasion, particularly where a person sets out to be dishonest, the use of purely objective, arithmetic tests to determine culpability of a civil offence is a radical departure from anything previously on the statute books. It should be realised that a serious misdeclaration penalty rests not on intent to deceive but on frequency and size of underdeclaration alone.

1.57 Cases of genuine dispute give equal cause for concern. Assume that a taxpayer completes his return in accordance with the generally accepted practice prevailing at the time, but a case decision, which may subsequently be appealed against in a higher court, comes to his notice. If the case held that an identical product or service to that which he is supplying has been held to be subject to VAT at the standard rate, as opposed to the zero-rate, he is then faced with the choice of either accepting that the decision is correct and increasing his prices by 15%, which if his competitors do not follow suit will probably result in a loss of business, or ignoring the decision and possibly facing a future penalty for serious misdeclaration if a higher court upholds the standard rated ruling. Again it is to be hoped that either Customs and Excise or the VAT tribunals might consider the 'reasonable excuse' escape route in these situations.

viii) 'Reasonable excuse'

1.58 In relation to claims that a person has a 'reasonable excuse' Customs and Excise have indicated only that each case will be treated on its merits and the initial claims by persons subject to potential penalties claiming 'reasonable excuse' will be monitored closely by the VAT Headquarters.

FA 1985, s 33(2), does however, provide two statutory rules on what will not be capable of being a reasonable excuse:

a) an insufficiency of funds to pay any tax due is not a reasonable excuse; and
b) when reliance is placed on any other person to perform any task, neither the fact of that reliance nor any dilatoriness or inaccuracy on the part of the person relied upon constitutes a reasonable excuse.

1.59 If the taxpayer has been clearly misdirected by Customs and Excise, the latter knowing the full facts, Customs and Excise normally apply a self-imposed estoppel provided the bad advice has been to the detriment of the taxpayer (see paras **4.15** and **4.16**). A situation may arise in future where a taxpayer has submitted the full facts to Customs and Excise, probably in the early years of VAT and obtained a favourable ruling in writing, which he subsequently acts upon in calculating his liabilities. If, some years later, Customs and Excise change their practice, possibly following a precedent case law decision on the point and publicise this in an amendment to a public notice, which the taxpayer receives, it is doubtful whether the VAT tribunals will support the view that the taxpayer will have a 'reasonable excuse' at a later stage. The importance of ensuring that changes in legislation or practice are given due consideration cannot therefore be overemphasised.

1.60 Practitioners should closely monitor the first cases which come before the VAT tribunals to establish what the tribunals will accept as 'reasonable excuse' and what they will not. In the very first case involving this concept, *L M Rhodes v Comrs C & E* LON/86/25, which was heard by Lord Grantchester in March 1986 the taxpayer earned commission running a debt collection agency and was late in notifying a liability to register for VAT. The taxpayer's representative argued that:

a) the rapid increase in turnover was not envisaged and the taxpayer was late in registering because she was totally engrossed in administering the business;
b) any VAT chargeable from the correct date of registration was recoverable by her clients as they were all registered for VAT;
c) there was no intent to avoid registration and she had contacted Customs and Excise voluntarily;

1.60 Civil penalties, interest and surcharges

d) the failure to register had not resulted in any loss of VAT revenue to the Crown as she had recovered the VAT from her customers;
e) the penalty was unjust in the circumstances.

However, in dismissing the appeal Lord Grantchester stated:

'In my opinion she [the taxpayer] has not put forward any excuse; she has only put forward mitigating circumstances. Ignorance of the law is no excuse . . . I regret that I cannot find any excuse in this case, let alone a reasonable excuse . . . and neither the Commissioners [of Customs and Excise] nor this tribunal has been entrusted with such a power to mitigate a fixed penalty.'

1.61 It is to be noted that although it was originally proposed to give Customs and Excise a general power, as recommended by the Keith Committee, to mitigate or remit any civil penalty, interest or surcharge for which a person became liable, during the passage of the 1985 Finance Bill through the Committee debates, representations were made that it was inherently unsatisfactory that Customs and Excise should have a greater power than the VAT tribunal and that it was essential that the tribunal should be given the power to review questions of mitigation decided by Customs and Excise. The Treasury minister, however, rather than deciding to allow the amendment which was being pressed, withdrew the clause allowing mitigation by Customs and Excise, on the grounds that the taxpayer had the escape route of 'reasonable excuse' for all penalties other than 'civil fraud' (HC Official Report, SC B, 18 Jun 1985, cols 614–620). Thus an appellant taxpayer who cannot convince Customs and Excise that he has a 'reasonable excuse' and who decides to appeal to a VAT tribunal is faced, except in cases of civil fraud, with an 'all or nothing' situation. The tribunal can only decide whether a penalty in such circumstances applies or whether it does not. By virtue of FA 1985, s 24(3), the VAT tribunal has no power to fix a penalty below that prescribed in the relevant legislation. Faced with such a situation an appellant, in seeking to avoid the imposition of a serious misdeclaration penalty, will have to argue on the basis of one of the following:

a) that his VAT liability has not been understated as Customs and Excise contend;
b) that VAT is understated, but only to a level which falls below the de minimis trigger limits;
c) that full information had been provided to Customs and Excise at a time when he was not under enquiry; or
d) that he has a 'reasonable excuse'.

With the onus on the appellant in this situation to discharge the burden of proof, the evidence which he is able to produce before the VAT tribunal, in some cases several years after the period in which the alleged underdeclaration occurred, will be of vital importance.

Failure to notify liability for registration (FA 1985, s 15(1)(a))

1.62 A person commits this offence if he fails to notify Customs and Excise within the time limits prescribed in VATA 1983, Sch 1, paras 3 or 4, that he is liable to be registered. (A specimen form VAT 1 for notifying registration is included in Appendix 7.)

The 1985 legislation 1.67

1.63 The penalty is 30% of the tax accruing between the time the registration should have been effected and the date when the failure was notified or discovered, with a minimum penalty of £50.

1.64 Under VATA 1983, Sch 1, para 3, a person is obliged to notify Customs and Excise that he is liable to be registered after the end of any quarter if the value of his taxable (ie standard and/or zero-rate) supplies:

i) in that quarter has exceeded £7,000; or
ii) in the four quarters then ending has exceeded £20,500.

In respect of i) above, if a person can satisfy Customs and Excise that his taxable supplies in that quarter and the next three quarters will not exceed £20,500 he will not be liable to be registered (Sch 1, para 1). Notification must be made within ten days of the end of the quarter and Customs and Excise must register the person with effect from the 21st day of the following quarter or from an earlier date as agreed between Customs and Excise and the person (Sch 1, para 3).

1.65 Under VATA 1983, Sch 1, para 4, a person is obliged to notify Customs and Excise that he is liable to be registered if, at any time, there are reasonable grounds for believing that the value of his taxable (ie standard and/or zero-rate) supplies in the period of one year beginning at that or any later time will exceed £20,500. Notification is to be made not later than the beginning of that period or from an earlier date as agreed between Customs and Excise and the person.

1.66 A penalty under this provision will not apply to a person if he has either been convicted of a criminal offence or he has suffered a penalty for 'civil fraud' (conduct involving dishonesty) in respect of the offence (FA 1985, s 15(5)).

1.67 A penalty applies only from 25 July 1985 (ie the date of enactment of FA 1985).

Example 1

(a) Registration applicable from	1 January 1986
(b) Registration notified to Customs & Excise on	1 July 1986
Arrears of net VAT between (a) and (b)	£3,000
Penalty (30%)	£ 900
Tax and penalty due to Customs & Excise	£3,900

Example 2

Registration applicable from	1 March 1985
Registration notified to Customs & Excise	1 October 1985
Arrears of net VAT between 1/3/85 and 24/7/85	£2,000
Arrears of net VAT between 25/7/85 and 30/9/85	£1,000
Penalty (30% of £1,000 from FA 1985)	£ 300
Tax and penalty due to Customs & Excise	£3,300

1.68 Under FA 1985, s 15(4), a statutory defence against the penalty is provided

1.67 Civil penalties, interest and surcharges

if the person can satisfy either Customs and Excise or, on appeal, a VAT tribunal, that he has a 'reasonable excuse' for the failure. Details of the first case decision (*L M Rhodes v Comrs C & E* LON/86/25) in which the taxpayer unsuccessfully claimed a 'reasonable excuse' are set out in para **1.60**.

1.69 A person exempted from registration under VATA 1983, Sch 1, para 11(2), because for example his supplies, although in excess of the statutory limits, are all, or predominantly, zero-rated, is also liable to the penalty if he fails to advise Customs and Excise of a material change in the ratio of his standard rated to zero-rated supplies, such that he would be required to be registered (FA 1985, s 15(1)(a)).

Commentary

1.70 On present evidence of some of the first offences under this provision the Customs and Excise policy is to notify the person at the time he is notified of his registration that his belated notification has rendered him liable to a penalty. He is also requested to provide within 30 days details of his net tax liability for the period of belatedness. If the person provides such details they are used as the basis for calculation and issue of a penalty assessment; if he does not, a penalty assessment is calculated by Customs and Excise, under the power conferred on them by FA 1985, s 21(1), from the best evidence available to them, and it will be issued from the local VAT office. Whatever the basis of the assessment issued it is subject to verification, and adjustment if necessary, at the time of the first control visit to the registered person.

1.71 It is understood that where companies in a VAT group registration have been accounting for VAT for a company which was inadvertently assumed to be a member of the VAT group, but which is subsequently discovered not to be in the VAT group, Customs and Excise will normally consider including the company in the group registration retrospectively, provided the conditions set out in VATA 1983, s 29, have been met throughout the proposed period of retrospection and it would not result in any revenue loss. It is further understood that when such retrospection is allowed Customs and Excise will not normally seek to issue a penalty assessment in respect of the late inclusion provided no arrears of VAT are due from that company.

1.72 Where a person is required to register immediately because he has good reason to believe that his taxable turnover in the twelve months then beginning will exceed the statutory threshold it appears that Customs and Excise will take a pragmatic approach in the issue of penalty assessments for late notification. Although Customs and Excise recognise that notification should be made to the local VAT office on the day that the person first believes his taxable turnover will exceed the annual threshold in the twelve months then beginning, it is understood that they will not issue a penalty assessment where the notification is completed at the proper time, but is not received by them until a few days afterwards, or is the subject of a genuine longer postal delay. Furthermore, where the belated notification exceeds such periods of grace and the person is issued with a penalty assessment, but disputes it, the person has the right to show 'reasonable excuse' to Customs and Excise and failing this, the right of appeal to a VAT tribunal (FA 1985, s 15(4)).

The 1985 legislation 1.78

The default surcharge (FA 1985, s 19)

1.73 A default surcharge of 5%, subject to a minimum of £30, rising in 5% steps to a maximum of 30% of VAT due will be leviable, from the date the provision is made effective (expected to be 1 October 1986), where:

a) VAT returns are submitted after the due dates;
b) VAT returns are not submitted at all; or
c) VAT due is paid after the due date.

1.74 A person will be in default in respect of a prescribed accounting period if, by the last date on which the VAT return is due (normally one month after the end of the period), either:

a) Customs and Excise have not received the return; or
b) Customs and Excise have received the return, but not the tax declared to be due on it (FA 1985, s 19(1)).

1.75 A person may not be liable to a surcharge on all occasions indicated in the previous paragraphs. If a person is in default in respect of any two accounting periods within a sequence of five accounting periods (or thirteen in the case of monthly VAT accounting periods) Customs and Excise will serve a 'surcharge liability notice' on the person. The notice will specify as a 'surcharge period' the period from the date of the notice to the end of the fourth (or twelfth in the case of monthly returns) period after the end of the later of the two accounting periods (FA 1985, s 19(2)).

1.76 The phased increase in the amount of surcharge is illustrated in the following table:

Default surcharge

Circumstance	Surcharge, greater of
First default in surcharge period	£30 or 5% of outstanding tax
Second such default	£30 or 10% of outstanding tax
Third such default	£30 or 15% of outstanding tax
Fourth such default	£30 or 20% of outstanding tax
Fifth such default	£30 or 25% of outstanding tax
Six or later such default	£30 or 30% of outstanding tax

'Outstanding tax' is the tax for the prescribed accounting period of default unpaid by the due date.

1.77 By virtue of FA 1985, s 19(3), Customs and Excise may issue a further surcharge liability notice on each default within an existing 'surcharge period', and this has the effect of extending the existing period to a date twelve months after the end of the return period for which the new default has arisen.

1.78 If a person, having received a surcharge liability notice, submits his returns and tax by the due dates throughout the surcharge period the notice lapses automatically and a further two relevant defaults are required before a further surcharge liability notice is sent to the person.

1.78 Civil penalties, interest and surcharges

Example

	Period ending	
	31 December 1986	default
	31 March 1987	no default
	30 June 1987	no default
	30 September 1987	no default
	31 December 1987	default
		Surcharge liability notice issued
Initial surcharge period	31 March 1988	no default
	30 June 1988	no default
	30 September 1988	default £30 or 5% surcharge
		Surcharge period extended
	31 December 1988	no default
Extended surcharge period	31 March 1989	no default
	30 June 1989	no default
	30 September 1989	no default
		Surcharge liability notice lapses

1.79 The default surcharge will not arise, however, and a person will not be regarded as in default, if Customs and Excise or, on appeal, a VAT tribunal, are satisfied that:

a) the return, or the tax, was despatched in a reasonable time and manner for it to be received by Customs and Excise within the appropriate time limit (FA 1985, s 19(4)(a)); or

b) there was a reasonable excuse for the return or tax not having been so despatched (FA 1985, s 19(4)(b)).

As noted earlier (see paras **1.58–1.61**) an insufficiency of funds to pay any tax due or the fact of reliance on, or dilatoriness or inaccuracy of a person relied upon are not reasonable excuses by virtue of FA 1985, s 33(2).

1.80 As an alternative to using this provision Customs and Excise will be able to apply a penalty under provisions relating to breaches of regulatory matters, ie failure to render a return or pay tax due by the due date (FA 1985, s 17).

Commentary

1.81 It is understood that Customs and Excise policy following implementation of this provision will be to record the postmark date together with the date of receipt for all returns and remittances sent to the VAT Central Unit at Southend.

1.82 It is worth remembering that persons paying by credit transfer rather than by cheque have the due date for both returns and the tax extended by seven days. This facility is described at para 77 of the VAT Guide (Notice No 700). Furthermore, the surcharge itself could be reduced by making payment on account (or eliminated altogether if the payment is equal to or exceeds the true VAT liability) although failure to furnish the return will still count as a default (FA 1985, s 19(1)(a)).

1.83 In the case of *Aikman v White* [1986] STC 1 the taxpayer completed a VAT return which included on it the instruction that it was to be returned once completed to the VAT Central Unit at Southend in the prepaid pre-addressed envelope provided. This was done, but apparently it never arrived at Southend. The taxpayer was subsequently charged with failure to furnish a VAT return as required under VATA 1983 and the VAT (General) Regulations 1980. The Court held that the word 'furnish' meant putting the return into the possession of Customs and Excise and that by giving the instruction on the return form VAT 100 Customs and Excise were adopting the Post Office as their agents. Accordingly, the return was 'furnished' when it was 'posted' in the prepaid envelope. The Customs and Excise appeal from the decision of the Sheriff acquitting the taxpayer in the lower court was therefore dismissed. Following this case Customs and Excise stated that they intended to make an amendment to Form VAT 100 to ensure that receipt by the Post Office cannot be regarded as receipt by Customs and Excise. For an example of a VAT return Form (VAT 100), see Appendix 3.

1.84 In the event of a postal strike or similar action Customs and Excise, after consultation with the Treasury, have the power to leave certain defaults out of account (FA 1985, s 19(6)(a)).

1.85 Although Customs and Excise anticipate that the default surcharge system will act as the major deterrent for those who persistently send in their VAT returns and/or tax late there is some concern that small businesses who supply goods or services to much larger organisations may be faced with the prospect of having to pay to Customs and Excise VAT which has not yet been collected by them due to the extended credit period frequently taken by certain of their customers, over which they have little control. It would be wise therefore to ensure that such adverse cash flow consequences are built into any financial plans of cash flow by, in particular, a new or existing small business.

1.86 Customs and Excise have issued a leaflet explaining the default surcharge procedure. The relevant section is reproduced in Appendix 4.

Repayment supplement (FA 1985, s 20)

1.87 A repayment supplement will be added to repayments of VAT reclaimed on returns in certain circumstances. The provision which is planned to become effective at the same time as the default surcharge (1 October 1986) requires Customs and Excise to pay a 5% supplement, or if greater, £30, if all the following conditions are met:

a) Customs and Excise have received a VAT return claiming a repayment to which a person is entitled within two months of the end of the relevant VAT accounting period (s 21(1)(a) and (b));
b) Customs and Excise have not issued written instructions for the repayment within 30 days of receipt of the VAT return (s 21(1)(c)); and
c) the amount of the repayment claimed on the return is not more than £100 in excess of the amount in fact due (s 21(1)(d)).

1.88 For the purpose of calculating the 30 days in b) above regulations may

1.88 Civil penalties, interest and surcharges

be made which prescribe that all of the following be left out of account:

a) the time taken for the raising and answering of any reasonable enquiry in connection with the return (s 20(2)(a));
b) the time taken by Customs and Excise for the correction of errors and omissions in the return (s 20(2)(b));
c) any period during which the person has failed to submit previous returns or to pay VAT shown as due on a previous return (s 20(2)(c)); and
d) any period during which Customs and Excise require the person to produce documents in support of the repayment or to provide security for the repayment and the person is arranging to provide them (s 20(2)(d)).

1.89 There is also provision under FA 1985, s 20(5), for any period to be left out of account by Customs and Excise. This will require a statutory instrument and is designed to cater for possible industrial action within the VAT Central Unit which might delay repayments.

1.90 The receipt of a repayment supplement will be disregarded for income and corporation tax purposes by virtue of FA 1986, s 53(2).

Commentary

1.91 In order to avoid paying the supplement it is not necessary for Customs and Excise to make the repayment within the 30 day period, merely to issue an instruction for the repayment to be made. Any delay between the issuing of the instruction within the Customs and Excise department and the actual date on which repayment is made does not count towards the 30 day period. It is understood that in practice Customs and Excise anticipate a maximum delay of seven days in these situations. In order that a person may check whether or not he qualifies for a supplement it is understood that Customs and Excise propose to print the date of the written instruction on the payable orders or on the advice notes where the payment is made directly into the person's bank account.

Example

A return for the quarter ending 30 June 1987 is submitted on 15 July 1987 showing a net repayment (ie excess of input tax over output tax) of £10,000. The return is received by Customs and Excise on 20 July 1987 but the written instruction to make the repayment is not issued until 10 September 1987.

As the written instruction was made later than 30 days after the receipt of the return and provided the conditions in the above paragraphs have been met, the person is entitled to a repayment supplement of £500 (ie 5% of £10,000) from Customs and Excise.

1.92 Customs and Excise have issued a leaflet explaining the repayment supplement procedure. The relevant section is reproduced in Appendix 5.

Interest (FA 1985, s 18)

1.93 From a date to be appointed by the Treasury (expected to be 1 July 1988) interest may be charged by Customs and Excise on assessments which relate to a VAT accounting period:

The 1985 legislation 1.94

a) for which either a return has been made, or an assessment has been issued (s 18(1)(a));
b) which exceeds three months and begins on the date from which the person was registered for VAT, or required to be registered (s 18)(1)(b)); or
c) at the beginning of which the person, having previously been exempted from registration, as he was making only or predominantly zero-rated supplies, failed to notify Customs and Excise of a material change in the nature of his supplies, such that he would be required to register (s 18(1)(c)).

In addition, interest may be charged:

d) if an assessment could have been made but the tax is recovered on a later return (s 18(3)); or
e) instead of recovering the tax due at b) above by way of assessment the tax is recovered on the first return (s 18(2)).

This provision will effectively provide commercial restitution to the Exchequer along the lines of that provided by the Taxes Management Act 1970, s 88, and is designed to deny the interest-free use of money overdue to the Exchequer. Even though the provision will not be effective until July 1988 Customs and Excise issued an information sheet on 1 June 1986 and this is included in Appendix 17.

1.94 Interest will be payable without any deduction of income tax (s 18(9)), at a rate to be advised by the Treasury (s 18(8)), and will run generally from the 'reckonable date' which is:

a) the due date for submission of the return for the period (s 18(7)); or
b) in the case of an assessment to recover tax which was incorrectly repaid by Customs and Excise, from seven days after Customs and Excise issued the written instruction authorising the repayment to be made (s 18(7)).

Interest will run until the tax is paid (s 18(1)–(7)). It should be noted also that the interest payable will not be an allowable deduction for corporation tax or income tax (by virtue of FA 1986, s 53(1)(b)).

Example 1

A VAT return for the period 1 January 1989 to 31 March 1989 is submitted as follows:

	£
Output tax declared	10,000
Input tax declared	5,000
Net tax declared	5,000

The return and tax are received by Customs and Excise on 30 April 1989.

On a subsequent control visit in June 1990 it is established by Customs and Excise that output tax should have been £12,000 and input tax only £4,000, and they issue an assessment on 30 June 1990 to recover the underdeclaration of £3,000. The assessment is paid on 31 July 1990.

Interest at the prescribed annual rate will be payable for the period 30 April 1989 to 31 July 1990 (ie for 15 months). The underdeclaration may also represent at least a serious misdeclaration and possibly 'civil fraud' if the person's conduct involved dishonesty for the purposes of evading VAT.

1.94 Civil penalties, interest and surcharges

Example 2

In the above example the person realises in July 1989 when he is preparing his VAT return for the period 1 April 1989 to 30 June 1989 that he has underdeclared tax of £3,000 on the previous return. He includes this as an adjustment on his June 1989 return and submits the return and tax with a covering letter explaining the adjustment on 31 July 1989.

Interest at the prescribed annual rate will be payable for the period 30 April 1989 to 31 July 1989 (ie for three months). Additionally, the covering letter explaining the adjustment should constitute full disclosure so as to avoid a serious misdeclaration penalty. This example illustrates that interest cannot be avoided on underdeclarations merely by paying the amount due prior to discovery and assessment of it by Customs and Excise.

Commentary

1.95 It is evident that from 1988 VAT returns and tax due will have to be accurately calculated and submitted by the due dates to avoid problems. For example, if a person does not charge VAT on certain supplies which he makes and in law such supplies are subject to VAT at the standard rate, he could be faced with the following situation when the point is discovered on a subsequent control visit:

a) an assessment for the arrears of tax due. As he will not have charged tax to his customers on the amounts received from them such amounts will be regarded as VAT inclusive and the arrears of VAT will effectively be paid out of the person's profits (unless he is able to recover from former customers the VAT which should have been charged);
b) an assessment for interest on the arrears of tax assessed; and
c) an assessment for a serious misdeclaration penalty of 30% of the tax if the trigger limits are exceeded, or a penalty assessment of between 50% and 100% of the tax due for 'civil fraud' (conduct involving dishonesty).

All the above elements will be included in a single notice of assessment, although the amounts relating to each item must be shown separately for checking purposes (FA 1985, s 21(4)).

Breaches of regulations (FA 1985, s 17)

1.96 The existing criminal penalties for regulatory offences, with the exception of the temporary retention of penalties for failure to render returns and failure to pay tax due, were replaced with civil penalties with effect from 25 July 1985.

1.97 The amount of the penalties, which may be collected by Customs and Excise by assessment, varies with the type and frequency of the default. Breaches of certain requirements will attract fixed penalties at a daily rate of £10, with £20 or £30 being substituted for previous offences of the same type (s 17(3)). In some cases there is an alternative daily penalty, if greater than the daily monetary rate, of one sixth, one third, or one half per cent of the tax due (s 17(5)). The amount of tax on which the percentages will be based is the tax shown as due on the return for the accounting period or, in the absence of a return, the amount assessed by the Customs and Excise as due (s 17(6)).

The 1985 legislation 1.102

Example

On a control visit Customs and Excise discover that a person has failed to maintain any proper VAT records or to retain copies of output tax invoices issued, although such records had been kept in the past. The commencement of the period of failure is established as being 1 January 1987 and the taxpayer complies with the relevant regulations with effect from 1 January 1988.

His failure to preserve records is liable to a sum of £500 (s 17(2)).

The failure to maintain any proper VAT records carries a penalty of £10 per day (no previous offences having occurred) ie 365 × 10 = £3,650 (s 17(3)(a)).

1.98 The table below sets out the main breaches and the penalties which may be applied:

Breach	Penalty
1. Failure to set up and maintain records (s 17(1)(b))	Fixed daily rate (ie £10, £20, £30)
2. Failure to preserve records (s 17(2))	£500
3. Failure to furnish information or to provide documents (s 17(1)(b))	Fixed daily rate
4. Failure to make a VAT return by the due date (s 17(5))	The greater of the fixed daily rate and the tax-geared percentage rate (ie ⅙%, ⅓% or ½%)
5. Failure to pay the tax due on a VAT return by the due date	As above at 4.
6. Failure to notify cessation of taxable supplies (s 17(1)(a))	Fixed daily rate
7. Breaches of any other regulation (s 17(1)(c))	Fixed daily rate

1.99 The provisions do not apply to any breach which occurred before 25 July 1985 and the penalties for failure to render a return or pay tax due will begin only on a date to be appointed by the Treasury (see FA 1985, s 12(8)). Also, none of the penalties apply if a person has either been convicted, or subject to a penalty for 'civil fraud' or serious misdeclaration, or subject to a default surcharge in respect of the same offence (s 17(10)).

1.100 By virtue of FA 1985, s 16(1), a person in breach of a walking possession agreement, which is used when Customs and Excise take distress action to recover VAT debts, is liable to a penalty of 50% of the tax or other amount specified in the distress warrant. This provision does not, however, apply to Scotland (s 16(5)).

1.101 The penalties do not apply if a person can satisfy Customs and Excise, or, on appeal, a VAT tribunal, that there is a 'reasonable excuse' for the breach (s 17(9) and s 16(4)).

1.102 It is understood that Customs and Excise policy in the initial stages of the new provisions will generally tend to be to issue written warnings for breaches of regulations and to set dates by which compliance must be met, imposing penalties only on the most regular and persistent offenders.

1.103 Civil penalties, interest and surcharges

1.103 Examples of regulations to which the penalties apply are reproduced in Appendix 6. By virtue of FA 1986, s 15, the provision was extended to cover breaches of Treasury orders made under the principal VAT legislation (VATA 1983) and regulations made under the ECA 1972. Examples of the Treasury orders covered are also included in Appendix 6.

Unauthorised issue of invoices (FA 1985, s 15(1)(b))

1.104 From 25 July 1985 a person who is not authorised to issue a tax invoice and who issues an invoice which purports to include VAT, is liable to a penalty of the greater of £50 and 30% of the purported tax (s 15(1)(b)). The amount shown as tax will also be recoverable by Customs and Excise under VATA 1983, Sch 7, para 6(2).

1.105 If a person can satisfy Customs and Excise or, on appeal, a VAT tribunal that he has a 'reasonable excuse' for the conduct, a penalty will not apply (s 15(4)). A person is not liable to a penalty under this provision if he is convicted of an offence or is assessed to a civil penalty for 'civil fraud' (ie tax evasion involving dishonesty) (s 15(5)).

1.106 Under FA 1985, s 15(2), an unauthorised person under this provision is anyone other than:

a) a registered taxable person;
b) a body corporate included within a VAT group registration (see VATA 1983, s 29);
c) a person carrying on the business of a deceased, bankrupt or incapacitated person;
d) an auctioneer or person selling goods under a power where goods are sold in satisfaction of a debt;
e) a person acting on behalf of the Crown.

The interaction of the penalties

1.107 In general the penalties are mutually exclusive, with the exception of interest on tax, and Customs and Excise will be able to choose which penalty to apply in any given circumstances. The order in which the penalty provisions are set out in the legislation suggests that this will depend on the amount of evidence which Customs and Excise may be able to obtain. The possible order of use may therefore be:

a) criminal penalties
b) 'civil fraud' penalties
c) serious misdeclaration penalty
d) penalty for breach of regulations

It should also be noted that by virtue of FA 1986, s 53(1), if a person is liable to a VAT penalty under FA 1985, ss 13 to 17, or interest under FA 1985, s 18, or a default surcharge under FA 1985, s 19, the payment will not be allowed as a deduction in computing any income, profits or losses for any tax purposes.

A survival checklist

1.108 The following is a checklist of considerations which may enable a person to avoid the imposition of the civil penalties, interest and surcharges introduced as a result of FA 1985.

1. Practice submitting accurate returns and tax by the due dates. If this cannot be achieved consult with Customs and Excise before the default surcharge applies. Exceptionally, Customs and Excise may allow the use of estimated figures on returns under the provisions set out in reg 61 of the VAT (General) Regulations 1985, SI 1985/886. Payments on account will also reduce the potential severity of the surcharge.
2. Review existing accounting systems to ensure that they are adequate to comply with the VAT legislation.
3. Review the VAT treatment, particularly as to liability (standard rate, zero-rate, exempt or outside the scope) of all products and services which are currently supplied. Take specialist advice on this or consult with Customs and Excise as necessary.
4. Consider carefully the liability to VAT of any new products or services offered. Ensure particularly that the VAT position is adequately covered in any proposed contracts which have been drawn up. If in doubt seek clearance in writing from Customs and Excise.
5. Do not forget to account for VAT correctly, if necessary, on any miscellaneous supplies made, eg management and other charges (especially between associated entities), second-hand asset disposals, contributions by employees for private usage of cars, canteen receipts, staff sales, etc.
6. Consider whether any exempt outputs made may be disregarded, or ignored under the de minimis regulations. If not, a person may be overclaiming input tax by not restricting input tax in accordance with VATA 1983, s 15, and the VAT (General) Regulations 1985.
7. Bring the circumstances of any underdeclarations of tax discovered to the attention of Customs and Excise immediately they are discovered and correct them on the next return. This may not necessarily avoid the imposition of interest from 1988 but may constitute full disclosure to avoid the serious misdeclaration penalty from 1988 and also remove suspicion that the error was made dishonestly with a view to evasion.
8. Consider any so-called VAT avoidance schemes with caution. Question whether they really work or might be challenged by Customs and Excise as ineffective. Do they really constitute evasion rather than legal avoidance of the tax? If in doubt seek specialist advice and, if necessary, obtain written clearance from Customs and Excise.
9. Are there any areas on which the benefit of the doubt has been given to the taxpayer which may require clarification?
10. Do any informal understandings or oral agreements thought to have been made in the past require clarification with Customs and Excise and confirmation in writing?
11. Are you aware of Customs and Excise changes of policy or practice affecting your VAT liabilities? Have the amendments to Customs and Excise public notices been considered?
12. Consider whether you are entitled to all the input tax which you are reclaiming, or less, or more, and take appropriate action to correct the position (eg petrol, business entertainment, etc).

1.108 Civil penalties, interest and surcharges

13. Educate staff and management alike to the need to consider VAT more carefully in the light of the potential penalties at stake.
14. Update staff regularly on VAT changes.
15. If unregistered for VAT, monitor closely the level of taxable turnover and register within the correct time limits.
16. In a group of companies are all the companies registered in a VAT group or separately? Check also for other entities, eg social club committees, which may constitute separate entities and may have taxable turnover in excess of the registration limits.
17. Train senior management and main board directors to discuss the VAT implications of any proposals before the proposals are implemented.
18. Confirm all oral advice given by Customs and Excise, either by telephone or on a control visit, in writing.
19. Do not be misled into regarding a control visit without adverse comment as giving a clean bill of health for periods prior to the visit. Customs and Excise may make a discovery of irregularities on a subsequent visit.
20. Arrange for at least one key person to have overall responsibility for VAT affairs and implications (a first reserve in case of illness, etc would also be a good insurance policy).
21. If an assessment is received from Customs and Excise for tax, and/or interest and/or penalties, consider whether it has been correctly based and issued within the correct time limits, or whether a 'reasonable excuse' may be claimed.
22. If a serious misdeclaration limit is triggered by an underdeclaration, review previous VAT accounting to establish whether input tax has been inadvertently underclaimed or output tax overdeclared and thereby keep the net underdeclaration below the trigger limits.
23. Consider the VAT implications of any direct tax saving schemes and vice versa. Some of these could result in the taxpayer paying more in VAT than is saved in direct tax and vice versa.
24. Ensure that all the relevant VAT records are preserved for the statutory six year period or a lesser period as agreed, in writing, with Customs and Excise.
25. As an insurance policy obtain an independent VAT review by appropriate specialists, who may question areas which have not been considered (and which may be discovered sooner or later on a control visit) or who may see certain areas in a different light. In certain cases the cost of such a review may more than pay for itself in terms of VAT savings which may be discovered or which may be planned for in future.
26. In a VAT group of companies ensure that all members of the group are complying with the VAT legislation and submitting accurate information to the representative member for completion of VAT returns (see also para **3.44**).
27. Constantly monitor and review VAT accounting systems and principles.

2 Criminal offences and penalties

The investigation of fraud to criminal standard takes time and absorbs manpower and for that reason fraud investigations are not commenced lightly.

Keith Committee 1983

2.01 Although the principal object of the 1985 legislation was to place the great majority of defaults into the newly created category of civil offences, practitioners and advisers should not lose sight of the fact that in serious cases prosecution under the criminal offence code will remain an alternative. In that respect it is important to realise precisely what criminal penalties remain with effect from FA 1985 and the modifications which have been introduced. Because many offences which may have been committed prior to enactment of FA 1985 may still arise for some years to come, it is also important to realise to what extent the offence may be subject to the previous criminal offence provisions. This section is therefore split into three parts, the first detailing the criminal code as it remains following the enactment of FA 1985, s 12, from 25 July 1985, the second considering the position prior to 25 July 1985, and the third covering procedural and other important implications such as compounding of proceedings.

THE POSITION FROM 25 JULY 1985

2.02 One of the first misconceptions frequently held is that VAT offences arise only under the VAT legislation. Analysis of the relevant legislation reveals that such offences can arise under VAT legislation, Customs and Excise legislation and even under the general criminal law.

a) Offences under VAT legislation

2.03 By virtue of VATA 1983, s 39(9), as amended, offences arising under the VAT legislation include any act or omission in respect of which a penalty is imposed. The acts or omissions and the penalties which may be imposed in respect of them are set out in VATA 1983, s 39, and FA 1985, s 10(4) (computer records), and are best illustrated in tabular form, followed by relevant explanations and comments. It will be noted that the penalties for summary conviction are expressed by reference to the 'statutory maximum' and levels of the 'standard scale'. The statutory maximum refers to the amount laid down in the Magistrates' Courts Act 1980, s 32(2) and (9). This was initially £1,000, but was increased by the Criminal Penalties Etc (Increase) Order, SI 1984/447, with effect from 1 May 1984 to £2,000. The standard scale refers to the scale of penalties set out in the Criminal Justice Act 1982, s 37(2). With effect from 1 May 1984 by virtue of the above statutory instrument, the penalties applicable under levels 1, 2, 3, 4 and 5 were respectively increased to £50, £100, £400, £1,000 and £2,000.

2.03 Criminal offences and penalties

Criminal offences and penalties

Offence	Maximum Penalty
1) Fraudulent evasion of VAT (VATA 1983, s 39(1)).	On summary conviction (ie before a magistrate): 1. A fine of the greater of 　a) the statutory maximum (ie £2,000); or 　b) three times the amount of the tax (see para **2.10** below); or 2. six months imprisonment; or 3. both 1. and 2. above. On conviction on indictment (ie trial by jury): 1. a fine of any amount; or 2. seven years imprisonment; or 3. both 1. and 2. above.
2) Use of documents which are false in a material particular (VATA 1983, s 39(2)(a)).	On summary conviction: 1. a fine of the statutory maximum (ie £2,000); or 2. six months imprisonment; or 3. both 1. and 2. above. On conviction on indictment: 1. a fine of any amount; or 2. seven years imprisonment; or 3. both 1. and 2. above.
3) Making statements which are false in a material particular (VATA 1983, s 39(2)(b)).	As at 2).
4) Conduct which must have involved the commission of an offence under 1)–3) above (VATA 1983, s 39(3)).	As at 1).
5) Receiving goods or services where the supplier evades the tax. (VATA 1983, s 39(4)).	A fine of the greater of: 　a) level 5 (ie £2,000) on the standard scale; or 　b) three times the amount of the tax.
6) Supplying goods or services without providing security (VATA 1983 s 39(5)).	A fine of level 5 (ie £2,000) on the standard scale.
7) Failure to furnish a return or pay tax shown to be due thereon within the prescribed time limits. (VATA 1983, s 39(8)).	1. A fine of level 3 (£400) on the standard scale, and 2. a fine for each day on which the failure continues, being the greater of: 　a) £10 per day, or 　b) ½% per day of the tax due or assessed to be due. *NB* See paras **2.32–2.34** below.

The position from 25 July 1985 2.08

Offence	Maximum Penalty
8) Failure to produce computer records or obstruction of a VAT officer authorised to inspect or copy such records (FA 1985, s 10(4)).	A fine of level 4 (£1,000) on the standard scale.

2.04 Before commenting on the above offences and penalties in some detail it should be noted that the main features remaining or implemented as a result of FA 1985 are as follows;

a) fraudulent evasion remains a criminal offence liable to be prosecuted through the courts (VATA 1983, s 39(1));
b) the maximum custodial sentence on indictment for such an offence has been increased from two to seven years by virtue of FA 1985, s 12(2);
c) the maximum alternative monetary penalty on summary conviction is three times the tax understated or overclaimed (VATA 1983, s 39(1));
d) input tax fraud, which could previously only be prosecuted under the Theft Acts, now becomes an offence contrary to VATA 1983 (VATA 1983, s 39(1A));
e) the issue of documents with the intent to deceive, which are false in a material particular, and knowingly or recklessly making statements, which are similarly false, also remain criminal offences (VATA 1983, s 39(2)).
f) failure to furnish a return by the due date, and failure to pay tax when due, remain criminal matters and may be prosecuted until the default surcharge is introduced on 1 October 1986 (see para **1.73**).

i) Fraudulent evasion of VAT (VATA 1983, s 39(1))

2.05 A person commits this offence and is liable to the appropriate penalties if he is knowingly concerned in either:

a) the fraudulent evasion of tax by him or any other person (s 39(1)); or
b) the taking of steps with a view to the fraudulent evasion of tax by him or any other person (s 39(1)).

2.06 Before a person can be liable under this offence it will be seen from the above that he must have acted knowingly. In other words, he must have had an intention to commit the offence (the 'mens rea'). Furthermore, on the authority of previous case decisions, in particular that of *Gaumont British Distributors Ltd v Henry* [1939] 2 KB 711, [1939] 2 All ER 808 such a state of mind must be proved by the prosecution.

2.07 It will be apparent, therefore, that a person who deliberately understates payment due to Customs and Excise for a prescribed accounting period may be liable under this provision.

2.08 Although mere failure to register for VAT ceased to be a criminal offence with effect from 25 July 1985 consequent on the repeal of the previous provision in VATA 1983, s 39(5), a person who deliberately decides not to register when he is liable and conceals the extent of his business, perhaps by

2.08 Criminal offences and penalties

failing to set up and preserve records, may be open to a charge of 'taking steps with a view to the fraudulent evasion of tax'.

2.09 By virtue of FA 1985, s 12(3), it is now specifically provided in VATA 1983, s 39(1A), that amounts overclaimed as follows may also amount to fraudulent evasion:

a) claims for payment of net input tax credits under VATA 1983, s 14(5);
b) a claim for refund of tax under the Do-It-Yourself Housebuilder's Scheme (VATA 1983, s 21);
c) a claim for refund of tax under the bad debt relief provisions (VATA 1983, s 22);
d) claims for repayment of tax under the EEC Eighth Directive Refund Scheme, to persons carrying on business in a member state other than the UK (VATA 1983, s 23).

Prior to 25 July 1985 it was necessary to prosecute such offences under the Theft Acts 1968 and 1978 (in England, Wales and Northern Ireland) or at common law (in Scotland).

2.10 In computing 'the amount of the tax' for the purposes of penalties set out in the table at para **2.03**, above, VATA 1983, s 39(1A), by virtue of an amendment introduced by FA 1985, s 12(3), indicates that the following are to be taken into account:

a) If a person's net tax position for a prescribed accounting period is such that net tax is due to Customs and Excise or net tax is due to be repaid by Customs and Excise to the person 'the amount of the tax' is the aggregate of the amount (if any) falsely claimed by way of credit for input tax and the amount (if any) by which output tax was falsely understated.
b) If the offence relates to a claim under b), c), or d), of para **2.09** above, 'the amount of the tax' will be the amount falsely claimed.

Example

Mr X, registered for VAT as a sole proprietor, calculates that his correct tax position for the VAT accounting period commencing on 1 January 1986 and ending on 31 March 1986 is as follows:

	£
Output tax	20,000
Input tax	10,000
Net tax due to C & E	10,000

Mr X deliberately decides to suppress various VAT invoices from his VAT records which results in his true output tax liability being understated by £2,000. At the same time he also deliberately decides to inflate his input tax by introducing into his VAT records certain fictitious VAT invoices. His input tax credit is thereby inflated by £3,000. He completes his VAT return for the period as follows, declaring his net tax due to Customs and Excise as:

	£
Output tax declared	18,000
Input tax declared	13,000
Net tax due to C & E	5,000

The position from 25 July 1985 2.15

For the purposes of the penalty provisions the 'amount of the tax' is the aggregate of £2,000 and £3,000, ie £5,000.

As the penalty is based on the statutory maximum (£2,000) or three times the amount of the tax (ie 3 × £5,000 = £15,000 in this example) the latter amount will represent the maximum monetary fine imposable on summary conviction.

It should be noted that if a conviction on indictment is obtained there is no statutory limit to the amount of the penalty which may be imposed.

2.11 In *R v McCarthy* [1981] STC 298, CA the defendant had been carrying on a business and making taxable supplies above the minimum compulsory registration limits, but had taken no steps to register for VAT. The Court of Appeal dismissed the appeal, rejecting the contention that the 'taking of steps' to evade tax involves the taking of positive steps.

ii) Use of false documents (VATA 1983, s 39(2)(a))

2.12 A person commits this offence if, with intent to deceive, he produces, furnishes, sends, or otherwise makes use of any document which is false in a material particular (s 39(2)(a)). Before such an offence can be committed therefore the person must not only have an intention to deceive, but also the document must be false in a material particular.

2.13 There would appear to be no definition of the phrase 'with intent to deceive' for the purpose of this offence but on the authority of Buckley J in *Re London and Globe Finance Corpn Ltd* [1903] 1 Ch 728, [1900–1903] All ER Rep 891 the generally accepted meaning is 'to induce a man to believe a thing is true which is false, and which the person practising the deceit knows or believes to be false'.

2.14 The case of *R v Tyson* (1867) LR 1 CCR 107, 37 LJMC 7 is relevant in considering whether a particular is material or not. It is concluded only that a particular may be material on the grounds that it renders something else more credible.

2.15 Five changes to VATA 1983, s 39, have been introduced by FA 1985. These are as follows:

a) The offence of using false documents with an intent to deceive is extended to include the situation where a false document is used to deceive a machine (VATA 1983, s 39(2C)), to cover the position where a false VAT return is submitted in order to obtain payment from the VAT Central Unit (FA 1985, s 12(5)).

b) The offence of using false documents with an intent to deceive is extended to include the situation where a person causes a false document to be produced, furnished or sent (FA 1985, s 12(5)).

c) A tax geared penalty is introduced as an alternative to the 'statutory maximum' for summary convictions where the document involved is a VAT return or a claim under b), c) and d), of para **2.09**, above, and a statement made knowing it to be false, or a false statement made recklessly, is contained in, or otherwise relevant to, such a VAT return or claim. The penalty is three times the input tax falsely claimed and/or the output tax falsely understated in relation to a return, or three times the amount falsely claimed (FA 1985, s 12).

2.15 Criminal offences and penalties

d) The maximum term of imprisonment on indictment is increased from two to seven years (FA 1985, s 12(2)), which, as with the term of imprisonment for fraudulent evasion of tax brings the penalty more into line with offences of comparable dishonesty charged under the Theft Acts and the Companies Act.
e) The offences detailed become arrestable offences (FA 1985, s 12(6)).

iii) Making statements which are false in a material particular (VATA 1983, s 39(2)(b))

2.16 A person commits this offence if, in furnishing any information for the purposes of VAT, he makes any statement which he knows to be false in a material particular or recklessly makes a statement which is false in a material particular (s 39(2)(b)).

2.17 The previous authorities on 'recklessness' were reviewed by Paull J in the case of *R v Grunwald and Others* [1960] 3 All ER 380, who concluded that the following three tests have to be satisfied before a statement could be held to have been made recklessly:

a) the statement had to have been made in fact;
b) it was a rash statement to make; and
c) the person who made the statement had no real basis of facts on which he could support the statement.

2.18 As regards documents which a person is required to sign under VAT legislation, the commonest of these being Form VAT 1 (Notification of Liability to be Registered) (see Appendix 7) and Form VAT 100 (VAT Returns) (see Appendix 3), it would appear that where an individual signs in good faith and unintentional errors or omissions have occurred, proceedings under this provision would only be possible if he had made the declaration which he is required to sign with a view to fraudulent evasion, or with intent to deceive, or recklessly.

iv) Conduct which must have involved the commission of an offence (VATA 1983, s 39(3))

2.19 A person commits this offence if his conduct must have involved the commission of one or more of the offences contained in VATA 1983, s 39(1) and (2), whether or not the particulars of the offence or offences are known.

2.20 In considering this offence the Keith Committee, during its examination of the use of various legislative provisions, noted that the purpose of this provision was to cover cases where it can be proved that an offence has been committed during a period spanning a number of prescribed accounting periods, but where it was not clear to what extent it was committed in any particular accounting period within the total period concerned. The Committee noted that such a case might arise where the aggregate tax evaded for the period of a year can be proved, for example, from sporadic deposits in a concealed bank account admitted to contain the proceeds of suppressed sales, but where the evasion cannot be allocated to particular quarterly tax returns. In those circumstances it can be proved that at least one of those returns must be false, since the aggregate tax declared on them is false, but not the precise extent of the evasion on each one.

2.21 The Keith Committee also noted that this offence was described in 1972, during the debate on the 1972 Finance Bill, as designed to offer benefits to both prosecution and defence in relatively serious cases of tax evasion, as an alternative (in suitable cases) to conspiracy charges, which except in Scotland must always be taken on indictment.

2.22 The contents of the HL Report, SC E, 14 June 1972, cols 836–861 indicate that the inclusion of this offence met with great resistance from the Opposition during the passage of the 1972 Finance Bill through Parliament, but was justified by the then Government as being necessary to cover the case outlined at para **2.19**, above. Thus under this provision the prosecution is not required to prove a conspiracy to evade tax, but only to prove that a VAT offence has been committed. Furthermore, the prosecution need not prove precisely when the offence took place or of what the offence consisted.

2.23 In 1972 ministerial undertakings were given that VATA 1983, s 39(3), was not aimed at relatively minor evasion by small businesses. The Keith Committee, in considering the statistics of prosecutions for 1981/82, noted that of 98 VAT fraud prosecutions during the year only 8 alleged offences within FA 1972, s 38(3) (subsequently replaced by VATA 1983, s 39(3)), and in six of those cases the VAT arrears alleged exceeded £10,000.

v) Receiving goods or services where the supplier evades VAT (VATA 1983, s 39(4))

2.24 A person commits this offence if he acquires possession of or deals with any goods, or accepts the supply of any services, having reason to believe that tax on the supply of the goods (including importation of goods) or services has been or will be evaded (s 39(4)).

Example

Mr X, an unregistered private individual employs a building contractor to carry out works of repair to his house. The contractor requests Mr X to pay for the work by 'cash' on the basis that no VAT will be added to the price. If Mr X agrees to this arrangement and believes that VAT will be evaded he is guilty of the offence covered by this provision.

2.25 In practice Customs and Excise would presumably be more interested in pursuing the building contractor rather than the recipient of the relevant supplies. The Keith Committee, in considering the 98 VAT fraud prosecutions in 1981/1982, noted that in that year there had been no prosecutions under FA 1972, s 38(4) (subsequently replaced by VATA 1983, s 39(4)). Be that as it may, it is doubtless considered worthwhile including the offence and the sufficiently high maximum penalty for their deterrent effects alone.

vi) Failure to provide security (VATA 1983, s 39(5))

2.26 Under VATA 1983, Sch 7, para 5(2), Customs and Excise are empowered, where it appears to them requisite to do so for the protection of the revenue, to require a taxable person, as a condition of his supplying goods or services under a taxable supply, to give security for the payment of any tax

2.26 Criminal offences and penalties

which is or may become due from him (s 39(5)). Thus, if Customs and Excise have reason to believe that a taxable person may not account for VAT or may be unable to pay the VAT due they may require security to cover any potential liability to VAT. The security to be given will normally be in the form of a bank guarantee.

2.27 A person becomes liable to the potential penalty if he supplies goods or services without giving security or further security in accordance with a direction made by Customs and Excise under VATA 1983, Sch 7, para 5(2). It is noted that in the year for which the Keith Committee considered prosecution statistics (1981/1982) there were no prosecutions for offences under this provision.

2.28 One of the reasons why there may not have been any prosecutions under this provision is that a person who receives a direction from the Customs and Excise to provide security may appeal to a VAT tribunal against the direction itself or the level of security required by virtue of VATA 1983, s 40(1)(n).

2.29 In recent years this facility has been used to a greater extent by businesses which have received such directions from Customs and Excise. In the majority of cases, however, the tribunals have dismissed the appeals and confirmed that the need for the level of security required by Customs and Excise was justified in the circumstances.

2.30 Typically, the appellant will have been involved in previous associated businesses which traded for a short while before being wound up owing substantial VAT arrears to Customs and Excise, which may not be recoverable. As an example, in the case of *Calmforce Ltd v Comrs C & E* LON/83/254 the company appealed against the Customs and Excise requirement for security. The company, represented by its director, asked for a reduction in the amount of the security required (£9,000). After hearing evidence as to the tax payable and outstanding under one of the previous companies with which the director had been associated, the tribunal upheld the Customs and Excise direction and dismissed the appeal.

2.31 In relatively few cases the amount of security required by the Customs and Excise has been reduced by the tribunal. In a case heard by the Cardiff VAT tribunal in 1979 (*S Evans v Comrs C & E* [1979] VATTR 194) Customs and Excise had required a scrap dealer to give security. The dealer appealed on the grounds that it was unlikely that a bank would act as security and hence the Customs and Excise action would drive him out of business. The appellant also claimed that he had arranged for an accountant to deal with his VAT returns in future. The tribunal, finding no evidence of fraud or evasion, allowed the appeal in order to give the taxable person a final opportunity to carry on his business without being required to give security.

vii) Failure to furnish a return or pay tax due within the prescribed time limits (VATA 1983, s 39(8))

2.32 Before outlining the position and related penalties it should be noted that FA 1985, s 19, provides for a default surcharge system to penalise those persistently late with their VAT returns and payments. Section 19(10) reveals that the provision will come into operation on a date to be appointed by the Treasury by statutory instrument. In a Customs and Excise Press Notice issued on 1 February 1986 Customs and Excise indicate that the target date for implementation of this provision is 1 October 1986.

2.33 FA 1985, s 12(8), indicates also that VATA 1983, s 39(8), will not apply to a failure (to render a return or pay tax due) which begins on or after a date to be appointed by the Treasury by statutory instrument: Following such date a person failing to render a VAT return or VAT payment by the due date may be liable to an automatic tax geared penalty for the failure or to a default surcharge, but not to a criminal penalty under VATA 1983, s 39.

2.34 For offences committed between 25 July 1985 and the date appointed by the Treasury under FA 1985, s 12(8), the person is liable on summary conviction to a penalty of level 3 on the standard scale (ie £400), together with a daily penalty during the period throughout which the failure continues of the greater of £10 and ½% of the tax due in respect of that period. 'Tax due' is the tax shown on the return (if furnished) or, in any other case, the tax assessed to be due by Customs and Excise. In the case of *Grice v Needs* [1979] All ER 501, Customs and Excise proceeded against two persons trading in partnership for penalties under VATA 1983, s 39(7), for failure to make returns by 31 January 1977. The information was laid before the court on 9 March 1977 and the case was heard on 18 April 1977. Fines of £25 plus daily penalties of £3 for 36 days between 31 January and 9 March 1977 only were imposed. Customs and Excise appealed, contending that the daily penalty should have continued up to 18 April, the date of the hearing. In the High Court it was held that in calculating the daily penalty the period ends with the date of the hearing if not previously terminated by the submission of returns.

b) Offences under Customs and Excise legislation

2.35 By virtue of the Customs and Excise Management Act 1979 (CEMA 1979), s 1(1), which states, inter alia, that an 'assigned matter' means 'any matter in relation to which the Commissioners are for the time being required in pursuance of any enactment to perform any duties' and VATA 1983, Sch 7, para 1(1), which states that 'the tax [ie VAT] shall be under the care and management of the Commissioners', it is apparent that VAT qualifies as an 'assigned matter' covered by the Customs and Excise Management Act 1979.

2.36 On similar lines to the VAT legislation, the general Customs and Excise legislation refers to various acts or omissions and sets out penalties which may be imposed. The omissions or acts which constitute 'offences' under the Customs and Excise legislation are:

a) bribing a Commissioner, officer or appointed or authorised person (CEMA 1979, s 15(2));
b) obstructing an officer performing various duties (CEMA 1979, s 16);
c) untrue declarations (CEMA 1979, s 167);
d) falsifying documents (CEMA 1979, s 168).

2.37 The penalties which apply to each of the offences in para 2.36 are respectively:

2.37 Criminal offences and penalties

a) On summary conviction a penalty of £1,000 with effect from 1 May 1984 (CEMA 1979, s 15(3)).
b) On summary conviction, a penalty of the prescribed sum, or up to 3 months imprisonment, or both; or on conviction on indictment, a penalty of any amount, or imprisonment up to 2 years, or both.
c) On summary conviction, a penalty of the prescribed sum, or up to 6 months imprisonment, or both; or on conviction on indictment, a penalty of any amount, or up to 2 years imprisonment, or both.
d) As at c) above.

c) Offences arising under criminal law

2.38 Examples of offences under the general criminal law which can be applied to acts or omissions in relation to VAT are:

a) Cheating the revenue (Theft Act 1968, s 32(1)(a)).
b) False accounting (Theft Act 1968, s 17).
c) Obtaining a pecuniary advantage by deception (Theft Act 1978, s 2).
d) Perjury (Perjury Act 1911, ss 1 and 5).

The penalties are as set out in the relevant legislation relating to each offence.

THE POSITION PRIOR TO 25 JULY 1985

2.39 The following table illustrates those offences which were contained in VATA 1983, s 39, together with the relevant penalties. As noted above many of these have been decriminalised and replaced by new civil penalties and those remaining after FA 1985 have generally been extended and the penalties increased.

Criminal offences and penalties under VATA 1983, s 39, prior to 25 July 1985

Offence	Penalty

1) Fraudulent evasion of VAT (VATA 1983, s 39(1))	On summary conviction (ie before a magistrate):
	1. a fine of the greater of:
	  a) the statutory maximum (ie £2,000); or
	  b) three times the amount of the tax; or
	2. six months imprisonment; or
	3. both 1. and 2. above.
	
	On conviction on indictment (ie trial by jury):
	1. a fine of any amount; or
	2. two years imprisonment; or
	3. both 1. and 2. above.

The position prior to 25 July 1985 2.39

Offence	Penalty
2) Use of documents which are false in a material particular (VATA 1983, s 39(2)(a)).	On summary conviction: 1. a fine of the statutory maximum (£2,000); or 2. six months imprisonment; or 3. both 1. and 2. above. On conviction on indictment: 1. a fine of any amount; or 2. two years imprisonment; or 3. both 1. and 2. above.
3) Making statements which are false in a material particular or recklessly making a statement which is false in a material particular (VATA 1983, s 39(2)(b)).	As at 2).
4) Conduct which must have involved the commission of an offence under 1)–3) above (VATA 1983, s 39(3)).	As at 1).
5) Receiving goods or services where the supplier evades the tax (VATA 1983, s 39(4)).	On summary conviction a fine of the greater of: a) level 5 on the standard scale (ie £2,000); or (b) three times the amount of the tax.
6) Failure to register (VATA 1983, s 39(5)(a)).	On summary conviction a fine of the greater of: a) a penalty of level 5 on the standard scale (ie £2,000); or b) three times the amount of the tax evaded by the failure.
7) Supplying goods or services in contravention of a security direction (VATA 1983, s 39(5)(b).	As at 6).
8) Unauthorised issue of invoices (VATA 1983, s 39(6)).	On summary conviction a fine of the greater of: a) a penalty of level 5 on the standard scale (ie £2,000); or b) three times the amount so shown.
9) Failure to keep records or furnish information and produce documents (VATA 1983, s 39(7)).	On summary conviction a fine of level 3 on the standard scale (ie £400), together with a penalty of £10 for each day on which the failure continued.

2.39 Criminal offences and penalties

Offence	Penalty
10) Failure to furnish a return or pay tax shown to be due thereon within the prescribed time limit. (VATA 1983, s 39(8)).	On summary conviction a fine of level 3 (ie (£400), on the standard scale together with a penalty of the greater of: a) £10 for each day on which the failure continues; and b) an amount equal to ½% of the tax due in respect of that period for each day on which the failure continues.

2.40 Of those offences which were decriminalised with effect from 25 July 1985 the following implications are worthy of note in relation to the period prior to 25 July 1985.

i) Failure to register or de-register (VATA 1983, s 39(5)(a))

2.41 Offences under this provision comprised:

a) failure to notify a liability to registration within the prescribed time limit (VATA 1983, s 39(5));
b) failure to notify, within the prescribed time limit, that taxable supplies had ceased (VATA 1983, s 39(5));
c) failure to notify any material change in the nature of supplies made or any material alteration in the ratio of taxable supplies made (VATA 1983, s 39(5)).

ii) Unauthorised issue of VAT invoices (VATA 1983, s 39(6))

2.42 Those persons listed under VATA 1983, s 39(6), as authorised to issue VAT invoices comprised:

a) a person registered under VATA 1983;
b) a body corporate included in a VAT group registration election under VATA 1983, s 29;
c) a person carrying on a business of a deceased, bankrupt or incapacitated person;
d) a person who sells another person's goods in satisfaction of a debt under a power vested in him;
e) a person acting on behalf of the Crown.

The offence will generally have been committed by a person who was liable to registration, but who had not registered and yet was issuing what purported to be VAT invoices.

iii) failure to keep records (VATA 1983, s 39(7))

2.43 Offences under this provision comprised:

a) failure to keep such records as Customs and Excise may have required (VATA 1983, s 39(7));
b) failure to preserve such records for such periods as Customs and Excise may have required (VATA 1983, s 39(7)).

iv) Failure to furnish information or produce documents (VATA 1983, s 39(7))

2.44 Offences under this provision comprised:

a) failure to furnish information within such time and in such form as Customs and Excise may have required (VATA 1983, s 39(7));
b) failure to produce, or cause to be produced, documents for inspection upon demand by a VAT officer (VATA 1983, s 39(7));
c) failure to permit a VAT officer to take copies of such documents, to make extracts from them, or to remove them (VATA 1983, s 39(7)).

v) Failure to comply with regulations (VATA 1983, s 39(7))

2.45 Included within this provision was failure to comply with any requirement imposed under 'any regulations or rules' made under VATA 1983. Theoretically, contraventions of this provision will have been committed if a registered person, for example:

a) failed to include all the details required to be shown on a VAT invoice (VAT (General) Regulations 1985, reg 13);
b) failed to issue a VAT invoice when requested (VAT (General) Regulations 1985, reg 12);
c) failed to notify a change of registration details (VAT (General) Regulations 1985, reg 4(3));
d) failed to make a provisional partial exemption restriction of input tax (VAT (General) Regulations 1985, reg 30).

This list could be extended to cover over 30 minor breaches of the various regulations and rules made under VATA 1983. In practice, it appears that Customs and Excise chose only to prosecute the most persistent defaulters and this was one of the reasons why the Keith Committee recommended decriminalisation of most of the regulatory contraventions.

2.46 The following table shows the classification by offence provision of the 98 offences of VAT fraud alleged in prosecutions during 1981/1982 as examined by the Keith Committee. Reference to (1), (2), etc are to sub-sections of FA 1972, s 38, which applied at the time.

Theft Acts and common law	13
Fraudulent evasion (1) with or without false returns (2)	38
Fraudulent evasion (3) with or without false returns (2)	8
False returns (2)(a)	13
False information (2)(b)	4
Failure to notify (5) and fraudulent evasion (1)	8
Failure to notify (5) and unauthorised issue of VAT invoices (6)	3
Failure to notify (5) only	10
Unauthorised issue of VAT invoices (6) only	1
TOTAL	98

Source: Table 39 of the report by the Committee on enforcement powers of the Revenue Departments.

2.47 Criminal offences and penalties

2.47 In the Customs and Excise annual report for the year ended 31 March 1985 it was revealed that during the year 176 prosecutions were carried out, of which 169 resulted in convictions. The courts imposed terms of imprisonment totalling 142 years, ranging between 1½ months and 4½ years. The number of cases compounded under CEMA 1979, s 152, was 445. The total sum of court fines, costs and compounded settlements amounted to £4,083,391 with tax arrears amounting to £23,349,124.

2.48 One of the major fraud problems which has faced Customs and Excise in recent years has been the dramatic increase in 'gold frauds'. With the increase in the price of gold, certain persons defrauded the Treasury of substantial sums of VAT by the practice of purchasing legal tender gold coins such as South African Krugerrands and the Canadian Maple Leaf, melting them down into gold bars, selling such bullion plus VAT, but pocketing the VAT instead of paying it over to Customs and Excise.

2.49 In the Customs and Excise report for the year ended 31 March 1985 it was stated that the special VAT accounting procedure introduced in November 1983 for transactions in gold between VAT registered traders, together with sustained surveillance and investigations of suspect dealers, restricted the scope for VAT frauds associated with gold, but that the problem had by no means been eliminated. During the year a number of cases which had been investigated in earlier years came to trial. Altogether 39 persons were convicted in respect of evasion totalling £14,410,000. They were sentenced to terms of imprisonment ranging from three months to six years, were fined a total of £318,000 and were made the subject of Criminal Bankruptcy Orders totalling £14,178,000. However, as the report indicates there is considerable doubt whether much of this £14 million or so will be realised. Although there is no direct evidence, say Customs and Excise, all the indications are that the major portion of the fraudulent profits are in the safe haven of inaccessible foreign bank accounts. A further 35 persons had been committed at the end of the year alleging the evasion of a total of £33,834,000. Also during the year a further 13 persons were charged with gold frauds involving the alleged evasion of £5,910,000 VAT.

COMPOUNDING

2.50 Under CEMA 1979, s 152(1), Customs and Excise may, as they see fit, 'stay, sist, or compound any proceedings for any offence under the Customs and Excise Acts.' This power is applicable to VAT by virtue of VATA 1983, s 39(9). It is not, however, applicable to offences in relation to VAT at common law, or under the Theft Acts. The latter offences therefore had to be prosecuted even if the use of compounding would have been considered appropriate were the offence under the Customs and Excise Acts. With the reclassification of VAT 1983, s 39, following amendment by FA 1985, s 12, Customs and Excise will, with effect from 25 July 1985, be able to compound proceedings for input tax fraud offences which could previously only be prosecuted under the Theft Acts.

Compounding 2.55

2.51 The power to compound criminal proceedings, ie settle out of court, has been used extensively for VAT enforcement purposes. A compounding settlement is effectively an agreement between Customs and Excise and the taxpayer and the terms of the agreement are embodied in writing. An example of a typical letter of offer and agreement was considered by the Keith Committee and this is reproduced in Appendix 8.

Example

Mr X deliberately suppresses certain VAT invoices from his VAT records and subsequently deliberately understates his output tax liability by a substantial amount. This is discovered on a routine VAT control visit. A VAT investigation of his affairs follows and Mr X admits to his actions and co-operates in the investigation.

Customs and Excise decide that the evidence obtained is sufficient to bring about a successful prosecution in the courts, but on being approached by Mr X's advisers they make a formal offer to compound proceedings on payment of a certain sum of money. Mr X agrees to this and the matter is settled without any recourse to court proceedings.

2.52 The above example describes a typical, albeit over-simplified, illustration of the stages which may follow discovery of alleged VAT fraud by Customs and Excise. A number of important considerations arise in relation to the practice of compounding criminal offences and these are set out in the following paragraphs.

2.53 Settlement takes the form of a contractual agreement freely entered into by the alleged offender, often on his own initiative, under which Customs and Excise, in return for the payment of an agreed sum of money, undertake not to pursue proceedings. Both parties are thereby saved the expense of a court hearing, the pressures on the courts are eased and the alleged offender is spared both the stress of a court appearance and a possibility of a criminal conviction.

2.54 A common misconception is that Customs and Excise resort to compounding when the evidence is considered too weak to support a prosecution in the courts. In evidence before the Keith Committee it was revealed that this is incorrect. Compounded settlements are offered only where Customs and Excise are satisfied that they have evidence to support their case to a criminal standard of proof (beyond reasonable doubt) if the offer is refused. Also in evidence it was revealed that no pressure one way or the other is exercised on the accused person and it is entirely a matter for his judgement as to whether he accepts the offer or decides to let the case go to court in the hope of securing an acquittal.

2.55 The practice of compounding was considered in the case of *Patel v Spencer* [1976] 1 WLR 1268 in which the judge commented:

'It is clearly in the public interest that . . . a discretion [to compound] has been conferred on the Commissioners, because once an offence has been detected it is salutary that it should be dealt with there and then if the Commissioners think it should be, without recourse to the courts. In no way can the Exchequer be the loser; there is payment of the compounded penalty . . . and the costs of court proceedings are avoided.'

2.56 Criminal offences and penalties

2.56 One area in which Customs and Excise have never offered to compound proceedings was in the area of 'regulatory' matters, the commonest of these being the prosecution of persons for failure to render VAT returns by the due date and of persons for failure to pay VAT due by the due date. Such proceedings were always taken summarily, and never compounded and in the past represented two thirds of all Customs and Excise prosecutions. Following the decriminalisation of these regulatory offences Customs and Excise will be empowered to impose civil penalties as described and commented on in Ch 1.

2.57 The following extract, from a table contained in the Keith Committee Report reveals that for the year 1980/1981 compounded settlements were offered in 528 out of 628 cases involving VAT offences.

VAT offence cases 1980–1981

VAT offences	Compounded	Prosecuted summarily	Prosecuted on on indictment
Failure to furnish returns	—	3,767(a)	—
Failure to pay tax	—	739(b)	—
Failure to keep or produce records	—	17(c)	—
Fraudulent evasion and other offences	528	62(d)	38

Notes:
(a) Includes 11 no convictions
(b) Includes 1 no conviction
(c) All successful
(d) Includes 3 no convictions

Source: Table 38 Report by the Committee on enforcement powers of Revenue Departments.

2.58 In evidence to the Keith Committee Customs and Excise indicated that they valued highly their prerogative to decide when prosecution is necessary and their powers to take alternative forms of action without prosecution. Further, in order to ensure that the merits of each case are considered efficiently and objectively Customs and Excise revealed that within their department the investigation of the case (by trained VAT investigation staff), the decision whether to prosecute and the conduct of the prosecution are all kept as separate functions.

2.59 Customs and Excise indicated that their policy was to compound whenever appropriate and the decision whether to prosecute or to offer such a settlement is taken on the merits of each case. The general factors taken into consideration are the gravity of the offence and the best interests of law enforcement and revenue. In some cases prosecution may be considered appropriate where the amount of tax evaded is considerable and heavy penalties on conviction might be expected. The need to deter other potential offenders by means of publicity of serious VAT fraud prosecutions is also a significant consideration. However, even in serious cases if an offender was

Compounding 2.63

dangerously ill so that the threat of proceedings might provoke a serious crisis in his health, or if there are other compassionate grounds, Customs and Excise have indicated that a decision to compound might still be reached.

2.60 Practitioners should note that in contrast to Inland Revenue practice, where a taxpayer is invited to make an offer in settlement at a level calculated to be appropriate for the inspector to recommend acceptance to the Board, the Customs and Excise practice is to calculate the sum which they find acceptable and themselves offer to compound proceedings in payment of the stated sum. In practice, the initiative to compound often comes from the taxpayer or his representative, although the formal offer to compound always comes from Customs and Excise.

Level of settlement

2.61 In evidence to the Keith Committee, Customs and Excise indicated that the starting point for penalties is generally equal to 100% of the tax evaded. Although Customs and Excise will normally claim that the terms for compounding are not negotiable, a taxpayer, or his professional advisers, should nevertheless put forward any mitigating factors and mention the degree of co-operation (if any) in the investigation, which will no doubt influence the final amount of the settlement offered. Indeed the Keith Committee noted that over the years the average penalty in compounded cases has fluctuated between 50–60% of the tax evaded. Practitioners should be aware that the settlement penalty is payable in addition to the arrears of tax which gave rise to the offence. Depending on the circumstances of each case it may also be possible to negotiate payment of the settlement penalty and the arrears over a period of time rather than as a single immediate payment, but Customs and Excise normally stipulate that if the taxpayer defaults in paying the agreed instalments they may well re-institute court proceedings.

2.62 An important point to note is that where proceedings have been commenced by the laying of an information in the courts it is rare for proceedings to be subsequently compounded. Experience shows that compounding will still be allowed in appropriate cases even though an information has been laid and the relevant summonses issued to the alleged offenders.

Publicity

2.63 A compounded settlement normally attracts no publicity for the taxpayer making it and this undoubtedly encourages most offenders to settle rather than to proceed to public trial with the potential adverse publicity and a possible criminal conviction. In certain serious cases, where a substantial sum may be offered but where Customs and Excise would prefer to prosecute for the deterrent publicity, a condition of agreeing to the settlement may be that the names of those making the settlement be published. Although the case referred to as 'Operation Nudger' which involved alleged evasion of VAT from amusement machines, was settled in this manner (see Customs and Excise Press Notice dated 19 August 1981) it is understood that such a condition is likely to be extremely rare. One of the Keith Committee's recommendations (Recommendation 38) was that the names of those making

2.63 Criminal offences and penalties

settlements in fraud cases should indeed be published in order that public perception of the scale of detected VAT fraud and the general deterrent effect should not be limited. During the consultation exercise following the Keith Committee's report this recommendation was almost universally opposed and the Government concluded in the paper 'The Collection of VAT' issued in November 1984 that were it to be adopted it would probably result in a large number of alleged offenders rejecting settlement offers or appealing to VAT tribunals and it was decided therefore not to implement it.

2.64 On occasions there has been criticism of an alleged Customs and Excise practice of issuing assessments in investigation cases before they have decided that there is sufficient evidence for a prosecution. If the taxpayer appeals to a VAT tribunal against the assessment Customs and Excise's policy is alleged to be to apply for the appeal to be stood over (ie postponed) pending the outcome of possible criminal proceedings. It has been claimed that if the taxpayer accepts a compound settlement there has been no opportunity for the VAT tribunal to review the assessment. In response to such criticism Customs and Excise have stated that where a taxpayer appeals to a VAT tribunal against an assessment when criminal proceedings are pending they would indeed normally apply for the appeal to be stood over until the prosecution had been heard. In their view this ensures that there is no rehearsal of the criminal evidence and consequent prejudice to a fair trial. They have stated further that if an alleged offender considers that the element within the offer to compound which represents assessed arrears of tax is excessive the person may seek a departmental review of it and he should put forward any further evidence which he can produce in support of his contentions that the amounts have been over-assessed. As explained in ch 4 such departmental reviews are normally conducted by a senior ranking officer who has not been involved in the case previously. As a final resort and if agreement still cannot be reached, the taxpayer has the option of rejecting the offer and subsequently challenging the assessed arrears in the court proceedings.

PROCEDURAL MATTERS

2.65 A number of procedural matters relating to criminal offences and the conduct of the proceedings should be borne in mind by practitioners and these are dealt with briefly in the following paragraphs.

Time limit

2.66 By virtue of CEMA 1979, s 147(1), and VATA 1983, s 39(9), proceedings for an offence committed prior to 25 July 1985 must be commenced not later than three years from the date when the offence is alleged to have been committed. The Keith Committee noted that if VAT offences were discovered years after the date of their commission, particularly given the increasingly extended intervals between regular control visits and when a repeated fraud is detected, often only the most recent part of the arrears of tax identified is in time for penalty proceedings or settlement under the three year rule. However, in practice it would appear that Customs and Excise have on occasions circumvented this in cases of serious fraud where there was a provable conspiracy. In such cases, Customs and Excise practice was to charge with the common law conspiracy to defraud Customs and Excise contrary to the Criminal Law Act 1977, s 1(1), rather than with conspiracy to commit an offence of fraudulent evasion of VAT. For common law offences it should be noted that there is no upper limit on the amount of any fine or terms of imprisonment and no time limit for commencing proceedings. The Customs and Excise choice for this route, where possible, is obvious. A further alternative, which Customs and Excise has also used in the past, is the common law offence of cheating the Revenue or conspiracy to do so, under the provisions of the Theft Act 1968, s 32(1)(a), again with unlimited penalties and no time limit for commencing proceedings.

Service of summons

2.67 A summons may be served on the person to whom it is addressed and it is deemed to have been duly served if it is delivered to him personally or left at his last known place of abode or business. In the case of a body corporate it may be left at the registered or principal office (CEMA 1979, s 146).

Institution of proceedings

2.68 Where an offence is alleged to have been committed jointly by two or more persons Customs and Excise may, by virtue of CEMA 1979, s 150(1), proceed against each person jointly and severally as they see fit. Under CEMA 1979, s 171(4), where an offence is alleged to have been committed by a body corporate with the connivance or consent of one or more of its officers, or was attributable to his or their neglect, Customs and Excise may take proceedings against both the officer(s) and the body corporate itself.

Onus and standard of proof

2.69 In proceedings for criminal offences tried summarily or on indictment the onus of proof is generally on Customs and Excise and the standard of proof is that guilt has to be proved beyond reasonable doubt (see ch 9 of the report by the Keith Committee, Cmnd 882).

Evidence

2.70 It should be noted that following the introduction of the new civil penalty for 'civil fraud' from 25 July 1985 statements and documents are not inadmissible in criminal proceedings merely because a person's attention has been drawn to the fact that Customs and Excise may assess an amount due by way of civil penalty instead of instituting criminal proceedings, or that their practice is to be influenced by a full confession of any dishonest conduct and the provision of full facilities for investigation, or that a civil penalty for

2.70 Criminal offences and penalties

dishonest conduct may be reduced based on the degree of co-operation given (FA 1985, s 13(5) and (6)). This effectively allows Customs and Excise to proceed on the basis of eventually assessing for a civil penalty, but with the right to change their minds at a later stage if they then prefer to take the criminal proceedings route (see para **1.35**).

2.71 A photograph of any document furnished to Customs and Excise for the purposes of VAT, and certified as such, is admissible in any criminal proceedings to the same extent as the document itself by virtue of VATA 1983, Sch 7, para 11(2). Furthermore, a copy of any document forming part of a taxpayer's records is admissible as evidence in criminal proceedings to the same extent as the records themselves by virtue of VATA 1983, Sch 7, para 7(3).

3 VAT control methods

The purpose of VAT control visits, which are made by appointment, is to make selective checks on the records and accounts of businesses and so to ensure that they are calculating and paying the correct amount of VAT on all of their taxable activities. For newly registered traders the visit also provides an early opportunity to resolve any practical problems which arise in the first year.

73 HC Official Report (6th series) written answers col *200*

INTRODUCTION

3.01 VAT is largely collected by reference to VAT returns (see Appendix 3) submitted by VAT registered businesses. As the table at para **3.02** below reveals, experience has shown that a significant proportion of returns and assessments (in the absence of returns) underdeclare tax due to Customs and Excise, whilst a small proportion give rise to overdeclarations of tax. Not surprisingly, therefore, significant resources and effort are devoted by Customs and Excise to verifying the tax liabilities of VAT registered businesses. This is carried out by various control procedures, some within the VAT Central Unit and local VAT offices, but mainly through a system of inspection referred to as 'control visits'.

3.02 The following table, compiled from a study of recent Customs and Excise annual reports, reveals that there has been a rising trend in the value of underdeclared tax discovered on control visits. Whether this has arisen because Customs and Excise control techniques are becoming more sophisticated or their officers better trained, or because businesses are unable or unwilling to concentrate sufficient resources to making accurate returns is difficult to gauge.

Years ended 31 March

	1980	*1981*	*1982*	*1983*	*1984*	*1985*
Number of control visits ('000s)	368.0	257.0[1]	358.0	335.0	350.0	370.0
Underdeclarations (£m)	84.0	145.8[2]	159.7	270.0	320.0	409.0
Overdeclarations (£m)	4.2	9.5	5.1	24.0	6.0	6.0

Notes

[1] Reductions in number of visits was due to Civil Service industrial action.
[2] The steep increase in underdeclarations may have been partly due to the fact that the previous standard rate (8%) and higher rate (12½%) of VAT were amalgamated into an increased standard rate of 15% from June 1979 and control visits during 1980/1981 were checking VAT returns submitted partly since the date of increase. In terms of numbers of underdeclarations discovered there appears to have been only a slight increase between 1980 and 1981.

3.03 Arguments have occasionally been advanced by various organisations that although the value of underdeclarations may appear significantly high, the amount of net tax involved is considerably less. This, it is argued, is due to the fact that much of the output tax underdeclared and subsequently assessed

3.03 VAT control methods

represents input tax, which may be deducted in the hands of other registered businesses. In reply to these contentions Customs and Excise indicated that they carried out an internal exercise to establish the amount of 'sticking' tax (ie tax which cannot be passed on to another registered trader and therefore 'sticks' with the person assessed). According to Customs the results revealed that less than 10% of underdeclarations related to non-sticking tax, whereas over 90% of underdeclarations provided a net gain to the revenue. The sources of the net gain are said to arise mainly from underdeclared retail takings, certain overclaims of input tax, computational errors and failure to account for invoiced output tax in the non-retail area.

3.04 Whatever the true net loss of revenue to the Exchequer in recent years there is no doubt that both the Keith Committee and the Government were concerned as to the number and frequency of underdeclarations discovered on control visits by VAT officers. The introduction of the 'serious misdeclaration' penalty, based on purely objective, arithmetic trigger limits of underdeclared or overclaimed tax (see ch 1) is undoubtedly designed to improve the accuracy of figures declared on VAT returns, thus improving the overall collection of VAT revenue.

3.05 From 1985 the importance of a correct understanding of Customs and Excise VAT control methods and, in particular what may happen on a control visit, cannot be over-emphasised. As outlined in ch 1, an error in VAT accounting which is allowed to continue may be discovered by a VAT officer on a control visit and may result in not only the arrears of tax having to be paid to Customs and Excise, but interest (from 1988) and possible penalties in addition.

ORGANISATION AND STRUCTURE OF CUSTOMS AND EXCISE

Board of Commissioners

3.06 The Customs and Excise is a department within the central Government administration and comes under the supervision of the Treasury. Day to day administration of the department is laid to a Board of Commissioners (VATA 1983, Sch 7, para 1(1)). Two members of this Board, which is headed by a Chairman, have direct responsibility for the administration and control of VAT in the UK, one being responsible for the collection and control of VAT and the other for VAT administration policy. These two Commissioners are often referred to as 'Directors', being in charge, respectively of the VAT Administration Directorate based mainly in London, and the VAT Control Directorate, based mainly at the VAT Central Unit in Southend on Sea, Essex. It should be noted that correspondence from Customs and Excise local and headquarters VAT offices will frequently refer to 'the Commissioners of Customs and Excise' or merely 'the Commissioners'. These terms are synonymous with 'Customs and Excise', as used mainly throughout this book, and should not be confused with either the General or Special Commissioners in direct tax appeal matters. The table below provides an illustration of the structure:

Introduction 3.09

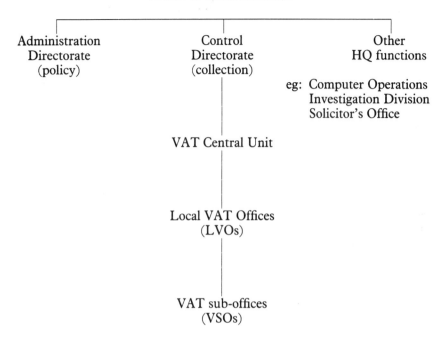

VAT Administration Directorate

3.07 The Commissioner through his administration staff (or directorate) is responsible for the policy aspects of VAT. The Directorate is sub-divided into divisions, each of which is controlled by an Assistant Secretary. These divisions deal with specific areas of policy such as the liability to VAT of specific supplies, retail schemes, partial exemption, international services, property and construction, etc. The Directorate is based in London, principally within the main Customs and Excise London Headquarters at Kings Beam House, Mark Lane, EC3.

VAT Control Directorate

3.08 The Commissioner responsible for the control of the VAT system is concerned mainly with the collection of the tax. The Directorate is split into divisions, each of which has responsibility for part of the process of monitoring the effective collection of VAT. The nature of this Directorate's work is such that it contains large numbers of clerical and some executive staff, dealing with the issue and receipt of returns and remittances. This Directorate is based mainly in Southend where the department's main computer installation is sited, and also in Bootle.

Other Directorates

3.09 Within the overall Customs and Excise organisation there are several specialist units within other directorates which provide advice and services to

3.09   VAT control methods

the VAT Directorates. These are principally the Solicitor's Office, who advise on legal matters and represent the department at VAT Tribunal hearings, the Investigation Division, which undertakes the investigation of large scale VAT fraud and the Computer Services Division which operates the VAT computers.

Local VAT offices

3.10 Local administration of the VAT system, in what is commonly referred to within Customs and Excise as 'the outfield', is undertaken by officers of Customs and Excise who control and monitor the application of VAT in a specific geographic area. They are frequently referred to incorrectly as 'VAT inspectors', their correct title being 'VAT officers'. The following table illustrates the structure of a typical local VAT office (LVO):

LVO structure

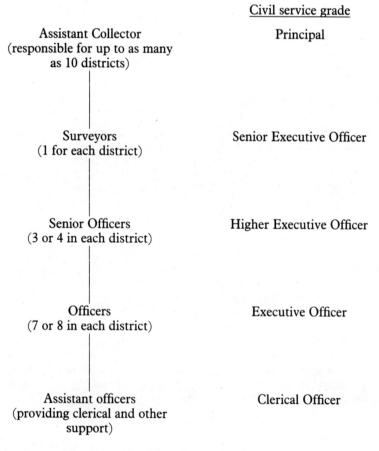

3.11 The local VAT offices have direct contact with VAT registered businesses and are responsible for ensuring that they comply with VAT law.

Each office is controlled by an Assistant Collector and normally comprises approximately 100 staff. Each office is split into districts, each district being under the control of a Surveyor and comprising approximately 4 staff at Senior Officer level. One or two of these districts are responsible for specialist functions such as local VAT enforcement (eg obtaining outstanding tax), local VAT registration procedures and records, or general enquiries. The other districts are concerned mainly with making routine control visits to registered businesses within their districts and dealing with any irregularities discovered.

VAT sub-offices (VSOs)

3.12 Due to the geographic size of some LVOs' territories it is necessary in various parts of the country to station a sub-office from which visiting staff can operate nearer to their area of work. Local business records are retained at the local VAT office and all specialist functions relating to the businesses visited from such sub-offices are performed at the local VAT office. It is understood that for economy and other reasons certain VSOs may be phased out.

CONTROL TECHNIQUES

VAT registrations

3.13 Nationally there is a VAT registration population of approximately 1.4 million. A local VAT office may be responsible for as many as 20,000 such registrations within its area, ranging from small retail outlets to large multinational and international corporations. They may be sole proprietorships, partnerships, limited companies, membership clubs or local or public authorities. They may be organised as groups, divisions or branches and be located in one place or in many places throughout the UK. Registrations are classified into over 300 different trade categories. Businesses involved mainly in exempt activities such as banking and insurance may also be registered because of subsidiary taxable activities. The aim of local Customs control is to visit all businesses within the local VAT office area over a period of time, although greater resources are devoted to those businesses or trade categories where large amounts of revenue may be at risk or where certain businesses have proved to be unreliable as regards VAT compliance in the past.

VAT control objectives

3.14 The control objectives may be summarised as being:

a) to enforce compliance with the VAT legislation;
b) to maximise the collection of VAT (both outstanding tax and additional tax underdeclared);
c) to protect the budgeted yield from the tax by preventive and deterrent effects; and
d) to maintain public acceptability of the tax.

3.15 VAT control methods

The role of the VAT Central Unit

3.15 VAT returns submitted to the VAT Central Unit are subjected to computer processing. Initially, a small proportion of all returns received have to be sent back to the registered person for correction or amendment, usually due to obvious arithmetical mistakes. Arithmetically correct returns are subject to a range of 'credibility' checks, which might include for example:

a) Withholding repayments of VAT claimed on a return if the size of the repayment exceeds certain parameters or if the person normally pays VAT to Customs and Excise rather than reclaims. The temporary inhibit on repayment will enable enquiries to be made either direct of the person or via the local VAT office. Often a sudden claim for repayment of VAT may arise if the person has purchased expensive new capital equipment, the VAT on which, together with other regular input tax, exceeds normal output tax;

b) The return details may be compared with the person's previous return details and those of other persons in a similar trade category. If the return details are within certain parameters verification will normally be left until the next control visit by the local VAT office staff. If, however, the details appear incredible in the light of the various parameters the return may be referred to the local VAT office for early verification by visiting staff.

Types of local visit

3.16 The legal basis for local control visits may be found within VATA 1983, Sch 7. In the early days of VAT the power of VAT officers to enter premises was generally seized upon by the popular media and one or two cases of alleged forced entry into premises, even into private homes, were responsible for the 'VAT man' image and subsequent open hostility between certain VAT officers and certain VAT registered businesses. When the original proposed powers of Customs and Excise in relation to VAT were being debated during the course of the 1972 Finance Bill the then Financial Secretary to the Treasury defended the proposed power against the vociferous challenges being made against it by interested parties as follows (HC Official Report, SC E, 12 June 1972, col 814):

'VAT, like purchase tax but unlike the taxes, including corporation tax, administered by the Inland Revenue, is essentially a tax on individual transactions which works on an invoice basis, rather than on accounts basis. It is therefore essential for officers to be able to enter premises to check returns against the original business documents relating to the transactions and also to check on stocks.'

Fortunately, after 13 years of VAT, relations between registered businesses, their professional advisers and Customs and Excise are reasonably good, although there are still many who harbour deep seated reservations and suspicions with regard to certain VAT control techniques.

3.17 Essentially there have been five different types of local visit used by Customs and Excise to date:

a) Educational/registration visit

In the early years of VAT, Customs and Excise's policy was to visit all newly registered persons. The purpose of such visits was:

Control techniques 3.17

i)   to educate the newly registered person on record requirements;
ii) to ensure that the person's accounting system was satisfactory for VAT purposes;
iii) to ensure that the person appreciated the VAT implications likely to affect his business; and
iv   to establish the likely frequency required for future visits.

However, due to staff cut-backs in recent years only a small percentage of newly registered persons are likely to be visited in this way. Customs and Excise consequently rely on the person and his accountant to ensure that the records are adequate for VAT compliance purposes. When the first control visit takes place the VAT officer will cover the above points and satisfy himself that the registration was effected properly and at the correct time. Given the new penalty provisions introduced by the Finance Act 1985 the person could suffer severe financial penalties if the notification was prepared incorrectly or he was late in registering. If a visit is not made by Customs and Excise and the newly registered person or his professional adviser are not clear on the VAT requirements in any area a visit should be requested, or if this is not possible, they should visit the local VAT office enquiry section themselves to discuss and resolve the problem. In this way any areas on which the person and Customs and Excise disagree will be dealt with and, it is to be hoped, resolved satisfactorily at an early stage.

b) Control visits

Although all visits by Customs and Excise VAT officers fall to be classified as 'control visits' the generally accepted meaning of a 'control visit' is the routine visit carried out periodically by a VAT officer to a registered person, in order to verify the accuracy of the VAT returns which have been submitted. The implications arising from such visits are discussed below at paras **3.20 – 3.45**.

c) Miscellaneous visits

These may be made at certain intervals for a variety of reasons including:
i)   verification of a particular repayment claim on a VAT return;
ii) verification of a VAT return which has failed certain checks by the VAT central computer;
iii) verification of a particular transaction in a chain of transactions between several registered persons;
iv) resolution of particular accounting or liability questions which have not been resolved by telephone or correspondence.

d) Distraint visits

Where a registered person fails to submit a VAT return and normally pays net tax to Customs and Excise the VAT computer will produce an assessment. If the return and tax are still not submitted the trader will be contacted by the local VAT office enforcement district and encouraged to submit the missing returns and tax. If this action is ignored, or a special arrangement with Customs and Excise is not reached, a VAT officer may visit the registered trader with a bailiff to distrain on any physical assets of the business under the provisions of regs 65 and 66 of the VAT (General) Regulations 1985, SI 1985/886. Initially a 'walking possession order' will

3.17 VAT control methods

normally be placed on the assets and if the tax is still not paid the assets will be removed and sold at auction in settlement of the tax debts.

e) Investigation visits

These may be instituted when serious fraud or evasion of tax, or other serious irregularities are suspected. The implications arising from these visits are discussed below at para **3.46**ff.

VAT staff

3.18 There are generally three grades of officers directly concerned with control visits:

a) Officers (Executive Officers)

This grade will tend to visit small to medium sized registrations. He or she may be a young person who has only recently taken up his or her first job after obtaining A levels or a university degree. They are not qualified accountants, although they will have received basic training on the operation of VAT and how to deal with accounts. At the other extreme the officer may be very experienced, particularly in control visits to certain categories of traders and will generally have a good general grasp of accounting systems.

b) Senior Officers (Higher Executive Officers)

This grade will tend to visit the larger, more complex businesses, where they may be faced with complex accounting systems and organisations managed by professionally qualified persons. In addition, they will also be responsible for the management of one or more officers.

c) Surveyors (Senior Executive Officers)

This grade manages districts within the local VAT office. Although a Surveyor will examine some of the visit reports of the officers and senior officers in his district, he may also accompany both types of officer on occasions in a supervisory role. In addition, these officers are responsible for management of the staff in the district and the smooth running of the control visiting programme.

VAT staff training

3.19 As mentioned above VAT officers are not qualified accountants, although they do have some training in basic bookkeeping. Certain VAT control staff may have attended more advanced accounting courses, giving them greater knowledge of accounting and auditing techniques. Such training is particularly relevant in the control of large payers of VAT as discussed at para **3.41**. As more businesses turn to computerised accounting Customs and Excise have also developed computer audit training for certain staff in local VAT offices. In general, a VAT officer will have spent some time on basic departmental training courses on VAT and basic bookkeeping and will have accompanied other more experienced officers on control visits, before he undertakes visits on his own. He will then develop his own knowledge and experience from such visits in consultation with his fellow officers and superiors. Additionally, certain officers who may be very experienced in controlling a particular trade category may run seminars within local VAT offices or prepare guidelines for use by other less experienced officers.

Control visits

Purpose

3.20 Control visits enable the officer:

a) to examine the VAT accounting records set up by a registered person;
b) to verify the returns which have been submitted, by checking all available evidence that tax has been accounted for accurately;
c) to ensure that the registered person understands VAT and is applying it correctly; and
d) to consider how frequently the business may need to be visited.

Frequency of visits

3.21 Once registered for VAT a person will be visited from time to time. The first visit will normally be within two years of being registered. The frequency of visits will depend on a number of factors including:

a) the size of turnover;
b) the complexity of the business activities;
c) the complexity of the accounting records;
d) the past compliance history of the business; and
e) unexpected variations in VAT return declarations.

Information available to the officer before the visit

3.22 The business will have been selected for a visit mainly by the VAT Central Unit who will supply the local VAT officer with the details of VAT returns submitted since the last visit, or since registration if it is to be the first visit. Additionally, the officer will have considered the permanent file on the business within the local VAT office and in particular the report made by the previous visiting officer.

Appointments

3.23 Although Customs and Excise are empowered to enter premises to make a VAT visit at any reasonable time by virtue of VATA 1983, Sch 7, para 10(1), as a matter of courtesy the officer will normally telephone or write to arrange a visit during normal office hours.

Duration of visit

3.24 For a small service business concerned with relatively simple and infrequent invoicing a visit may only take a few hours; for a large or complex organisation visits may last two or three days on a fairly frequent basis.

3.25 VAT control methods

The visiting officer

3.25 As explained previously the small businesses will tend to be visited by a VAT officer, the more complex businesses by senior officers. Occasionally, an officer or senior officer may be accompanied by his superior to assist him in the visit or in a supervisory capacity.

Place of production of the records

3.26 Customs and Excise will normally want to visit the principal place of business in order to examine and discuss the business activities and the records at the same time. If the records are not normally kept at the principal place of business the officer may require them to be produced there for the visit or he may agree to inspect them elsewhere. In law, however, he is able to insist on the records being produced at the principal place of business by virtue of VATA 1983, Sch 7, para 8(2)(b).

Conduct of the visit

3.27 When the officer first arrives he will need to talk to the person in charge of the VAT affairs of the business. After that, as long as there is a responsible person who can answer any questions and provide any further information required, he will normally be able to continue his work, even if the person in charge is not there. At the end of the visit the officer may want to discuss the outcome with the person in charge.

3.28 The officer will want to look at the way the business operates, including how goods received and supplies made are recorded and how the business deals with cash coming in and going out of the business. He will also want to inspect the premises to establish whether the VAT returns have been accurately representing the level and nature of the business activities.

3.29 The main duties of a VAT officer on a routine control visit will be:

a) to carry out certain basic checks relating to the registration details and any changes in circumstances since the last visit;
b) to check the VAT accounts and subsidiary records in order to verify the VAT returns submitted. If VAT returns have not been submitted and assessments issued from the VAT Central Unit have been paid he will check the correct liability and issue an additional assessment for any further tax due;
c) to review the business generally to satisfy himself as to the credibility of the VAT returns in light of both the business being carried on and the annual accounts prepared for the business;
d) to carry out more in-depth checks if he is not satisfied with the credibility of the VAT returns;
e) to inspect the premises;
f) to be alert for signs of evasion of tax or other fraud;
g) to discuss any apparent discrepancies or irregularities with the person in charge of the VAT affairs;
h) to assess underdeclarations of tax (and interest and penalties as applicable) and correct over-declarations of tax;

Control techniques 3.32

i) to resolve any points of difficulty with the person in charge of the VAT affairs.

Discovery of errors

3.30 The officer will normally try to settle everything during the visit, but more information may be needed before a particular point can be resolved. If the person in charge of the VAT affairs cannot readily explain apparent discrepancies he may need to research the problem and explain or provide relevant information as soon as possible. In certain cases the officer may want to examine the VAT records at the VAT office. If this happens the VAT officer should be asked to provide a receipt for the records which are taken away. Customs and Excise normal policy is to return them within one month, but if they are required for the immediate carrying on of the business the officer must normally arrange for suitable copies to be given within a reasonable time under the rules laid down in VATA 1983, Sch 7, para 10B. If an apparent discrepancy cannot be resolved the officer may either issue an assessment during the visit or following any period of time he has allowed for a satisfactory explanation to be provided. If an assessment has been issued but satisfactory information is subsequently produced the assessment will be waived.

Disputes

3.31 If a person disagrees with an officer's assessment or decision it should be discussed with the officer. If agreement still cannot be reached a person may write to the local VAT office asking Customs and Excise to reconsider the assessment/decision. Clearly, the reasons why the person disagrees should be stated and any further information or facts which the person or his professional advisers consider may not have been taken into account should also be provided. The person may also be able to appeal to the independent VAT tribunals. The subject of disputes and appeals is dealt with in more detail in ch 4.

Reliance on control visits

3.32 Unfortunately, satisfactory visits are no guarantee against subsequent assessments covering periods prior to the visit, although it may be possible to exert moral pressure on Customs and Excise to restrict any future assessments to periods following the visit if Customs and Excise had access to all the relevant facts at the time of the visit but did not technically 'misdirect' the person. In their own leaflet entitled 'Visits by VAT officers' (700/26/85) Customs and Excise state:

'It is your responsibility to account for VAT correctly. The officer will not normally have time to look at all of your records or every aspect of your business. So you can't assume that you are accounting for VAT correctly on everything just because he doesn't find any errors. It is in your own interest to ask the officer about anything you are unsure of.'

In order to avoid such situations the contents of para **3.39**, below, may be of assistance. Many registered persons have incorrectly assumed that a VAT control visit without adverse comment is effectively giving them a 'clean bill of health'. Certain organisations have in the past called for a system of inspection

3.32 VAT control methods

certificates to be given to taxpayers following a control visit. These, it has been proposed, would absolve taxpayers from liability for any simple, genuine error, which was not detected, but would not cover them if they had been fraudulent. Although such a proposal sounds attractive, it is doubted whether it will ever be agreed in practice, as it would be virtually impossible, so the Treasury and Customs and Excise would argue, to establish whether an error discovered on a subsequent control visit had been made genuinely and also whether the VAT officer had been given all the relevant information at the time to enable him to have discovered it previously.

Advice given by a control officer

3.33 During a routine control visit VAT officers will normally raise questions about the person's VAT affairs. The following should, however, be borne in mind:

a) It is in the person's own interest to obtain subsequent written confirmation of any oral advice given by the officer, to ensure that no midunderstanding has occurred and to protect the taxpayer from a future assessment (and possibly interest and penalties) under Customs and Excise 'misdirection' policy if the advice given was incorrect in law.

b) The officer cannot be expected to be an encyclopaedia on the most esoteric aspects of VAT. He may have to seek the advice of his local office or the VAT Administration Directorate if the point involves a question of complex liability.

c) Even if he is able to answer he may be providing his opinion only, rather than stating the correct legal position. VAT officers do not always appear to have been provided with or absorbed details of the many frequent changes in both the legislation and Customs and Excise headquarters policy on certain aspects. They may neither be particularly aware of recent VAT tribunal or High Court decisions which have overruled Customs and Excise former views. It is as well, therefore, to check the up-to-date position with specialist VAT advisers.

Dealing with questions from a control officer

3.34 The VAT officer's questions will be aimed at establishing the accuracy of the VAT returns which have been submitted. Care should be taken that only correct answers are given and that no inaccurate off-the-cuff remarks are made, for example, regarding pricing policies, as it may subsequently prove difficult to persuade the VAT officer that this was an inaccuracy. If a person genuinely cannot answer a question he should say so and take steps to obtain the necessary information to provide an accurate reply to the question.

3.35 Many VAT officers are young and inexperienced and may be as wary of the businessman as he is of them. It should be remembered that VAT officers are not trained bookkeepers and tact and a reasonable attitude by both the registered person and his professional adviser may do much to ease relationships and overcome what may appear to be an overbearing attitude on the part of the VAT officer. Certain VAT officers may occasionally appear to be officious. If it is thought that an officer has exceeded his authority or acted improperly he should be asked for an explanation. If the person is still not satisfied and wishes to complain the most direct way is to write to the Assistant Collector in charge of the local VAT office, who will investigate the complaint and advise the person of the result.

The role of the accountant or professional adviser

3.36 A person may wish to have his accountant present if he is best able to explain the business records and accounting systems. Normally, the accountant will not need to be present on a routine control visit, but if a dispute arises or the VAT officer wishes to return for a further visit to discuss apparent discrepancies it would be as well to arrange for the accountant or VAT adviser to be present. Additionally, the accountant and VAT adviser should be able to review the accounting systems and technical aspects on a more regular basis than Customs and Excise, in order to prevent disputes from arising in the first place.

Annual accounts

3.37 Where such accounts or other financial statements exist VAT officers will normally require to see them as a cross-check on declarations made on VAT returns. By virtue of VATA 1983, Sch 7, para 8(4), a VAT officer is entitled to ask for production of any profit and loss account and balance sheet relating to the business. For example, they will compare net sales as declared on VAT returns with the turnover as shown in the annual accounts and also compare inputs with expenditure items shown in the accounts.

Action by the control officer following the visit

3.38 The VAT officer's action following the visit will include:

a) the writing of a report on those areas checked and the irregularities dealt with. This will remain in the permanent folder for the business and it will be used by the next visiting officer, which may not necessarily be the same officer;
b) corresponding with the person if further information is required or to resolve or confirm a point which was put to him during the visit;
c) the setting of an assignment value on the VAT central computer. This is based on a system of points for complexity of business, size of turnover, complexity of accounts, previous compliance history (including a judgement made on the latest visit) and likely revenue risk. The assignment value will then influence the frequency and scope of future control action and visits;
d) normally only in serious cases of suspected fraud Customs and Excise may use their powers under FA 1972, s 127, to disclose information to the Inland Revenue. It should be noted that a control or investigation visit may be instituted as a result of disclosure of information from the Inland Revenue to Customs and Excise;
e) the issuing of an assessment to collect underdeclared tax, if this was not done on the visit. In evidence to the Keith Committee Customs and Excise

3.38 VAT control methods

revealed the reasons for underdeclarations of VAT assessed in the year ended 31 March 1982 as follows:

Reason for underdeclaration	Percentage of total underdeclarations (by value)
Inadequate central assessment	15
Output tax errors	
a) Understatement of sales	12
b) VAT liability error	6
c) Error in VAT retail scheme, other than understatement of sales	4
d) Other output tax errors	30
	52
Input tax errors	33
Total	100

Action by the registered person following the visit

3.39 It is recommended that the person's action should include:

a) making a record of the points discussed and any areas covered by the VAT officer during the visit. This may prove invaluable in any future dispute with Customs and Excise;

b) confirming in writing with Customs and Excise any oral advice given by the officer or any 'understandings' which the officer is thought to have agreed to;

c) implementing directly any directions given by the officer to correct inadequacies in the VAT records or VAT accounting systems; the person would be well advised to discuss these with his professional adviser to consider the correctness or otherwise of the direction and its effect on other tax or accounting implications.

d) discuss any dispute arising on an assessment issued with a VAT specialist immediately to establish whether the assessment is correctly based, both arithmetically and in law, and whether it has been issued within the legal time limits. If it is not possible to do this immediately the person should consider lodging a protective appeal with a VAT tribunal and request a VAT specialist to consider and assist in negotiating with Customs and Excise, as it may be possible to settle the matter without recourse to a VAT tribunal hearing.

Control of large payers

3.40 In the Customs and Excise Annual Report for the year ended 31 March 1985, it was reported:

'In recent years, particular attention had been paid to the time taken for those traders with the greatest VAT liability to pay the tax which was due. These efforts were more than repaid by a reduction in payment delays and in the amount of tax outstanding. In the light of the recommendation made by the Keith Committee that the department should take further steps to enhance the VAT enforcement regime, a number of traders

Control techniques 3.44

whose VAT performance is regularly monitored in this way was increased during the year to a total of just under 8,000. Delays in 1984/85 were reduced by an amount equivalent to a once and for all saving of £23 million with a corresponding and continuing saving in interest charges.'

3.41 It is also well known that Customs and Excise have been centralising responsibility for VAT collection for large companies. This includes greater co-ordination to ensure that large groups of companies with locations in different parts of the country are controlled effectively. In particular certain large companies have been given searching questionnaires calling for, inter alia,

a) details of company hierarchy to establish who is ultimately controlling it;
b) details of subsidiary and associated companies;
c) details of business activities; and
d) volumes of accounting data.

3.42 It would appear that certain VAT officers have been issuing these questionnaires to companies for completion and return to the VAT office, others may not formally have given the questionnaire to the company, but may have asked sufficient questions direct of company personnel to have completed it themselves. The information so obtained is then used to co-ordinate control efforts to best effect.

3.43 It has also been noticed in recent years that if a major accounting or liability error is established in a company within a certain trade sector, this has tended to be reported to Customs and Excise headquarters and an instruction is subsequently issued to all other VAT offices to target and check the point in other known companies in that business sector. This is where the specialist VAT adviser should be of assistance, as he may be generally aware of areas which have been challenged by Customs and Excise and will include these in any review of accounting systems and VAT compliance which he is requested to undertake.

3.44 One of the many problems facing large organisations, particularly VAT groups of companies, which may include companies engaged in many different activities and locations, is that the person who ultimately signs the VAT returns for the group cannot be totally certain that all outputs and inputs have been accounted for correctly. This may be particularly the case in rapidly expanding groups of companies where busy and inexperienced staff may have responsibility for compiling the figures for inclusion in the group's returns. Often a member of staff within a remote subsidiary may not appreciate that the information being supplied to its parent company is being included in the group's VAT returns. In certain cases where major underdeclarations of VAT have subsequently been discovered the person signing the VAT return is put under some pressure by Customs and Excise to explain how and why the errors occurred. Faced with this possibility certain large organisations have already altered their VAT reporting systems to ensure that:

a) each subsidiary within the VAT group submits the VAT information to the parent in writing and confirms that the information is both correct and complete;
b) only experienced staff are engaged in compiling VAT figures and are given the necessary resources to keep up to date and comply with VAT legislation;

3.44 VAT control methods

c) circulars explaining the relevant VAT rules are distributed to all personnel within appropriate accounting sections of the organisation;
d) one person is given overall responsibility for VAT matters and is authorised to consult professional VAT advisers as a matter of course to ensure that the group's VAT interests are protected as far as possible;
e) VAT is included on all checklists in the decision making process of running the group.

3.45 With the introduction of the serious financial, often tax-geared, penalties in FA 1985 the implications have been taken seriously by many large organisations, but undoubtedly many may still be completing VAT group returns without any close control or monitoring of the figures being included in them. The potential loss of revenue from such lack of control has been a source of concern to Customs and Excise in the past and is one of the reasons why they have been deploying more resources in recent years to the control of large payers.

Investigation techniques

Credibility checks

3.46 During the course of control or investigation visits it is common for Customs and Excise officers to use one or more of the following methods to establish the credibility or otherwise of the figures declared on VAT returns:

a) examining sample batches of invoices to ensure that the correct rate of tax has been charged;
b) checking that such invoices have been correctly posted to the VAT records;
c) checking that the page totals have been calculated correctly;
d) checking calculations of retail schemes or used goods schemes to ensure that correct calculations have been carried out;
e) examining supplementary evidence such as orders, sales correspondence, bank statements, annual accounts;
f) in the absence of sufficiently detailed records, particularly with small businesses, comparing annual drawings with estimated expenditure to maintain the life style of a person;
g) test purchasing followed by subsequent checks to establish whether all sales have been declared;
h) observing point of retail sales to determine whether all cash sales have been rung up correctly in the till;
i) comparing VAT returns with annual accounts, which may reveal that a cash difference has been added to sales in the profit and loss account to overcome a discrepancy between recorded cash expenditure and recorded cash income. Customs and Excise may infer from this that the outputs have been underdeclared on VAT returns and this may form the basis of a subsequent assessment;
j) comparing pricing policies against recorded purchases to estimate 'assumed takings' followed by comparison of such figures with declarations on VAT returns. This method of credibility check is often referred to as a 'mark-up exercise', as it checks the amount by which a person marks-up purchased items to arriving at selling prices. Provided the person has correctly recorded all purchases this often provides an indication of whether sales have

been correctly recorded or suppressed. Such methods have, however, been the source of frequent disputes between registered persons and Customs and Excise and many VAT tribunals have had to apply subjective judgements to the evidence presented by both parties. The subject of the strengths and weaknesses inherent in 'mark-up exercises' are discussed further in paras **3.50ff**;

k) making calculations based on the relationship which may exist between an element of expenditure within the business and the level of sales such as:
i) the relationship between petrol purchased and the takings declared by a taxi driver compared with a test period of takings and fare-paying mileage;
ii) the relationship between numbers of meals served in restaurants and the average price of meals declared;
iii) the relationship between gallons of water consumed in a launderette and the average number of gallons used for each wash.

VAT tribunal decisions

3.47 Any business which is challenged by Customs and Excise as to the apparent incorrectness of recorded takings following such exercises would be well advised to consider the weaknesses which have been highlighted in certain of the many case decisions reached by VAT tribunals over the years, as it may be easy to overlook the reason underlying an apparent low recorded takings level when compared with the Customs and Excise evidence. For example, in the case of *Gloucester Old Boys Rugby Football Social Club v Comrs C & E* CAR/77/133, 100 Taxation 148 Customs and Excise had issued an assessment related to an apparent shortfall in the recorded bar takings. Before the tribunal it was revealed that the bar was staffed by its own members on a voluntary basis and that such staff were allowed free drinks. Although the tribunal considered that the Club was run inefficiently, with a distinct lack of control, it made the important observation:

'VAT is a tax on supplies made by a taxable person and not a tax on inefficiency.'

The question which should be addressed therefore in each case is not whether a person is capable of achieving a certain level of takings but whether, taking into account all relevant factors, the person could have been expected to achieve such a level. If all relevant factors are not taken into consideration the assessment may well prove to be excessive. With the addition of interest and penalties it is anticipated that many more appeals will be made to VAT tribunals in attempts to dislodge the underlying assessment and hence the interest and penalties.

Treatment of underdeclarations

3.48 Underdeclarations of VAT through a mistake or carelessness and smaller suspected frauds will normally be dealt with simply by assessment and recovery of the tax underdeclared, with the addition of interest (from 1988) or civil penalties as applicable. If fraud is suspected it may initially be investigated by the control officer, who may continue the investigation either himself or jointly with a specialist investigator. In more serious frauds the matter may be dealt with solely by the specialist investigation staff. The following table from the Keith Committee Report reveals the number of cases subject to criminal investigation during 1981/82 and whether they were investigated by the local VAT office staff, the Collection Investigation Unit (a regional area of the Investigation Division), or the Headquarters Investigation Division staff.

3.48 VAT *control methods*

VAT fraud cases concluded in 1981/82

	Investigated by			
	LVO	CIU	ID	TOTAL
Prosecution	36	47	15	98
Compounded settlement	235	229	29	493
Arrears of tax only	153	211	60	424
TOTAL	424	487	104	1,015

3.49 The powers of Customs and Excise investigation staff to obtain information and documents and other related implications are discussed in ch 5.

'Mark-up' exercises

3.50 Most retail businesses will tend to have a definite policy with regard to achievement of profit margins. For example, a publican may follow the prices charged by managed houses operated by his brewer; a restaurateur may add a fixed mark-up to the basic cost of his ingredients; an electrical retailer may charge the manufacturer's recommended price, and a newsagent will charge the cover price for newspapers and magazines. Given that there is such a relationship between purchases and sales a retailer's purchase records may be used as a starting point for calculating assumed sales for a given period.

Assumed sales

3.51 Assumed sales represent the cost of goods sold during the period plus the calculated gross profits thereon, with allowance being made for various factors which may have reduced gross profit. The following formula illustrates the calculation required:

$$A = (C-S) \times (1 + M) - R$$

where

A = the value of assumed sales;
B = the cost of goods purchased for resale during the period;
S = cost of 'stock losses' during the period arising from pilferage, wastage, gifts, etc;
M = average mark-up applied by the trader;
R = value of reductions in selling prices which may have been made during the period, eg by way of discounts or bargain sales.

Cost of purchases

3.52 The cost of goods purchased for resale during the period is normally ascertainable from the person's purchase records. It may be necessary to classify purchases between various categories of goods in order to obtain a weighted average mark-up.

3.53 To ensure strict accuracy purchases must be adjusted for opening and closing stocks. In the past VAT tribunals have refused to make any allowance

Control techniques 3.56

for stock adjustments unless the increase or decrease in stocks can be quantified (see *Arora v Comrs C & E* [1976] VATTR 53).

Stock losses

3.54 Stock losses can occur even in the best run businesses and can arise due to a number of factors. For example, goods can be stolen, be consumed in the business in one way or another, be short delivered, or become unsaleable due to damage. It is therefore necessary to estimate the cost of stock losses during the relevant test period in order to avoid inflating the value of assumed sales.

Pilferage

3.55 Losses arising from pilferage are to a certain extent based on estimates, although it will normally be necessary to produce some evidence that pilferage is taking place, or is likely to have taken place, before Customs and Excise will agree to an allowance being made. In the case of *Kazemi v Comrs C & E* EDN/77/40, 101 Taxation 497, an allowance had been given where a restaurateur produced statistics demonstrating that takings remained constant, but purchases were reduced, after staff had been dismissed. In certain other cases VAT tribunals have inferred from the facts that pilferage must have occurred and have accordingly given an allowance. For example, this has occurred where staff supervision was lax (see *Scanlon v Comrs C & E* LON/76/59, 99 Taxation 22), where the layout of the shop premises was conducive to theft (see *Kazemi v Comrs C & E* (cited above)), where the volume of business made it difficult to prevent shoplifting (see *Cole Bros of Malden Ltd v Comrs C & E* LON/82/136, unreported), where contractors were left unsupervised (see *Lovat Road Hotel v Comrs C & E* MAN/75/26, 95 Taxation 359) and where no one was responsible for stock control (see *Scanlon v Comrs C & E* cited above). In general, no allowance will be given unless some evidence that pilferage has taken place is produced (see *Goode v Comrs C & E* LON/77/118, 100 Taxation 148). The tribunal must also be satisfied that it is stock, and not cash, that has been stolen. It is necessary to account to Customs and Excise, for the tax element of stolen takings because a supply has taken place, but if stock has been lost or destroyed no supply can have taken place. VATA 1983, Sch 7, para 4(6), places the burden of proof for showing that the loss relates to stock on the trader (see *Furby v Comrs C & E* MAN/77/316, 102 Taxation 104). For example, in *Benton v Commissioners of Customs and Excise* [1975] VATTR 138, it was held that output tax is due once a supply has been made, and it therefore makes no difference whether the takings are stolen or used to pay cash expenses; output tax was still accountable to Customs and Excise on the value of the supply.

Wastage

3.56 Details of waste must normally be estimated from the available information, eg from detailed records kept during a test period. The wastage in public houses has been examined in depth in a number of cases (see, for example, *Roocroft v Comrs C & E* MAN/76/110, 98 Taxation 266). It is also evident that wastage can vary considerably from day to day in certain trades (see *Brown v Comrs C & E* LON/80/109, unreported, in relation to a wholesale florist).

3.57 VAT control methods

Consumption of trading stock in the business

3.57 Trading stock may also be consumed by the business, eg a petrol station will use business petrol in the business vehicles (see *Ross v Comrs C & E* MAN/76/98, unreported). It is therefore vital that such factors are taken into account when a mark-up computation prepared by Customs and Excise is being checked. However, it should be noted that by virtue of VATA 1983, Sch 2, para 5, stock used for non-business purposes is generally a supply for tax purposes valued at cost (see *Lam v Comrs C & E* LON/82/183, unreported).

Weighted mark-up

3.58 The normal gross profit measurement used by accountants expresses gross profit as a percentage of sale price. A mark-up is the gross profit of an item expressed as a percentage of cost of purchases, which is more relevant to mark-up computations as the basis of calculation is the value of purchases. Mark-ups are calculated by reference to the selling price of goods (found on price tickets, exhibited price lists, etc). It is vital that cost and selling prices are converted to the same tax basis, ie VAT inclusive or VAT exclusive or the calculation will be distorted. Gross profit is the difference between the two prices.

3.59 Most retailers sell more than one category of goods and often different mark-ups are applied to each category. In calculating a retailer's average weighted mark-up it is necessary to avoid giving undue emphasis to the mark-up of any particular category. The weight applied to the various mark-ups for each category is usually the cost of the respective purchases of each category of goods made during the test period.

3.60 In the past VAT tribunals have rejected assessments based on arithmetical rather than weighted averages (see *Parson's Nose v Comrs C & E* LON/77/263, 101 Taxation 61). They have also rejected assessments based on inadequate, and unrepresentative or inaccurate samples (see *Serendipity v Comrs C & E* MAN/77/284, 101 Taxation 374) and assessments based on a sample from one category where two or more categories of goods were sold (see *Richardson v Comrs of C & E* CAR/79/133, unreported).

Calculation of understated output tax

3.61 An assessment will normally be prepared by Customs and Excise on the basis of an understatement of tax representing the difference between output tax calculated from assumed sales and output tax which has been declared on the retailer's VAT returns.

3.62 It will be realised that the method of calculation will vary according to the nature of the business and the records available. The following example illustrates the computation of tax underdeclared by a retail business selling two categories of goods, both of which are taxable at the standard rate.

Example

The following is obtained from the business records, price lists, test checks, and information given by the retailer. The average reduction in sale prices due

Control techniques 3.66

to discounts and sales is 10%. Output tax declared by the trader during the period is £10,195. The rate of tax in force during the period was 15%.

	Cost of purchases (VAT excl)	Average class mark-up	Stock losses
Category A	£50,000	10%	2%
Category B	£25,000	30%	1%

Assumed sales calculation:

	£
Category A: 98% of £50,000 × 1.10 =	53,900
Category B: 99% of £25,000 × 1.30 =	32,175
	86,075
Less: discount and sales reduction (10% of £86,075)	8,607
VAT excl value of assumed sales	£77,468

Understated output tax:

	£
Output tax due: £77,468 @ 15%	11,620
Deduct: output tax declared	10,195
Assessment:	£1,425

Changes in tax rate

3.63 If the rate of tax has changed during the period it will be necessary to calculate assumed sales for periods before and after the change in order to obtain the correct tax due at each rate.

Effect of inflation

3.64 In the case of *Nolan v Comrs C & E* [1977] VATTR 219, the VAT tribunal considered that some allowance should have been made for inflation. As stock was turned over by the trader once a year, and no adjustment was made to retail prices once fixed, outputs for an accounting period had been incorrectly fixed by reference to inputs of an accounting period which had ended 12 months previously. The tribunal considered that 'the assessment should have been made in that way in the first instance'.

Variations in mark-up

3.65 Although a mark-up is calculated at a given point in time, it is then applied to a period which may consist of several prescribed VAT accounting periods. However, the pattern of trade may have changed during the period: for example, the mix of goods sold may have changed, or the pricing policy may have been altered, and in each case this may affect the average weighted mark-up during the period.

3.66 VAT tribunals have in the past been critical when mark-ups calculated from a short test period have been applied to an earlier period for assessment purposes, particularly when the earlier period is of long duration (see *Rawcliffe*

3.66 VAT control methods

v Comrs C & E MAN/82/134, 103 Taxation 306). However, the practice was approved by the Divisional Court (see *Van Boeckel v Comrs C & E* [1981] STC 290, [1981] 2 All ER 505) and, as one tribunal Chairman pointed out, the duration or timing of any test period will always be open to criticism on one ground or another (see *Lees Chinese Food Centre v Comrs C & E* MAN/82/134). Thus, a retailer who believes that the period selected by the VAT officer is unrepresentative, is at liberty to prepare alternative calculations based on a period which he considers to be more representative. The VAT tribunal then has the task of adjudicating between the rival calculations.

3.67 If a retailer believes that the average weighted mark-up has varied during the assessment period he must generally be able to produce some evidence which indicates his belief (see *Shaw's Bar v Comrs C & E* EDN/76/28, 100 Taxation 363). Unless selling prices in force at specific times during the assessment period have been retained this may prove difficult if not impossible. In the case of *Stockman v Comrs C & E* LON/79/347, 106 Taxation 458 the Chairman commented:

'The tribunal wishes to emphasise the importance of traders keeping records of price changes particularly in the licensed trade. Price lists are normally displayed in bars and it seems to us to be a comparatively simple matter to retain a price list when it is substituted by a new one. The old list can be put in a file that could be quite small even if several such changes took place in a year.'

Mark-up calculations inappropriate

3.68 If a business is conducted without any regard to specific mark-ups, an assessment prepared on this basis would be inappropriate. For example in the case of *Green v Comrs C & E* LON/76/207, 99 Taxation 380 a supplier of linen goods fixed sale prices by reference to what the market would bear, and the mark-up varied on similar goods according to whether they were sold wholesale or retail, and how favourable the terms of purchase had been. The accounting records were accepted in preference to Customs and Excise mark-up calculations.

The views of VAT tribunals

3.69 Despite the problems associated with their preparation, VAT tribunals have consistently accepted the mark-up calculation as a proper method of assessing output tax due (see *T Brookes and Co Limited v Comrs C & E* MAN/77/236, 101 Taxation 184). The justification for their use was aptly summed up in the case of *Robinson v Comrs C & E* MAN/76/48, 102 Taxation 152:

'The method of obtaining a hypothetical mark-up over a test period in order that it may then be applied to the whole period of assessment is one which has frequently been approved by these Tribunals. Of necessity there are imponderable factors inherent in its adoption, and in every case its use requires careful scrutiny by a tribunal: it is apparent that a trifling error in the calculations for a comparatively short test period will be magnified many times in the longer period of an assessment and that it cannot replace precision in the books and accounts. But where the books and accounts are themselves suspect it is difficult to see what other method can be employed for the purposes of an assessment.'

4 Disputes and appeals

The love of justice is, in most men, nothing more than the fear of suffering injustice.

La Rochefoucauld

4.01 Inevitably, with a tax which is collected essentially on a self-assessment basis, with VAT registered persons responsible for declaring and paying over their net VAT liabilities to the authorities, disputes arise as a matter of course. As explained in ch 3 Customs and Excise employ a variety of methods to test the credibility or otherwise of VAT return declarations, with a view to ensuring that the collection of VAT revenue for the Exchequer is maximised. On the other hand, the person registered for VAT does not want to declare or pay over more tax than that properly due under the VAT legislation. This chapter considers how practitioners may best deal with dispute situations and considers the role of the VAT tribunals in resolving such disputes.

4.02 Before considering appeals to VAT tribunals, which many businesses and their advisers still regard as a last resort in any dispute with Customs and Excise, it is worth examining some of the stages which often precede a formal appeal to a VAT tribunal.

How disputes arise in practice

4.03 Assuming that a person registers for VAT correctly and submits his returns and tax by the due dates most disputes will emanate from a control visit by a VAT officer to check the accuracy of the declarations made on VAT returns. In the absence of any returns having been submitted the VAT officer will be checking or assessing what he regards as the correct tax payable, in order to issue additional assessments, if necessary, over and above any assessments issued automatically from the VAT Central Unit. In certain instances it may be established that the person has declared and paid too much tax, in which case the person will receive a welcome repayment of tax. In most instances, however, where a VAT officer alleges errors in VAT returns these will involve alleged underdeclarations and possible underpayments of VAT. The VAT officer may allege:

a) that output tax has been underdeclared;
b) that input tax has been overclaimed; or
c) that a combination of a) and b) has occurred,

resulting in too little tax having been declared or paid over to Customs and Excise.

4.04 The errors may have occurred due to:

a) an error in the VAT accounting system;
b) a technical error in applying the VAT legislation; or
c) action on an incorrect ruling given by a VAT officer during a previous visit.

4.05 Disputes and appeals

Accounting errors

4.05 In the case of errors in the accounting system it will be necessary to establish from the VAT officer the precise nature of the apparent error and either satisfy the officer of the correctness of the system or correct the system immediately to ensure that VAT is accounted for correctly in future. In the latter case an assessment to collect arrears of VAT which may have arisen before the error was discovered can be anticipated.

Technical errors

4.06 In the case of technical errors the person will need to satisfy himself that Customs and Excise interpretation of the VAT legislation is correct. This in itself can prove to be an enormous hurdle for the businessman who may not be able to gauge whether the Customs and Excise view is correct in law. In many cases therefore the businessman will turn to his professional adviser who will need to be well versed in the technicalities of the relevant legislation, which includes not only UK VAT law, but also European Community Directives on VAT. The professional adviser should also be experienced in dealing with disputes on similar points in practice.

4.07 In the case of 'misdirection' by a VAT officer during a previous visit or during other previous contact with Customs and Excise it will be necessary to satisfy the latter that the person has in fact been 'misdirected' in the past. If this is accepted Customs and Excise administrative practice, but not the law, may protect the person from an unwelcome assessment, interest and penalties. This practice is considered in detail at paras **4.15** and **4.16**, below.

Dealing with dispute situations

4.08 In 1983 a meeting was held between representatives of Customs and Excise and the accountancy bodies at which a number of procedural matters relating to the resolving of disputes between traders and Customs and Excise were considered. These included difficulties which might arise in resolving disputes locally and the consequent need for adequate liaison between officers of Customs and Excise and accountants. Following the meeting Customs and Excise wrote to the accountancy bodies and an extract from the letter is set out below:

'Local discussions

Our general position is that we seek to resolve disputes by local discussion so far as this is possible. It is firm policy that local staff should explore all reasonable possibilities of informal settlements in a dispute with a taxpayer prior to issuing an assessment. A special section in Public Notice No 700 sets out the options available to taxpayers who disagree with a decision made by the department. Our instructions issued to officers clearly state that any schedules containing facts, figures and calculations relating to assessments must be made available to the taxpayer or to their representatives. It has always been our intention that any dialogue should continue beyond the lodgement of a formal appeal, so that any new facts which may come to light can be properly considered. It is certainly not our intention that negotiations should proceed only via our Solicitor's Office once an appeal has been lodged and this is not, in our experience, a view that is commonly held amongst appellants. Once the Solicitor's Office is involved in a case which is the subject of appeal to a tribunal, before any agreement is reached by

Disputes and appeals 4.10

informal means the local staff may naturally find it desirable to check with the solicitor concerned: but this does not stop local settlement taking place.

Whilst we instruct our staff to have this continuing dialogue with taxpayers and their representatives, there will undoubtedly be occasions where further discussions will not be profitable, and ultimately each side to the discussion must judge the stage at which such contacts are unlikely to reach agreement. In such circumstances, it may sometimes be said, often with the benefit of hindsight, that certain cases might have been settled informally if more time for discussion had been allowed, or if they had been referred to a higher level. We are always prepared to look at such cases on an individual basis, with a view to learning lessons from them. But to put the matter into perspective, only 30% of the appeals lodged with the tribunals actually come to a hearing, which together with the large number of disputed assessments which are settled without lodgement of appeal gives a fair indication of local management's success in implementing the policy.

Liaison between the Department and Accountants

Linked with the subject of disputes and appeals you also raise the general question of liaison between officers of this Department and accountants. Although the registered traders must be our principal contact, it is normal practice to maintain details of his professional advisers in our local records. Officers are encouraged to include such advisers in any discussions particularly when accounting problems arise. This policy is included in both our departmental training courses and in the written instructions issued to local VAT officers.'

Action prior to issue of an assessment

4.09 In whatever way a dispute arises the person registered for VAT is likely to be given an early indication by the VAT control officer of apparent errors or discrepancies, which if not resolved to his satisfaction might result in the issue of an assessment. If Customs and Excise have given only an indication or opinion that an error has occurred, it is not possible to enter a formal appeal to a VAT tribunal until the stage at which Customs and Excise issue an appealable decision or ruling, which it is their policy to provide in writing. Prior to such a formal decision being given, therefore, it is in the person's interest to consult professional advisers in order to put forward all relevant information to satisfy Customs and Excise before a decision (which can include an assessment) is given. In this way the issue of an assessment may be avoided, or an assessment which may involve a lesser sum than anticipated which is not in dispute, may be issued.

4.10 Frequently an assessment may be threatened on the basis of Customs and Excise dissatisfaction with declared retail takings, following a credibility check of the type described in ch 3. If this is the case the person and his professional adviser should consider any reasons for the apparent discrepancy between declared and alleged takings and discuss these with the VAT officer either at the conclusion of the control visit or in subsequent correspondence or during a further meeting with Customs and Excise before the stage of issuing an assessment is reached. In this connection it would be worth considering some of the reasons which have been put forward in precedent VAT tribunal decisions, as the reasons for apparent discrepancies may not be immediately obvious even to the person intimately involved in running the business. Also on this point the need for exercising caution in replying to Customs and Excise questions on control visits regarding pricing policies and other important aspects of how the business is run cannot be over-emphasised, as it is all too

4.10 Disputes and appeals

easy for persons to provide information which is either subsequently proved incorrect or is subject to qualification.

Example

During a control visit a VAT officer asks a sole proprietor of a small clothing retailers what pricing policy is applied.

The sole proprietor indicates that purchases are generally marked-up by 100% to arrive at selling prices, with a two week sale each summer when goods are discounted by 50%.

Based on this information the VAT officer carries out a mark-up type credibility check which indicates that takings declared may have been understated.

During subsequent discussions with the proprietor and his professional adviser it is established that the 100% mark-up is in fact applied to VAT exclusive purchase prices to arrive at VAT inclusive selling prices. After adjusting for this the true mark-up from VAT exclusive purchase prices to VAT exclusive selling prices is found to be only 74%. In addition, the proprietor recalls that during one of the years under review the summer sale lasted for four weeks and not the usual two weeks in order to make way for substantial new designs.

Taking these factors into account the assumed takings figure is only marginally above declared takings and the VAT officer decides that the discrepancy is insufficient to support an assessment in the circumstances.

4.11 On other occasions a VAT officer may doubt whether a particular supply of goods or services being made attracts VAT at the zero-rate, as the person may have assumed, or whether it is in fact standard rated. Conversely, a supply which has been treated as zero-rated may be viewed by the VAT officer as being exempt, with the result that input tax should have been restricted for partial exemption reasons. The VAT officer may refer the matter to the VAT Administration Directorate for its views and the Directorate will then give a ruling on how it interprets the VAT legislation on the point at issue.

4.12 It is important to note that although the letter received from the local VAT office may include the phrase 'the Commissioners have decided . . .', this is a reference to 'the Commissioners of Customs and Excise' (ie Customs and Excise themselves) and not an appellate body which has considered the matter and found in Customs and Excise favour. The ruling given is, in effect, only a Customs and Excise interpretation of the legislation and may not necessarily be correct. If such a ruling is received it is still possible to discuss or correspond with Customs and Excise as to how or why they have reached their decision and if some new information can be supplied or the point approached from a different angle, perhaps by reference to previous case decisions, it may still be possible to persuade Customs and Excise that their initial ruling is untenable.

Completion of VAT returns pending resolution of a dispute

4.13 A situation may frequently arise where the person and his professional advisers share one view of the law and Customs and Excise take a different view, such as to cause a dispute. Whilst negotiations, which may be protracted

Disputes and appeals 4.16

if complex liability issues are involved, are taking place, the question arises as to how to complete VAT returns in the meantime. If the returns are prepared on the basis of Customs and Excise views and these are subsequently proved to be incorrect in an appeal decision, the generally accepted principle which holds that tax paid under a mistake in law is generally not recoverable may prevent any subsequent claims for repayment of the tax (see, for example, *National Pari-Mutuel Association Limited v R* (1930) 47 TLR 110). On the other hand if the returns are completed on the basis that no tax is due and Customs and Excise views are eventually upheld in the court this would almost certainly then involve an assessment with interest charges (from 1988) and possible penalties.

4.14 Faced with such a difficult choice a possible solution is to complete and submit the returns on the basis of Customs and Excise views, but to make it clear in a covering letter with each return that Customs and Excise views are not accepted and that any payment being made is made under protest. This should enable the person to claim a subsequent repayment from Customs and Excise if the point is decided against Customs and Excise in the courts. In this connection practitioners should consider the terms of Customs and Excise Press Notice No 1099 issued in May 1985 following the judgment of the European Court of Justice in the case of *Direct Cosmetics Limited v Comrs C & E* [1985] STC 479, that directions issued on the company under the provisions of FA 1972, Sch 3, para 3 (subsequently replaced by VATA 1983, Sch 4, para 3) were invalid.

Misdirection

4.15 In some cases which result in a dispute a person will claim that he was acting in accordance with a previous VAT officer's oral or written instructions. The position in law is that if a VAT officer instructs a person incorrectly, Customs and Excise may in law issue an assessment to recover any arrears of tax understated if they subsequently realise their error. Recognising the inequity in this situation Customs and Excise have agreed to an extra-statutory concessionary treatment, whereby the arrears which are properly due in law may be waived. It is important, however, to appreciate the limited circumstances in which this may be applicable, as countless claims of 'misdirection' have proved unsuccessful in the past. The circumstances in which the concession may be applicable are those referred to in the statement made in the House of Commons in 1978 by the then Secretary to the Treasury (954 HC Official Report (5th series) col 426):

'If a Customs and Excise officer, with the full facts before him, has given a clear and unequivocal ruling on VAT in writing or, knowing the full facts, has misled a registered person to his detriment, any assessment of VAT due will be based on the correct ruling from the date the error was brought to the registered person's attention.'

4.16 Three important considerations arise from this statement. Firstly, whether Customs and Excise have been provided with the full facts. Secondly, if there has been oral misdirection, how the person is to establish evidence of this. It is dangerous to rely on any oral advice given by Customs and Excise, unless confirmation of it is also obtained in writing, as without the latter it may be impossible to establish precisely what the officer did say at the time (which

4.16 Disputes and appeals

may be several years previously) or whether this included an element of misdirection. Thirdly, the misdirection must normally have been to the person's detriment, which Customs and Excise appear to interpret as not including the situation of a person who has been advised incorrectly that he may reclaim input tax (eg on a new car) to which he is not entitled. Although the person may have received the amount and spent the money on other items Customs and Excise will tend to claim that the person was never entitled to such money in the first place and that the misdirection has not been to the person's detriment. This may be contrasted with the situation where a person may not have charged VAT due to Customs and Excise misdirection and is subsequently unable to recover such VAT from former customers. Such misdirection has clearly been to his detriment. In the former case it may be possible to exert moral pressure on Customs and Excise to settle the matter satisfactorily, depending on the circumstances of each case.

Waiver of tax

4.17 Occasionally, depending on the circumstances, Customs and Excise may also consider waiving VAT which has not been charged or which has been undercharged for the following reasons:

a) where it can be established clearly that had VAT been properly charged the recipient would have been entitled to recover the VAT in full as input tax. Such an argument may meet with some resistance at local VAT office level depending on the circumstances. If the circumstances of the case warrant it the matter may be worth pursuing to Customs and Excise VAT Administration Directorate, but not the VAT tribunal, as the latter are bound by the terms of the law despite any sympathy they may feel for the appellant in the situation;
b) where tax has not been properly charged through a genuine misunderstanding, particularly if Customs and Excise views on the point as expressed in their Public Notices or leaflets are ambiguous or otherwise unclear. Similar comments as at a) above, however, apply. In this connection see the decision of the VAT tribunal in the case of *Boots Co plc v Commissioners of Customs and Excise* LON/85/600 regarding retail and business promotion schemes, in which the Tribunal Chairman, although dismissing the appeal, commented:

'I hope that the Commissioners and the Commission of the European Community will consider the difficulties which have been raised by this appeal in the light of the legislation as it now stands. I include in that consideration by the Commissioners their Public Notice No 727 which is far from easy to understand and does not state what the Commissioners now contend to be the rules governing sales promotion schemes by retailers.'

Extra-statutory concessions

4.18 Practitioners and businesses alike should be aware of those circumstances in which extra-statutory concessions may be available. These, including details of the 'misdirection' and 'misunderstanding' concessions referred to above, are contained in Customs and Excise Notice No 748 entitled 'Extra-statutory Concessions', the relevant VAT sections from which are reproduced in Appendix 9.

Disputes and appeals 4.21

In exceptional cases where the liability of a supply depends on the customer's status practitioners should consider whether the public statement made by Customs and Excise in Press Notice No 1032 is of assistance. In that notice Customs stated that:

'As a general principle, the determination of liability of VAT is the responsibility of the taxpayer. In certain special cases the VAT liability of supplies of goods or services depends on the status of the customer receiving them. This can present problems for the supplier where the customer, innocently or otherwise, wrongly represents his status. Where this happens the Commissioners of Customs and Excise will not hold the supplier responsible for failing to charge the correct amount of tax, provided they are satisfied that the supplier:

— acted in good faith; and
— made normal and prudent checks and enquiries about the status of the customer and of any documentation or certification provided by him.'

Appealable decisions

4.19 If the discussions and negotiations with Customs and Excise prior to the issue of a formal decision or assessment do not resolve the dispute and Customs and Excise issue such a decision or assessment, it will be necessary to consider whether the decision or assessment is appealable to a VAT tribunal, and if so, whether this action should be taken and within what time limits.

Departmental review

4.20 Whilst a formal appeal should be lodged with a VAT tribunal within 30 days of the decision or assessment being issued, it is possible to postpone an early formal hearing of the appeal once lodged, by requesting Customs and Excise in writing also within the 30 day period to carry out a 'departmental review'. The decision or assessment will then be reviewed by an officer, normally of a higher rank than the officer who issued the disputed decision or assessment, during which any new information, which the person or his professional advisers can supply, will be considered. In cases of doubt the local VAT office reviewing officer may submit the matter to the VAT Administration Directorate. This review may take only a few weeks or on occasions several months if complex liability matters are involved, but ultimately Customs and Excise may:

a) withdraw the assessment or decision in total;
b) reduce the assessment or modify the decision; or
c) confirm the assessment or decision in full.

If a) occurs then the dispute will have been resolved, but if b) or c) is the outcome, the person will normally be allowed a further 21 days within which to appeal to a VAT tribunal, if this has not already been done, and this will be included in the letter advising the results of the review (see r 4 of the Value Added Tax Tribunals Rules 1986, SI 1986/590).

Protective appeals

4.21 It is, however, wise for a number of reasons to consider lodging a protective appeal at the earliest possible opportunity, even though it may be

4.21 Disputes and appeals

hoped that matters can be settled without recourse to a formal tribunal hearing. The reasons for such action are that:

a) by virtue of FA 1985, s 25, it is possible to negotiate a settlement with Customs and Excise which has the force of law when it is concluded;

b) whilst negotiating costs in achieving a satisfactory settlement may be recoverable from Customs and Excise, this applies only to costs of, incidental to and consequent upon an appeal (r 29 of the VAT Tribunals Rules 1986);

c) the lodging of an appeal may concentrate Customs and Excise minds and may result in a more thorough and searching review of the disputed decision or assessment;

d) a protective appeal may be withdrawn at any time (r 16 of the VAT Tribunals Rules 1986), but this should always be done well before any date is fixed for a formal hearing of the dispute.

4.22 Whether to pursue the dispute ultimately to a formal VAT tribunal hearing will nevertheless depend on a number of factors, including the strengths and weaknesses of the arguments, the costs and the potential publicity, all of which are discussed later in this chapter.

Prevention of disputes

4.23 In a self-assessment tax system such as VAT the maxim that 'prevention is better than cure' should not be overlooked. With the standard rate of VAT at the fairly high level of 15% (although even this is lower than in most other European Community countries) on turnover, not on profits or gains, errors on VAT in the past have been costly. With the introduction of interest and potential penalties in addition to tax arrears it is even more essential to prevent disputes occurring.

Survival checklist

4.24 At the end of ch 1 a detailed checklist aimed at surviving the incidence of the penalties has been included. In addition the points covered in the following paragraphs may also generally prevent a dispute regarding the tax from arising in the first place.

Notification of errors

4.25 In August 1982 the accountancy bodies published a guidance statement, following discussions with Customs and Excise, on the notification of errors in VAT returns. This is important to consider not only in relation to the business itself, but also so that the professional adviser may be seen to have acted correctly in the matter of errors discovered. The following is an extract from the statement:

'The Customs and Excise authorities have indicated that, if as a result of an error there is an underdeclaration of VAT of more than £1,000, the taxpayer should nevertheless not wait until the next return is due to be made but would be well advised to inform his local VAT office immediately he discovers the error in order to avoid suspicion that the error was deliberate. It follows that a member who discovers such an error should advise his client accordingly. The same principle applies where there is an overdeclaration of tax repayable of more than £1,000. For his own protection, in the event of the matter coming to the notice of the Customs and Excise authorities before the client has disclosed it, the member should ensure that his records of his advice to his client are such as to rebut any allegation that the member himself was knowingly concerned in the commission of an offence.'

This statement, although written against a background of criminal sanctions, still applies in the context of the post FA 1985 criminal and civil sanctions.

Acquiring knowledge of VAT offences and errors

4.26 Members of the Institute of Chartered Accountants in England and Wales would do well to consider the ethical guidelines laid down in the *Members Handbook* regarding advice to be given in the event of offences or errors being discovered and the implications which need to be considered if the person is unwilling to disclose the error to Customs and Excise. The relevant section is 1.306 (paras 98 to 119).

Time to pay

4.27 In the past a business which had completed its VAT returns and discovered that it was financially unable to pay the amount of tax due, perhaps because the VAT charged had not been collected from customers or the money had been used to settle other debts, was able in certain circumstances to negotiate with Customs and Excise to pay the VAT due on the return over a period of months following the due date for payment of the tax. With the introduction of the default surcharge system for late payment it remains to be seen whether this procedure will be allowed for only the first two late payments within a two year period, which will then lead to the issue of a surcharge liability notice and potentially further onerous debts by way of surcharges, or whether these may be suspended exceptionally in cases of extreme financial hardship. It is understood that Customs and Excise will normally expect the person to obtain funds from commercial sources to meet his VAT liabilities based on the view that it is not for Customs and Excise to fund a business through delayed payment of VAT due to them.

Decision making and checklists

4.28 Attention should be given to ensuring that all relevant personnel within a business organisation, whether small or large, are adequately aware of the basic principles of VAT and that when making business decisions they should consider what the VAT implications are. In larger organisations, as stated in ch 1, at least one person should acquire a reasonable knowledge of the technical aspects of VAT legislation and have ready access to a professional VAT specialist to advise on the more complex areas. Any checklists used in the decision making process should include VAT as a matter of course.

4.29 Disputes and appeals

Interaction of VAT and direct taxes

4.29 Both practitioners and businesses should be aware of the fact that all the tax aspects, both indirect and direct, of commercial transactions must be considered. Unfortunately, with the impact which taxes frequently have on the viability of commercial transactions a business will often consider that the 'tax tail is wagging the commercial dog' rather than vice versa. In other words, a transaction which appears commercially viable is rendered unprofitable due to the tax implications and it is often the latter rather than the former which influences the decision making process. However unfortunate that may be, general practitioners need to be acquainted with all the tax implications which might impinge on a transaction if they are to be able to advise properly. Failing this, they should at least know the basic principles, know how and when to recognise a potential problem area and have access to a specialist tax adviser. VAT planning strategies are outside the scope of this book, but it should be borne in mind that VAT cash flow implications as much as the absolute impact of VAT need to be considered adequately in relation to any direct tax implications.

Customs and Excise Public Notices and leaflets

4.30 Customs and Excise publish a number of Public Notices and leaflets on various subjects from the basic 'VAT Guide' (Notice No 700) to the more specialist leaflets on complex technical aspects. Although these provide good reference of Customs and Excise views on many situations, they should be regarded as only a statement of Customs and Excise interpretation of the legislation, which may not always be correct, with the exception of certain sections of the VAT Guide and certain other notices, which effectively extend the VAT legislation. Also, in view of the fact that Customs and Excise practice and hence the content of the notices frequently have to be revised in the light of decided cases, practitioners and businesses should ensure that the most up-to-date version of the notice or leaflet, including any amendments, are consulted. With the flood of amendments and case decisions which are a feature of the VAT system this is another area where the professional VAT specialist should be of assistance. A list of those notices and leaflets available from Customs and Excise local VAT offices is provided in Appendix 10.

Entering into transactions

4.31 It is often all too tempting to enter into transactions without ensuring that the VAT implications are adequately considered, either in the wording of draft contracts or on an oral basis if there is no written agreement as to the arrangements. In the case of *J D Wynn v Comrs C & E* LON/85/467 the appellant had paid for goods with the apparent addition of VAT, without demanding tax invoices, which it was said by the vendors would be provided later. From the decision it appeared that the vendors misled the appellant into believing that they were registered for VAT and Customs and Excise subsequently issued an assessment to collect 'input tax' overclaimed by the appellant as a result. In his summary the Chairman of the tribunal said:

'This is a clear case where the appellant erred in his judgement not to insist on receiving immediate tax invoices at the time of the transactions. But no doubt he found convenient the credit which these traders allowed him, and also the initial convenience of trading on a sale or return basis. It seems likely, however, in this case, that a demand for an immediate tax invoice would have resulted in no transactions taking place. We have some sympathy for the appellant in his predicament, but in truth he has only himself to blame.'

'Equity' or 'letter of the law'

4.32 In the case of *International Warranty Co (UK) Ltd v Comrs C & E* EDN/85/28 the appellant's sole business at the time of a VAT control visit was the sale of exempt warranties or insurance to motorists. Customs and Excise therefore issued an assessment for incorrect recovery of input tax. At the tribunal hearing the appellant produced no legal argument as to why he considered he should be allowed to retain the VAT in dispute, relying instead on 'equity rather than letter of the law'. As there was no dispute that Customs and Excise were entitled in law to make the assessment the tribunal dismissed the appeal in the following terms:

'In these circumstances, we have no hesitation in refusing the appeal. It is our duty to apply the law and not to give effect to broad considerations of equity, or reasonableness, unless the law itself makes them directly relevant to the question in issue, which it does not in this instance. In any event, even if it were legitimate to have regard to such considerations here, we are not persuaded that their admission would lead us to allow the appeal.'

Appeals

4.33 In this section the author considers the role of the VAT tribunals in the VAT system and the procedures which will be encountered if an unresolved dispute reaches the stage of formal appeal.

Role of the VAT tribunals

4.34 Value Added Tax tribunals were set up in 1972 with the sole function of determining appeals against the decisions of the Commissioners of Customs and Excise. Their constitution and procedures are governed by VATA 1983, Sch 8 (as amended), and by the Value Added Tax Tribunals Rules 1986, SI 1986/590. They are independent of Customs and Excise and are under the control of the Lord Chancellor. Prior to 1 April 1986 administrative responsibility for the VAT tribunals was with Customs and Excise, but with effect from 1 April 1986 administrative responsibility for VAT tribunals in England, Wales and Northern Ireland was transferred from Customs and Excise to the Lord Chancellor. Responsibility for the tribunals in Scotland was transferred on the same date to the Secretary of State. As this was envisaged at the time of the 1985 Finance Bill consequential provisions were included in the legislation at that stage.

4.35 At present there are tribunal centres in London and Manchester with a centre in Edinburgh covering Scotland and Northern Ireland. All appeals are co-ordinated by the headquarters of the Value Added Tax tribunals which is in London.

4.36 Disputes and appeals

Composition of a tribunal

4.36 Each VAT tribunal has a legally qualified Chairman who may sit alone or with one or two part-time members. The composition of the tribunal for a particular appeal lies with the decision of the President of the VAT tribunals. Where the appeal is exclusively a question of law, a Chairman will often sit alone, but where there is a dispute involving questions of facts or figures, part-time members usually sit with the Chairman and normally they will have some particular expertise which is relevant. For instance, in a mark-up assessment case one member of the tribunal is likely to be a qualified accountant. The aim is to give a sympathetic and understanding hearing of any case so that, as far as possible, justice can be done. It should be stated, however, that tribunals are to a large extent bound by the letter of the law, unless they are reviewing the use of a discretion given to Customs and Excise. This means that although tribunals may well sympathise with an appellant and even comment that they feel there may have been an element of misdirection by Customs and Excise, or that they hope Customs and Excise will view the appellant's predicament compassionately, often they have no choice but to dismiss appeals because tax is properly payable in law.

Statistics

4.37 In the Customs and Excise annual report for the year ended 31 March 1985 it was revealed that in 1984/85, 1,213 appeals were lodged against decisions of Customs and Excise relating to VAT. 308 appeals of all kinds were heard by the tribunals. Of these, 226 appeals were dealt with following full hearings and 82 others were dismissed at preliminary hearings following applications from Customs and Excise. During the year 567 appeals were withdrawn.

An analysis of the tribunals decisions is as follows:

a) allowed in full	45
b) allowed in part	20
c) disallowed	210
d) decisions pending and appeals part heard	33
	308

4.38 The above statistics reveal that many 'protective' appeals are in fact withdrawn without recourse to a full hearing, either because a dispute is settled with Customs and Excise or the potential appellant and his professional advisers, on reflection, believe that the chances are too remote to make it worthwhile proceeding.

4.39 However, the statistics also give the impression, from the small number of cases in which appeals are allowed in full or in part, that the tribunals tend to find in favour of Customs and Excise. It must be said that the number of cases which reach the tribunals, which in hindsight should not have been heard because there was really no hope of success, does tend to give a misleading impression. With many of the appeals heard by tribunals involving disputes on so-called 'mark-up' assessments, where Customs and Excise have alleged underdeclaration of takings, rather than points of technical VAT law, there have been calls in the past for the VAT tribunals to be split into a two-tier system on the same basis as the General and Special Commissioners in the direct tax system. Under such a system it is claimed that one tier could hear computational type appeals and the other could hear appeals on more technical matters arising from the VAT legislation. Although the Government did at one stage consider whether the General and Special Commissioners could be merged with the VAT tribunals in view of the fundamental differences within the two systems this possibility was rejected and no further moves to split the VAT tribunals into two tiers have been made.

Access to tribunals

4.40 In evidence to the Keith Committee certain representations were made that VAT tribunals were less accessible than the 486 divisions of the General Commissioners. The President of the VAT tribunals, in his evidence to the Keith Committee, pointed out, however, that appeals were heard at a number of addresses which were within 80 miles of any place in England and Wales, but rather more miles in Scotland, and that the tribunal were willing to sit in other places on request. With a sharp increase in the number of appeals anticipated in the light of the new penalty provisions it remains to be seen whether the existing tribunals are able to cope or whether a revised system may well become necessary at an early stage.

Grounds for appeal

4.41 Appeals lie to a tribunal only if they fall within the express provisions of VATA 1983, s 40(1), as amended by FA 1985, s 24. From this, it follows that there can be no appeal until a decision in writing has been given by Customs and Excise. Numerous grounds of appeal are listed in VATA 1983, s 40(1); in essence the decision must relate to one or more of the following:

a) an assessment or the amount of an assessment;
b) the registration or cancellation of the registration of any person as a taxable person;
c) the tax chargeable on the supply of goods and services or on an importation of goods;
d) the amount of any input tax allowable;
e) the proportion of any supplies which may be taken as taxable supplies eg by a partially exempt trader;
f) the amount of a refund for a person constructing a new home;
g) a refund of tax in respect of a bad debt;
h) a refund of tax paid on an importation for private purposes of goods belonging wholly or partly to another;
i) a refusal to allow group registration or a change in group registration;
j) a refusal to exempt a trader from registration or to allow voluntary registration as a taxable person;
k) a direction that the value of supplies shall be their open market value instead of the consideration paid for them;
l) a refusal to allow a retailer to use one of the special schemes;
m) a requirement in relation to invoices produced by a computer;
n) a requirement that a trader should provide security for any tax payable by him;
o) the liability to a penalty or surcharge;

4.41 Disputes and appeals

p) the amount of any penalty, interest or surcharge (it should be noted that by virtue of FA 1985, s 24(2), the tribunal cannot reduce any penalty below the statutory minimum unless it finds that the offence has not been committed or it accepts the defence of 'reasonable excuse' in which case no penalty will apply);
q) the making of an assessment on grounds of evasion or dishonest conduct.

Giving notice of appeal

4.42 Under r 4 of the Value Added Tax Tribunals Rules 1986 a notice of appeal must be received at the appropriate tribunal centre within 30 days of the disputed decision or within 21 days of an extension of such time as agreed in writing by Customs and Excise. If the time limit has expired, the notice of appeal should be served together with a notice of application for an extension of time. The notice of appeal must contain the following information:

a) the name and address of the appellant;
b) the address to which the disputed decision was sent;
c) the address of the VAT office which issued the disputed decision;
d) a copy of the decision or details of it;
e) the grounds of appeal.

Although it is not essential to use the official form a printed form of notice of appeal and all other tribunal documents, copies of which are reproduced in Appendix 11, can be obtained on application to any tribunal centre or VAT office.

Pre-appeal conditions

4.43 By virtue of VATA 1983, s 40(2), an appeal cannot be entertained by a tribunal unless all the returns and tax relating to the relevant returns have been submitted. Customs and Excise may subsequently challenge these returns and raise an assessment for further tax due. An appeal against such an assessment can normally be made without depositing further tax due with Customs and Excise, but the payment or deposit is required if the assessment relates to:

a) the tax chargeable on the supply of any goods or services or on the importation of goods;
b) an assessment under VATA 1983, Sch 7, para 4(1) or (2) (incorrect or incomplete returns or incorrect repayments in respect of a period for which the appellant has made a return, or an assessment under sub-para (6) (failure to account for goods)).

If Customs and Excise, or on appeal, a VAT tribunal, is satisfied that financial hardship (and this means hardship, not merely inconvenience) may result, they are empowered to waive the requirement for the deposit in a) or b) above by virtue of VATA 1983, s 40(3)(b). A notice applying for non-payment or non-deposit on the grounds of hardship should accompany the notice of appeal when it is lodged.

Statement of case

4.44 Rules 7 and 8 of the VAT Tribunals Rules 1986 set out the rules and time limits requiring Customs and Excise to produce a statement of their case

Disputes and appeals 4.49

which is copied to the appellant. If there is a hardship application under r 11(4), Customs and Excise must also state their grounds of opposition in writing and a copy is sent to the appellant. If Customs and Excise contend that all the requirements precedent to an appeal have not been fulfilled, they are required to serve notice to this effect on the tribunal centre and a copy will be sent to the appellant (r 6). It will be seen in rr 7 and 8 that different rules apply to FA 1985, s 13 appeals, 'reasonable excuse' appeals, and 'other' appeals.

Documents

4.45 Rule 20 of the VAT Tribunals Rules 1986 sets out the rules and time limits within which the appellant must produce a list of books and documents which he intends to refer to at the hearing. Any document, etc, not so listed may be refused production at the hearing. Attached to the list should be an indication of a time and place where Customs and Excise may inspect the documents. Similarly, Customs and Excise will produce a list and will make available books and documents on request by the appellant. Copies of the lists will be sent by the tribunal centre to each of the other parties.

Preliminary hearings of opposed matters

4.46 These cover the following matters and are normally heard in private:

a) hardship applications;
b) applications for extension of time within which to serve a notice of appeal and a hardship application;
c) applications by Customs and Excise for appeals to be struck out or dismissed because they cannot be entertained.

In the case of a hardship application, it is essential that the appellant brings evidence of assets, liabilities, income and expenditure with supporting documentation. The appellant should attend in person in addition to his representative, if any.

Witness statements

4.47 A witness statement may be served at the appropriate tribunal centre within the time limits set out in r 21 of the VAT Tribunals Rules 1986. If the other party objects, notice of objection must be given in writing within 14 days of the date of serving of the witness statement; it is then essential for the witness to attend the hearing since the statement cannot now be used or read at the hearing. See r 22 of the VAT Tribunals Rules 1986.

Non-compliance with a direction or summons issued by a VAT tribunal

4.48 A person who fails to comply with a summons or direction issued by a VAT tribunal may be fined by the tribunal up to a maximum of £1,000 by virtue of VATA 1983, Sch 8, para 10, as amended by FA 1985, s 28.

Date of hearing

4.49 If either party is not ready by the time required in the Tribunal Rules, an extension of time may be granted by the tribunal. As soon as the tribunal centre decides that the case is ready for hearing, or as soon as the tribunal feels

4.49 Disputes and appeals

that sufficient time has been given for the preparation of the case, the date and place of the hearing is fixed. If the appellant has good reason for not wanting a particular date or period, he should acquaint the tribunal staff accordingly and they will endeavour to assist. Once the date is fixed, the appellant and his representatives should attend. Failure to do so may result in the award of costs against the appellant.

Postponement of hearing

4.50 When a date for hearing has been fixed it will be postponed only for good reason. Application for postponement should be made by telephone immediately the situation is apparent and confirmed in writing at once to the tribunal centre. Postponement is entirely a matter for discretion of the tribunal who may, in cases of illness, require medical evidence.

The tribunal environment

4.51 The diagram on p 87 illustrates the layout of a typical tribunal room indicating the location of the various parties involved.

Conduct

4.52 When appearing before a VAT tribunal it is wise to remember that it is similar to a court of law and evidence is given on oath. A person who is unfamiliar with the formalities may expect to be assisted by the tribunal over rules of evidence and other legal niceties, but the presentation of the facts and the examination of witnesses is entirely his own responsibility. Those addressing the tribunal or giving evidence should take with them books and papers required for the hearing and would be well advised to study the VAT Tribunals Rules 1986 which came into effect on 1 May 1986 and which are set out in full in Appendix 12.

Order of events

4.53 The order of events as set out in r 27 of the VAT Tribunals Rules 1986, but which may be varied at the discretion of the tribunal, is as follows:

a) opening address, on behalf of the appellant;
b) evidence-in-chief, cross-examination and re-examination of witnesses for the appellant;
c) respondent's (ie Customs and Excise) opening address;
d) evidence-in-chief, cross-examination and re-examination of witnesses for Customs and Excise;
e) summing-up on behalf of Customs and Excise;
f) closing speech on behalf of the appellant;
g) decision of the tribunal, which may be given on the day of the hearing or may be reserved until later.

In appeals relating to FA 1985, s 13, the procedure will be as per r 27(2) of the 1986 Rules.

4.54 It is normal practice for the appellant or his representative to present his

Disputes and appeals 4.51

The tribunal room

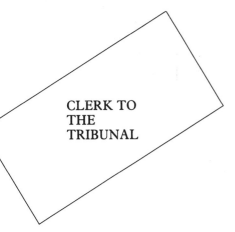

4.54 Disputes and appeals

case first and having opened the case by stating the decision of Customs and Excise which is disputed and the reasons why, the appellant or his representative should state what the appeal is about, the way the business is conducted and the reasons why it is felt that the appeal should succeed, quoting precedent tribunal cases wherever possible.

4.55 Following this, if necessary, the appellant should be called as a witness, followed by any other person who may be able to assist the appeal. The appellant's representative should question the witnesses in order to extract from them replies which might assist the case, but it is to be noted that only evidence given from the witness box is taken into account by the tribunal and hearsay evidence will not be admitted. Both the tribunal and the Customs and Excise solicitor may cross-examine the witness, following which further questions may be put to clarify matters which may have been dealt with in the cross-examination.

4.56 Customs and Excise will then present their case in a similar sequence, calling their own witnesses, who may be cross-examined by the appellant or his representative. The Customs and Excise representative will then close their case by making a summary address to the tribunal.

4.57 Finally, the appellant (or his representative) has the opportunity to close his case by making a summary address to the tribunal. During this address the appellant or his representative should marshal his arguments, indicating the findings of fact which he contends have been established by the evidence and suggest the findings which the tribunal should reach on those facts.

4.58 Only in the simplest cases is the decision likely to be given orally by the tribunal at the conclusion of the hearing. In most cases the tribunal will announce that it reserves its decision and a written copy of the decision will be sent to both parties some time after the hearing. Although a detailed analysis of the way in which VAT tribunals have heard points of principle in precedent cases is outside the scope of this book, the following two points are worthy of brief mention regarding the question of how the VAT tribunal is likely to interpret the VAT legislation.

Interpretation of VAT legislation

4.59 In interpreting VAT legislation, VAT tribunals sometimes refer to the case of *Brutus v Cozens* [1972] 2 All ER 1297. This was a case where the issue was whether an individual had been guilty of 'insulting behaviour' and in the House of Lords the meaning of the word 'insulting' had to be considered. The following principle is revealed in the decision, per Lord Dilhorne:

'Unless the context otherwise requires, words in a Statute have to be given their ordinary natural meaning and there is in this Act, in my opinion, nothing to indicate or suggest that the word "insulting" should be given other than its ordinary natural meaning.'

In the same decision, per Lord Reid:

'The meaning of an ordinary word of the English language is not a question of law . . . it

Disputes and appeals 4.61

is for the Tribunal which decides the case to consider, not as law, but as fact, whether in the whole circumstances the words of the Statute do or do not as a matter of ordinary usage of the English language cover or apply to the facts which have been proved.'

It should also be borne in mind that the VAT tribunals do not generally accept arguments advanced on the basis of decided cases under direct tax legislation. For example, in the VAT case of *A C S Eccles and Co v Comrs C & E* EDN/85/71 the appellant's representative attempted to justify the VAT treatment on the authority of a decided direct tax case. In reply the Chairman indicated:

'We may say at once that we do not accept the application of the special provisions of the Income Tax Acts, dealing as they do with capital and income, as being any guide to the interpretation of the Value Added Tax Act 1983, and we agree with the view of the tribunal on that point in the case of *Sir Ian MacDonald of Sleat v Commissioners of Customs and Excise.*'

Effect of EEC Directives

4.60 In the important case of *UFD Limited v Comrs C & E* [1981] VATTR 199 the President of the VAT tribunals, in considering the proper meaning of words within the UK VAT legislation made an historic statement that after considering a recent European Court of Justice case it seemed to the tribunal that:

'On this appeal and henceforth in all appeals involving issues of liability, the tribunal should consider the relevant provisions of the (EEC) Council Directives to ensure that the provisions of the United Kingdom legislation are consistent therewith.'

Since that decision many appellants have sought to rely on the provisions of the EEC VAT Directives in dislodging an assessment made under UK VAT law. In general where a point of law is involved and there is a conflict between the national UK law and European Community law, the latter will be held to prevail whenever the EEC Directive is clear and unconditional. By way of example, practitioners should study the decision of the tribunal in the case of *Yoga for Health Foundation v Comrs C & E* LON/82/228, [1983] VATTR 297 and the subsequent decision of the High Court in the case [1984] STC 630.

The decision

4.61 Decisions are signed by the Chairman and contain full reasons. They are available to the public and are circulated to leading tax and accountancy journals who often comment on them and reproduce extracts from the decision. The official reports of certain cases are published by HM Stationery Office under the title 'Value Added Tax Tribunal Reports'. Decisions are not normally given at the conclusion of the hearing unless the matter is relatively straightforward and no point of law is involved. However, if commercial considerations require a quick decision, it is sometimes possible to announce the decision at the conclusion of the hearing and for the parties to be promised reasons in writing as soon as possible. Owing to the wide publication of the

4.61 Disputes and appeals

tribunal decisions and the detailed scrutiny which they attract, most tribunals prefer to reserve their decision so that they may give care and thought to the actual wording of the decision to ensure clarity and unambiguity.

Costs

4.62 Under r 29 of the VAT Tribunals Rules 1986 the successful party may apply for costs but the costs must be 'incidental to and consequent upon the appeal'. It follows therefore that the only charges which are allowable are those directly connected with the appeal; any charges in respect of the period before the appeal was lodged are not generally allowable. Costs may be awarded by the tribunal or the tribunal may direct that the costs be taxed by a Taxing Master of the Supreme Court.

4.63 As regards the Customs and Excise policy in asking for costs of unsuccessful appeals by taxpayers before the VAT tribunals a parliamentary answer in 1978 (958 HC Official Report (5th series) written answers cols 92–93), later published in 1979, revealed the following:

'Mr Robert Sheldon [the then Secretary to Treasury]: Customs and Excise now have more than five years experience using the Tribunal system to deal with a wide range of questions relating to VAT, some of great legal complexity which would otherwise be appropriate to the High Court. The machinery has proved flexible in handling not only issues of principle but also smaller cases where the informality of the proceedings have made it possible for taxpayers to argue their own cases without representation. In the light of the review, the Commissioners have concluded that, as a general rule, they should continue their policy of not seeking costs against unsuccessful appellants; however they will ask for costs in certain cases so as to provide protection for public funds and the general body of taxpayers. For instance, they will seek costs of those exceptional tribunal hearings of substantial and complex cases where large sums are involved and which are comparable with High Court cases, unless the appeal involves an important general point of law requiring clarification. The Commissioners will also consider seeking costs where the appellant misused the Tribunal procedure – for example, in frivolous or vexatious cases, or where the appellant has failed to appear or to be represented at a mutually arranged hearing without sufficient explanation, or where the appellant has first produced at a hearing relevant evidence which ought properly to have been disclosed at an earlier stage and which could have saved public funds had it been produced timeously. In all cases the question whether or not costs should be awarded will, of course, remain entirely within the discretion of the tribunal concerned and the amount of any such award will be fixed either by that tribunal, or by the High Court, as provided by tribunal procedure rules. The Council on Tribunals has been consulted and sees no objection to this proposed policy, subject to its having the opportunity to monitor its effect.'

4.64 In the case of *Streamline Taxis (Southampton) Ltd v Comrs C & E* LON/85/499 which considered the straightforward question of whether supplies from a vending machine on the appellant's premises were subject to VAT at the standard rate, Customs and Excise, following dismissal of the appeal, applied for costs. The costs applied for were only a nominal £50 but the Customs and Excise representative contended that this was because the appeal had, in their view, been made for frivolous or vexatious reasons. The reason given for their view was that they had supplied the appellant with a copy of a similar decision in a precedent case and yet the company still maintained its appeal. The tribunal, however, deciding this point commented:

Disputes and appeals 4.68

'We do not consider that the facts of the appeal as recorded in the decision establish with sufficient clarity that the facts of that case are identical with the present one. Accordingly we do not regard this appeal as being so frivolous or vexatious as to justify an award of costs in favour of the Commissioners and we decline so to do.'

Interest

4.65 Under VATA 1983, s 40(4), where the appellant is successful in his appeal and the deposited tax must be repaid, interest is awarded on the sum involved, at a rate to be fixed by the tribunal. Similarly, Customs and Excise may ask for interest on any unpaid tax which becomes due as a result of the decision.

Further appeals

4.66 An appeal from a decision of the tribunal lies on a point of law only to the High Court of Justice in England and Wales, the Court of Session in Scotland, the High Court of Justice of Northern Ireland and the Staff of Government Division on the Isle of Man. Further information concerning such an appeal is normally set out in the letter sent to the appellant or his representative with the decision of the tribunal. See Appendix 13.

In the Customs and Excise Annual Report for the year ended 31 March 1985 it was revealed that during the course of the year five appeals by appellants against decisions of the tribunal were heard by a single judge of the Queen's Bench Division. Of these two were allowed and three dismissed. There were three appeals by tribunal appellants against judgments in the Queen's Bench Division to the Court of Appeal. One appeal was allowed, two were dismissed.

The impact of the FA 1985 provisions on VAT tribunal appeals

4.67 The following are the changes which were brought about by virtue of FA 1985:

a) extension of the list of grounds for appeal to include disputes regarding penalties, interest or surcharges (s 24);
b) power given to the VAT tribunals to increase certain assessments on appeal (s 24(5));
c) a formal procedure whereby appeals may be settled, with the force of law, between an appellant and Customs and Excise without recourse to a VAT tribunal hearing (s 25);
d) provision for certain appeals from VAT tribunal decisions to lie direct to the Court of Appeal, rather than initially to the High Court (s 26);
e) the burden of proof in an appeal against a 'civil fraud' penalty to be on Customs and Excise and not on the appellant (s 27);
f) the introduction of penalties for failure to comply with certain directions of a VAT tribunal (s 28);
g) enforcement of certain decisions of a VAT tribunal, as if they were judgements of the High Court in England and Wales, with similar provisions for Scotland and Northern Ireland (s 29).

4.68 In connection with c) above, although many appeals have been settled by agreement between the appellant and Customs and Excise in advance of

4.68 Disputes and appeals

hearings in the past, there was no formal procedure under the law for this. An appeal to a VAT tribunal may now be settled by agreement, which must be confirmed in writing, and the person has 30 days from the date of the agreement or confirmation in which to resile from the agreement. Once that time limit has passed, the agreement including any terms regarding costs, has the same status as a decision of a VAT tribunal and can be enforced accordingly (FA 1985, s 25).

5 Powers

The Keith Committee were much concerned to balance the proposed strengthening of the powers of the Customs and Excise in certain respects with increased protection for the taxpayer.

'The Collection of Value Added Tax', November 1984

INTRODUCTION

5.01 Those practitioners and VAT specialists who have been closely involved with VAT since the era of FA 1972, which introduced VAT into the UK, were concerned at the contents of the Keith Committee recommendations on VAT powers when they were published in early 1983. There were many warnings from such interested commentators that the adoption of the recommendations would increase the already extensive powers of Customs and Excise to an unacceptable level and tilt the balance far too much in favour of Customs and Excise as against the general body of taxpayers.

5.02 In order to understand the concern regarding Customs and Excise powers in relation to VAT it is necessary to consider the fierce opposition which was a feature of the debates on the 1972 Finance Bill. Historically, Customs and Excise have always enjoyed extensive powers to deal with smuggling and illicit production of spirits. Some of these powers date back centuries when the need for such powers may well have been justified to deal with the determined smuggler and others who often resorted to violent means in their fight to evade the duties and taxes of the day. At the time of the 1972 Finance Bill, however, there were many who questioned whether Customs and Excise really needed or should be allowed such extensive powers, such as a general right of entry, with a tax which would embrace over one million registered persons, many of whom would be carrying on business from their own private residences.

5.03 Whilst there is no doubt that public opinion is wholeheartedly in support of measures which prevent evasion and abuse to the detriment of other taxpayers, Customs and Excise have over the last few years successfully argued their case, first before the Keith Committee and also the Government, for even greater powers to enforce compliance with VAT legislation. Practitioners who have studied the Keith Committee's recommendations, the 1984 Consultation Document, the 1985 Finance Bill and finally the Finance Act 1985 cannot have failed to notice the strengthening of the powers of Customs and Excise in relation to VAT.

5.04 Before the powers available to Customs and Excise in relation to VAT are examined in detail it is worth considering precisely what the impact of FA 1985 has had on such powers. The main changes set out below have been divided into those which might be regarded as strengthening or maintaining

5.04 Powers

Customs and Excise powers and those which might be regarded as offering increased protection for the taxpayer.

Changes benefiting Customs and Excise

a) Introduction of a new 'civil fraud' offence, which allows Customs and Excise an alternative between criminal penalties or civil penalties, the latter generally requiring less evidence and proof (FA 1985, s 13);
b) an increase in the maximum term of imprisonment for criminal offences from two years to seven years (FA 1985, s 12(2));
c) the introduction of a range of new civil penalties to penalise non-compliance ranging from breaches of numerous regulations to serious misdeclaration, the latter offence being determined by arbitrary objective tests (FA 1985, ss 14–17);
d) the introduction of a new default surcharge to enforce timely payments of VAT due (FA 1985, s 19);
e) the introduction for the first time of the power to charge interest on discovered understatements or overclaims of VAT in all circumstances (FA 1985, s 18);
f) an increase in the period for which VAT records are required to be retained from three years to six years (FA 1985, Sch 7, para 2);
g) the power to issue assessments for penalties, surcharges and interest and enforce payments as if these were tax (FA 1985, s 21);
h) an extended time limit to issue assessments in civil fraud cases (FA 1985, s 22(4));
i) power to assess tax-geared penalties up to two years after the tax due has been finally determined (FA 1985, s 22(2));
j) power to increase assessments in the absence of returns to amounts greater than would otherwise have been assessed (FA 1985, Sch 7, para 1(3));
k) greater powers to obtain information, search persons, remove documents, open gaming machines, etc (FA 1985, Sch 7, paras 4–6);
l) a new penalty for breach of a walking possession order (FA 1985, s 17);
m) abolition of the need for ex parte leave of a VAT tribunal to be sought to assess back beyond six years, subject to a new twenty year cut off (FA 1985, s 22);
n) power to increase an assessment to correct arithmetical errors in the original assessment (FA 1985, s 22(7));
o) new powers regarding access to computer systems, including the power to demand co-operation of persons in charge of computers (FA 1985, s 10);
p) a power of arrest in respect of VAT fraud (FA 1985, s 12(6));
q) search warrants still to be authorised by magistrates and not the higher judiciary (FA 1985, Sch 7, para 5);
r) the power of VAT tribunals to mitigate the level of penalties generally restricted (FA 1985, s 24(2));
s) the power of VAT tribunals to increase assessments (FA 1985, s 24(5));
t) Customs and Excise proposed power to mitigate penalties, surcharges and interest restricted (see Clause 23 of 1985 Finance Bill which was not enacted).

Changes benefiting taxpayers

a) Repayment supplement, subject to numerous conditions, if Customs and Excise delay repayments of VAT (FA 1985, s 20);

Powers under VAT legislation 5.06

b) right of appeal to VAT tribunals against penalties, surcharges and interest, but on an 'all or nothing' basis and subject to restrictions (FA 1985, s 24(1));
c) certain appeals from VAT tribunals to lie direct to the Court of Appeal rather than initially to the High Court (FA 1985, s 26);
d) increased safeguards on the issue of search warrants (FA 1985, Sch 7, para 5);
f) formal arrangements to settle appeals by agreement with Customs and Excise and facility to resile from such an agreement (FA 1985, s 25).

POWERS UNDER VAT LEGISLATION

5.05 In the following paragraphs the existing powers of Customs and Excise which arise from the VAT legislation are analysed. A feature of such powers is that in many cases the primary legislation allows Customs and Excise to make regulations to cover certain circumstances. The regulations (or secondary legislation), which are in the form of statutory instruments, then allow Customs and Excise to make further rules, some of which are contained only in their Public Notices (eg retail schemes, record requirements, etc). A further feature is the amount of discretionary power given to Customs and Excise by such phrases as 'if the Commissioners are satisfied', 'as the Commissioners think fit' and 'as the Commissioners may direct'. Whether such discretionary powers may be challenged by the taxpayer if he disagrees with them is considered at para **5.60**.

Registration (VATA 1983, s 2(5))

5.06 By virtue of VATA 1983, s 2(5), various powers relating to registration for VAT arise within VATA 1983, Sch 1:

a) if the quarterly limit of taxable turnover for compulsory registration has been exceeded, but the taxpayer believes that his taxable turnover in a full year will not exceed the annual limit, compulsory registration is not necessary, but only 'if the Commissioners are satisfied' on the evidence available or put forward by the taxpayer (VATA 1983, Sch 1, para 1);
b) if a person who is registered for VAT considers that his taxable turnover in the next year will not exceed the statutory minimum (normally fixed at £1,000 below the minimum registration limit) the person may cease to be registered, but only 'if the Commissioners are satisfied' (VATA 1983, Sch 1, para 2);
c) Customs and Excise have the power to agree an earlier date for registration than is strictly necessary from application of the compulsory time limits (VATA 1983, Sch 1, paras 3 and 4);
d) a person who intends to make taxable supplies at some time in the future may be allowed to register under VATA 1983, Sch 1, para 5, but
i) only if the person 'satisfies the Commissioners';
ii) subject to such conditions as Customs and Excise think fit to impose;
iii) from a date to be agreed with Customs and Excise;
iv the conditions imposed may subsequently be varied by Customs and Excise;
v) the provisional registration may be cancelled;
e) Customs and Excise have the power to agree a date of cancellation of

5.06 Powers

registration other than that strictly necessary under the law 'if they are satisfied' or 'if they think fit' (VATA 1983, Sch 1, paras 8, 9, and 10);

f) Customs and Excise have the power to allow exemption from registration, but only if the person satisfies Customs and Excise of certain facts and only if Customs and Excise see fit to allow exemption (VATA 1983, Sch 1, para 11(1)(a));

g) Customs and Excise may allow a person to be registered voluntarily, even if his taxable turnover does not exceed the compulsory registration limits, but only if they think fit and subject to such conditions, which may subsequently be varied, as they think fit to impose. For the conditions which apply see Customs and Excise Press Notice No 763 issued in September 1982 (VATA 1983, Sch 1, para 11(1)(b));

h) Customs and Excise are empowered to require notification of registration in such form and containing such particulars as they may prescribe in regulations (VATA 1983, sch 1, para 14). The regulations which apply are regs 4–11 of the VAT (General) Regulations 1985, SI 1985/886 which contain further rules relating to registration. Effectively the regulations enable Customs and Excise to insist on a person using the required form VAT 1 (reproduced in Appendix 7) to notify registration. The regulations also set out some of the conditions which Customs and Excise impose in certain registration cases.

By virtue of FA 1986, s 10, where two or more persons are carrying on what purports to be separate businesses for the avoidance of VAT registration Customs and Excise may issue a direction that those persons are to be treated as one taxable person.

Time of supply (VATA 1983, s 5)

5.07 By virtue of s 5, Customs and Excise may direct, following a request by a taxable person, that the time of supply may be treated as being other than that prescribed by the law. They may also make regulations determining the time of supply of certain goods or services in certain circumstances. For the numerous special cases see regs 17–28 of the VAT (General) Regulations 1985.

Input tax (VATA 1983, s 14)

5.08 Customs and Excise are empowered to make regulations regarding the evidence required to support claims for input tax (see reg 62 of the VAT (General) Regulations 1985).

Partial exemption (VATA 1983, s 15)

5.09 Customs and Excise are empowered to make regulations to secure a fair and reasonable attribution of input tax when a person makes both taxable and exempt supplies and for treating all supplies as taxable in certain circumstances (see regs 29–37 of the VAT (General) Regulations 1985).

Exports (VATA 1983, s 16)

5.10 Customs and Excise may make regulations setting out those goods, and under what conditions, which may be zero-rated on export. Zero-rating will

Powers under VAT legislation 5.15

also be allowed only if Customs and Excise are satisfied that the goods have been or are to be exported (see regs 49–57 of the VAT (General) Regulations 1985).

Second-hand goods relief (VATA 1983, s 18)

5.11 If the conditions laid down in Treasury orders, or imposed by Customs and Excise in pursuance of such orders, are satisfied, a reduced amount of VAT is payable on supplies of certain second-hand goods. This refers to the margin schemes whereby VAT is payable only on any profit margin made on resale of the goods. For the relevant orders see the following:

a) VAT (Cars) Order 1980, SI 1980/442
b) VAT (Special Provisions) Order 1981, SI 1981/1741
c) VAT (Horses and Ponies) Order 1983, SI 1983/1099.

It should be noted that in the orders the relief does not apply unless a person keeps such records and accounts as Customs and Excise may specify in a notice published by them, or which they may recognise as sufficient (eg see VAT (Special Provisions) Order 1981, art 4(3)(c)). The notices referred to are obtainable from local VAT offices (eg Notice No 712 'Second-hand Works of Art, Antiques and Scientific Collections').

Imports (VATA 1983, s 19)

5.12 Customs and Excise may make regulations providing for the remission or repayment if they think fit, of tax chargeable on certain imports in certain circumstances (see regs 38–48 of the VAT (General) Regulations 1985).

Refund of tax (VATA 1983, s 20)

5.13 Under various orders Customs and Excise may determine the time and form of claims by certain bodies (eg local authorities) for refund of tax incurred on expenditure (see the VAT (Refund of Tax) Order 1973, (No 2) Order 1973, and Order 1976).

Refunds to 'Do-It-Yourself' Housebuilders (VATA 1983, s 21)

5.14 Provided a person complies with the conditions and requirements in regulations made by Customs and Excise a person who is constructing a dwelling may obtain a refund of tax incurred on certain goods incorporated in the dwelling (see VAT ('Do-It-Yourself' Builders) (Relief) Regulations 1975, SI 1975/649).

Bad debts (VATA 1983, s 22)

5.15 If a person makes a claim at a time and in a form as specified in regulations made by Customs and Excise and satisfies the general conditions laid down in s 22, he will be entitled to VAT bad debt relief (see VAT (Bad Debt Relief) Regulations 1978, SI 1978/1129).

5.16 Powers

Repayment of tax to those in business overseas (VATA 1983, s 23)

5.16 Customs and Excise may make repayment of UK VAT incurred by those in business overseas, but only as the scheme provides and subject to conditions laid down in the regulations (see VAT (Repayment to Community Traders) Regulations 1980, SI 1980/1537).

Goods imported for private purposes (VATA 1983, s 26)

5.17 If Customs and Excise are satisfied that to disallow a claim for refund of tax on goods imported for private purposes would constitute double taxation they may allow relief from such tax.

Refunds to government departments (VATA 1983, s 27)

5.18 Customs and Excise are empowered to determine the form and manner of claims for refund of tax incurred by other government departments.

Groups of companies (VATA 1983, s 29)

5.19 Customs and Excise are empowered to refuse an application for group registration (s 29(4)), or to include further members in an existing VAT group (s 29(5)), but the legislation indicates that they shall not do so unless it appears to them necessary to do so for the protection of the revenue. It should be noted from s 29 that Customs and Excise cannot refuse to allow a company to leave a VAT group or an application to disband a group. Under s 29(6) Customs and Excise may terminate VAT group treatment if the relevant control criteria cease to be satisfied. An application for VAT group registration or to include a further member is normally to be made not less than 90 days before the relevant date, but Customs and Excise are able to allow shorter notice under s 29(7).

Divisional registration (VATA 1983, s 31(1))

5.20 If Customs and Excise see fit they may allow a company to register in the names of the separate divisions.

Unincorporated bodies, personal representatives (VATA 1983, s 31(2), (3), (4), (5)

5.21 Customs and Excise may make regulations regarding the responsibilities of persons carrying on a business in partnership or by a club, association or organisation, or who act as personal representatives of a deceased, bankrupt or incapacitated person (see regs 9, 10 and 11 of the VAT (General) Regulations 1985).

Powers under VAT legislation 5.28

Agents (VATA 1983, s 32)

5.22 Under s 32(1), Customs and Excise are able to direct that any agent, manager or factor who is resident in the UK and who has acted on behalf of a person who is accountable for any tax, is to be substituted for that person. This power is particularly relevant to practitioners who may be asked to act as 'VAT agents' for overseas traders. Although in correspondence Customs and Excise have stated that their policy, in the event of a default of VAT by the overseas person, would not be to seek payment of the VAT from the VAT agent, if the latter is acting only in an accountancy capacity, the existence of the power and the risk that it might nevertheless be used, has led many practitioners to refuse to act as VAT agents for overseas traders.

5.23 Under s 32(4), Customs and Excise are also empowered, if they think fit, to treat a supply of goods or services via an agent, who acts in his own name, both as a supply to the agent and as a supply by the agent.

Transfer of going concerns (VATA 1983, s 33)

5.24 Customs and Excise may make regulations to secure continuity in cases where a business carried on by a taxable person is transferred to another person as a going concern (see reg 4(5)–(8) of the VAT (General) Regulations 1985).

Supplies of dutiable goods in a warehouse (VAT 1983, s 35)

5.25 Customs and Excise may make regulations to enable goods supplied in a warehouse to be removed without payment of tax (see regs 38–57 of the VAT (General) Regulations 1985).

Trading stamp schemes (VATA 1983, s 37)

5.26 Customs and Excise may make regulations modifying the value of goods under certain trading stamp schemes (see VAT (Trading Stamps) Regulations 1973, SI 1973/293. Also see VAT (Treatment of Transactions) (No 1) Order 1973, SI 1973/325, which complements the regulations made).

Disclosure of information for statistical purposes (VATA 1983, s 44)

5.27 Customs and Excise may disclose certain information which they hold to the Business Statistics Office of the Department of Trade and Industry.

Valuation (VATA 1983, Sch 4)

5.28 Schedule 4 empowers Customs and Excise to make directions substituting different values for VAT purposes in certain circumstances. Such powers are claimed to be available by Customs and Excise under derogations allowed by the EEC Sixth Directive (77/388/EEC), the direct effect of which has been discussed in ch 4. In the case of *Direct Cosmetics Limited v Comrs C & E*

5.28 Powers

[1985] STC 479 the European Court of Justice, ruling in favour of the taxpayer, indicated that the power set out in FA 1972, Sch 3, para 3, (subsequently VATA 1983, Sch 4, para 3) had been invalid since 1981, as it did not comply with the Sixth Directive provisions on a technicality. Subsequently, Customs and Excise indicated that they had sought to re-establish the validity of the power with the European Commission and new directions made under VATA 1983, Sch 4, para 3, were re-issued during 1985 to persons affected. Preliminary appeals by two such persons affected by the new directions (*Direct Cosmetics Ltd v Comrs C & E* LON/85/377 and *Laughtons Photographs v Comrs C & E* LON/85/428), again challenging the validity of the new directions have been referred to the European Court of Justice for a preliminary ruling and the cases are expected to be heard during 1986 or early 1987.

Administration, collection and enforcement (VATA 1983, s 38)

5.29 VATA 1983, s 38, states that 'Schedule 7 to this Act will have effect with respect to the administration, collection and enforcement of the tax'. Many of the Customs and Excise powers in relation to VAT are therefore contained in Sch 7 and regulations made under that Schedule; the more important of these are set out in the following paragraphs.

Keeping of records (VATA 1983, Sch 7, para 7)

5.30 VATA 1983, Sch 7, para 7, gives Customs and Excise numerous powers relating to records to be kept by taxable persons. Sub-para 7(1) states that 'every taxable person shall keep such records as the Commissioners may require'. Effectively, this means that where a public notice contains a requirement as to records it has the force of law. Section VIII of the VAT Guide (Notice No 700) sets out general requirements regarding records for all taxable persons. The Retail Scheme and Second-hand Scheme Notices set out requirements regarding records for those affected by them. In practice, Customs and Excise do not insist that the person keeps his records or accounts in any particular form (with the exception of certain strict rules regarding second-hand schemes) provided they are able to satisfy themselves from the record system that the returns which have been submitted are accurate.

5.31 Under VATA 1983, Sch 7, para 7(2), as amended by FA 1985, VAT records must be retained for six years instead of the previous three years. This change was not retrospective, so that records up to 24 July 1985 need to be kept for VAT purposes for only three years, but records from 25 July 1985 must be kept for the new six year period. If the new rule causes registered persons substantial inconvenience the problem should be discussed with the local VAT office, who may be willing to consider a concessionary arrangement.

Power to require the production of records (VATA 1983, Sch 7, para 8(2))

5.32 Schedule 7, para 8(2), enables Customs and Excise to require anyone 'concerned in whatever capacity' with the making of supplies, or a person to

Powers under VAT legislation 5.37

whom they are made, to furnish information to Customs and Excise. This provision was amended by FA 1985 to include supplies of services (as well as supplies of goods) and to introduce a power to require that the records be produced either at the principal place of business of the person or at such other place as Customs and Excise may reasonably require. Pending further legislation Customs and Excise have undertaken not to disturb the existing legal professional privilege available to clients of solicitors. VATA 1983, Sch 7, para 8(4), specifies that Customs and Excise are empowered to inspect any profit and loss account and balance sheet relating to the business.

Power to copy or remove records (VATA 1983, Sch 7, para 8)

5.33 VATA 1983, Sch 7, para 8(4A–4C), empowers Customs and Excise to copy records or to remove them at a reasonable time and for a reasonable period. A receipt must be provided by Customs and Excise if requested. If a lien on the records is claimed their removal by Customs and Excise does not break it. Under Sch 7, para 10(3)(b), Customs and Excise are able, following the issue of a search warrant, to seize records or anything else which may be required as evidence for possible proceedings in respect of fraud.

Power to inspect computer systems (FA 1985, s 10)

5.34 FA 1985, s 10, enables Customs and Excise to check the operation of any computer used to keep VAT records. By virtue of s 10(4) computer users and those in charge of equipment must afford reasonable assistance to Customs and Excise to enable them to check such records. There would appear to be no provision for compensation if an inexperienced officer corrupts or destroys data held on a computer system, but it is understood that Customs and Excise intend to allow only officers who are experienced with such systems to check their operation.

Power to take samples (VATA 1983, Sch 7, para 9)

5.35 Customs and Excise are empowered to take samples in order to determine how the goods or materials of which they are made should be treated for VAT purposes (eg whether they should be standard rated or zero-rated).

Power to open gaming machines (VATA 1983, Sch 7, para 9A)

5.36 This power was inserted by FA 1985, Sch 7, para 4, and enables Customs and Excise to open a gaming machine and check the takings.

Powers of entry and search (VATA 1983, Sch 7, para 10)

5.37 Three separate powers are given to Customs and Excise by this provision:

a) the power to enter premises used in connection with the carrying on of a business, at any reasonable time, for the purposes of exercising any powers under the VAT legislation (eg control visits);
b) the power to enter any premises, at any reasonable time, if Customs and Excise have reasonable cause to believe that they are being used in connection

5.37 Powers

with a taxable supply of goods and to inspect the premises and any goods found on them;

c) the power to enter (if necessary, by force) at any time and search premises and persons found on such premises and to remove documents and other items found on the premises. A search warrant issued by a justice of the peace in accordance with para 10(3) must be issued before this power may be used.

Power to require security and production of evidence (VATA 1983, Sch 7, para 5)

5.38 For the protection of the revenue, Customs and Excise may require a taxable person to:

a) produce documents supplied to him relating to the tax as a condition of allowing or repaying any input tax;
b) give such security for the amount of the payment as appears appropriate to them as a condition of making a repayment of tax for a prescribed accounting period; or
c) give security, or further security, of such amount and in such manner as they may determine, against a payment of any tax due or which may become due as a condition of the person supplying goods or services under a taxable supply.

Although an appeal may be made against the security demanded under c) above, any person who supplies taxable goods or services without giving the security demanded is liable to a penalty.

Power to distrain for payment (VATA 1983, Sch 7, para 6)

5.39 By virtue of VATA 1983, Sch 7, para 6(4), Customs and Excise may make regulations for authorising distress (or poinding in Scotland) where a person refuses or neglects to pay tax due. Where the tax due is the result of an assessment issued by Customs and Excise under VATA 1983, Sch 7, para 4(1) and (2)(b), distress cannot be levied until 30 days after the tax becomes due (ie the period during which an appeal against the assessment can be lodged. The goods seized must be kept for five days to enable the person neglecting or refusing to pay time to settle the oustanding amount by other means. This is normally achieved by a walking possession order being placed on the goods and if the debt remains unpaid at the end of the necessary period the goods are sold by public auction and any surplus remaining, after deduction of the sum due, plus costs and charges, will be restored to the owner of the goods distrained. The relevant regulations which have been made are regs 65 and 66 of the VAT (General) Regulations 1985.

5.40 The VAT (General) (Amendment) Regulations 1985, SI 1985/1560, which came into force on 1 January 1986, transferred the authority to issue a warrant for the forcible entry of premises to levy distress from a collector of Customs and Excise to a magistrate; this gave effect to a recommendation made by the Keith Committee in 1983. However, a further statutory instrument, SI 1986/305, entitled 'The VAT (General) (Amendment) (No 2) Regulations 1986' which came into effect on 1 April 1986 amended reg 65 by revoking the power of an authorised person to apply to a justice of the peace for the issue of a warrant to effect forcible entry to premises for the purposes of levying such a distress. This followed Parliamentary Counsel's advice that express statutory authority is required to enter premises by force for the purposes of levying distress and that VATA 1983 does not provide such authority (see Customs and Excise Press Notice No 1091).

Power to assess tax due (VATA 1983, Sch 7, para 4)

5.41 Under the VAT system tax is payable on the basis of figures declared on periodic VAT returns (see Appendix 3 for an example of a VAT return). Returns must be submitted and tax paid within certain limits: see regs 58–64 of the VAT (General) Regulations 1985. These regulations obviate the need for a system of formal assessments to collect tax due from registered persons. However, Customs and Excise are empowered under VATA 1983, Sch 7, para 4, to issue assessments if necessary as follows:

a) when a person fails to make a return (para 4(1)); for an example of a typical assessment from Customs and Excise in these circumstances, see Appendix 14);
b) when a person fails to keep any documents and afford facilities necessary to verify returns submitted (para 4(1));
c) if it appears to Customs and Excise that returns which have been submitted are incomplete or incorrect (para 4(1)); for an example of a typical assessment form used by Customs and Excise in these circumstances, see Appendix 15;
d) where tax, which should not have been repaid, has been repaid to any person (para 4(2));
e) where input tax credit, or an excess of input tax credit over output tax due, for a prescribed accounting period has been incorrectly paid to any person (para 4(2));
f) when a person is unable to prove that goods which have been supplied to him or imported by him are available to be supplied or have been lost or destroyed (para 6);
g) to assess liabilities to penalties, interest or surcharges (FA 1985, s 21).

5.42 Assessments under a), b), c) and f) above must be made to the best of Customs and Excise's judgement (VATA 1983, Sch 7, para 4(1) and (6)). The proper meaning of 'best judgement' was considered in the case of *Van Boeckel v Comrs C & E* [1981] STC 290, [1981] 2 All ER 565. Three principles arose from that case as follows:

a) there must be material before Customs and Excise on which to make their judgement;
b) they must make a value judgement on the material before them, doing so honestly and bona fide; and
c) although their decision as to the amount of the assessment must be reasonable and not arbitrary, they are under no obligation to do the work of the taxpayer by carrying out exhaustive investigations, but if they do make investigations, they must take into account the material disclosed by them.

5.43 Under VATA 1983, Sch 7, para 4(5), an assessment under para 5.41, a)–d),

5.43 Powers

above, for any prescribed accounting period cannot be made after the later of:

a) two years after the end of the prescribed accounting period;
b) one year after evidence, sufficient in the opinion of Customs and Excise to justify the making of the assessment, comes to their knowledge but in any case not more than six years after the end of the prescribed accounting period; or
c) where the taxable person has died, three years after death.

5.44 Under FA 1985, s 21, Customs and Excise may assess and notify any amount due by way of penalty or default surcharge under FA 1985, ss 13–17, and 19, or interest under FA 1985, s 18, and unless the assessment is withdrawn or reduced, the amount is recoverable as if it were tax due.

5.45 Where any penalty must be calculated by reference to tax which was paid late and that tax cannot be readily attributed to one or more prescribed accounting periods, Customs and Excise may allocate the tax due to such period or periods as they determine to the best of their judgement (FA 1985, s 21(3)). Further, where penalties or interest accrue on a daily basis, the assessment must specify a date to which the penalty or interest is calculated (FA 1985, s 21(5)).

5.46 By virtue of FA 1985, s 22, an assessment for any relevant period in the case of evasion of tax, conduct involving dishonesty, serious misdeclaration and interest cannot be made after the later of the following:

a) where tax has been lost as a result of conduct involving dishonesty:
i) 20 years after the end of the relevant period;
ii) 2 years after the tax due for the relevant period has been finally determined; or
iii) where the taxable person has died, three years after the death;
b) where tax has been lost in circumstances giving rise to a penalty for registration irregularities or unauthorised issue of tax invoices:
i) 20 years after the event giving rise to the penalty; or
ii) where the taxable person has died, three years after the death;
c) in respect of assessments for serious misdeclaration, interest and default surcharges:
i) six years after the end of the relevant period;
ii) two years after the tax due for the relevant period has finally been determined; or
iii) where the taxable person has died, three years after the death;
d) for assessments relating to breaches of walking possession agreements or breaches of regulatory provisions:
i) six years after the event giving rise to the penalties; or
ii) where the taxable person has died, three years after the death.

Power to make further assessments

5.47 Customs and Excise are empowered to make further assessments as follows:

a) where, after an assessment has been made under para **5.41**, a) – d), above,

further 'evidence of facts', sufficient in the opinion of Customs and Excise to justify the making of an assessment, comes to their knowledge (VATA 1983, sch 7, para 4(5));
b) if it appears to Customs and Excise that the amount which ought to have been assessed exceeds the amount which was so assessed, the further assessment must be made under the same provisions and within the same time limits as the original assessment (FA 1985, s 22(7)). This power is designed to cater for arithmetic errors in the original assessment.

Power of arrest (VATA 1983, s 39(3A))

5.48 By virtue of an amendment introduced by FA 1985, s 12(6), where Customs and Excise have reasonable grounds for suspecting that a fraud offence has been committed, they may arrest anyone whom they have reasonable grounds for suspecting to be guilty of the offence. In answer to serious concern by representatives of taxpayers a ministerial assurance was given that this power would be used only in respect of the most serious cases and then only by specialist investigators (see Customs and Excise Press Notice No 1029 issued in August 1985).

Recovery proceedings

5.49 Tax due from any person is recoverable as a debt due to the Crown by virtue of VATA 1983, Sch 7, para 6(1). Both the VAT legislation and the general law provide Customs and Excise with numerous powers to recover tax due to them:

a) the power of distraint (VATA 1983, Sch 7, para 6(4));
b) the power to take civil recovery proceedings in the High Court or county court (VATA 1983, Sch 7, para 6(1));
c) the power to make use of garnishee proceedings, attachment of earnings orders, or interlocutory injunctions (known as a Mareva injunction following the first case in which it was granted: *Mareva Compania Naviera SA v International Bulk Carriers SA* [1980] 1 All ER 213, (1975) 2 Lloyd's Rep 509);
d) by virtue of the fact that VAT is a preferential debt in a bankruptcy, liquidation or receivership, Customs and Excise may secure their position by presenting a bankruptcy or winding up petition in appropriate cases (IA 1985, Sch 4, para 2);
e) where a taxable person has left the jurisdiction of the UK courts but is still within an EEC member state, Customs and Excise may request the competent authority of the relevant state to take recovery proceedings on their behalf in the national courts of that state (FA 1977, s 11 and FA 1980, s 17).

Disclosure of information to the Inland Revenue (FA 1972, s 127)

5.50 Customs and Excise power to exchange information with the Inland

5.50 Powers

Revenue arises under FA 1972, s 127, which is still extant. For some years a trial scheme was operated on this basis in the Leeds area and following encouraging results reported to the Keith Committee the latter recommended that this practice be extended nationwide.

Disclosure of information to European Community member states (FA 1978, s 77 and FA 1980, s 17)

5.51 Under FA 1978, s 77, and FA 1980, s 17, Customs and Excise are empowered to disclose VAT information to tax authorities in other member states. This power is subject to the safeguard that Customs and Excise must be satisfied that the competent authority of the receiving state is bound by equal rules of confidentiality with regard to the information disclosed.

Power to recover tax due to European Community Governments (FA 1977, s 11)

5.52 Under FA 1977, s 11, Customs and Excise are empowered to take enforcement proceedings in respect of debts for VAT incurred in European Community member states.

Power to compound proceedings (CEMA 1979, s 152(1))

5.53 Under the Customs and Excise Management Act 1979, s 151(1), Customs and Excise may, as they see fit, 'stay, sist or compound any proceedings for any offence under the Customs and Excise Acts'. This power is applicable to VAT by virtue of VATA 1983, s 39(9). The implications and application of this power are discussed in detail in ch 2.

Civil powers (FA 1985, ss 13–17)

5.54 FA 1985, ss 13–17, and FA 1986, ss 14 and 15 introduced a range of new civil powers and penalties available to Customs and Excise. These are set out and discussed in detail in ch 1.

COMMENTARY

5.55 In the preceding paragraphs the main powers of Customs and Excise in relation to VAT have been highlighted. In view of the extensive and comprehensive nature of such powers, which have been further strengthened by FA 1985, the following paragraphs consider certain implications of which practitioners and businesses should be generally aware. These are:

a) what to do if Customs and Excise appear to have exceeded their powers;
b) the right of appeal against Customs and Excise use of discretionary powers;
c) the right of judicial review of Customs and Excise actions;
d) the implications of professional privilege.

What to do if Customs and Excise appear to have exceeded their powers

5.56 If a taxable person believes that Customs and Excise may have exceeded their powers, the first step should be to discuss the matter with the head of the local VAT office, who will provide the reasoning behind any action or proposed action by Customs and Excise in any set of circumstances and also the detailed statutory authority under which Customs and Excise believe they may act as they wish to or have so acted. The taxable person should naturally consider whether Customs and Excise are within their powers and this will normally involve consulting a VAT specialist. The latter will be able to consider whether the particular power being quoted has been subject to scrutiny by the courts in the past and what the outcome was. If the power has not been challenged it should be possible to determine whether there is a right of appeal to a VAT tribunal to consider the issue. Over the years certain notable cases have considered the extent of Customs and Excise powers in particular in relation to assessments and records.

5.57 In a recent case, *Hedges and Butler Ltd v Comrs C & E* (unreported) it was held by the High Court that Customs and Excise had exceeded their powers relating to Excise records. The case was heard in the Queen's Bench Division of the High Court on 19 December 1985 and resulted in the court ruling that the power of Customs and Excise officers under the Customs and Excise Management Act 1979, s 93, to demand production of all documents relating to the business of the occupier of, or owner of goods kept in, an Excise warehouse, does not extend to other aspects of the business, which are unconnected with the Excise warehouse.

5.58 The fact that VAT is a European tax not just a UK tax is a feature which should also be considered closely. VAT is a Community harmonised tax which requires that member states mirror in their own national law the mandatory elements of Community law. Although Art 22(8) of the EEC Sixth Directive (77/388/EEC) does not contain mandatory provisions in that it specifies only that 'member states may impose other obligations which they deem necessary for the correct levying and collection of the tax', the question of whether VAT is chargeable on any particular supply of goods or services should be considered in relation to the Sixth Directive. For example, in the case of *Direct Cosmetics Ltd v Comrs C & E* [1985] STC 479, Customs and Excise's right to demand VAT on an uplifted value by virtue of FA 1972, Sch 3, para 3 (subsequently VATA 1983, Sch 4, para 3), was held to be invalid under the Sixth Directive because the underlying UK VAT legislation was ultra vires. Thus Customs and Excise had no legal authority to require the taxable person to comply with directions made under the UK provisions.

The right of appeal against discretionary powers

5.59 Although Customs and Excise enjoy wide powers to make regulations and to exercise their discretion in many circumstances under such regulations, it should be borne in mind that certain of the discretionary powers are restricted by the wording of the legislation. For example, in considering

5.59 Powers

whether to allow a VAT group registration Customs and Excise may only refuse an application where it appears to them necessary to do so 'for the protection of the revenue' (VATA 1983, s 29(4)). In other words, there has to be an underlying reason before they may exercise such powers. However, in other instances the wording of the legislation is more general such as 'as the Commissioners see fit'.

5.60 The question of whether and to what extent Customs and Excise discretion may be challenged was considered in detail in the case of *Comrs C & E v J H Corbitt (Numismatists) Ltd* [1980] STC 231. In that case Customs and Excise considered that the records kept by the taxable person, who dealt in old coins and medals, were not sufficient for the margin schemes, whereby VAT is payable on the profit margin only. Customs and Excise further contended that their decision was not subject to review by a VAT tribunal. The tribunal held that it did have the jurisdiction to review the decision, but the High Court reversed this. The High Court's decision was subsequently reversed in the Court of Appeal, but restored by the House of Lords, who held that to give the VAT tribunal the right to review Customs and Excise's use of their discretion to accept records would enable it to supervise Customs and Excise to ensure that they had exercised their discretion reasonably. The House of Lords concluded that had that been the intention of Parliament the legislation would have indicated this clearly, which it did not. Following this decision, however, an amendment was made to the legislation by FA 1981, s 15, which effectively allows a VAT tribunal to review such powers of discretion as set out below.

5.61 By virtue of VATA 1983, s 40(6), in an appeal which is made under VATA 1983, s 40(1), and which is against a decision by Customs and Excise which depended on a prior decision taken by them, the fact that the prior decision may not be an appealable matter under s 40(1), does not prevent the tribunal from allowing the appeal on the grounds that it would have allowed an appeal against the prior decision. For example, in the case of *Pinetree Housing Association Ltd v Comrs C & E* [1983] VATTR 227 the VAT tribunal held that under this power it had jurisdiction to review Customs and Excise's decision to refuse an application for intending trader registration (see VATA 1983, Sch 1, para 11(1)(b)). The question which it sought to answer was whether Customs and Excise had exercised their discretion in a way in which no reasonable body of Commissioners could have acted. On the evidence the tribunal concluded that Customs and Excise had acted unreasonably and allowed the appeal. In most cases where an appeal is under this provision the decision falling within s 40(1) is likely to be an assessment by Customs and Excise, which has been issued as a result of a prior decision by Customs and Excise in the exercise of their discretionary powers.

Judicial review

5.62 Where VAT tribunals have no power to review a decision of Customs and Excise, eg where a taxable person claims that conditions imposed by Customs and Excise are invalid, a person has the right to apply to the High

Court for judicial review under the Supreme Court Act 1981, s 31. Applications for orders under this power are governed by RSC Ord 53.

5.63 Initially, leave must first be obtained to make an application for judicial review. The application for leave is made ex parte to a judge by filing the following in the Crown Office of the High Court:

a) Notice No 86A, which must contain, inter alia, details of the relief sought and the grounds on which it is sought; and
b) an affidavit which verifies the facts relied on.

It should be noted that the application should be made within three months of the date of judgment, order or proceedings against which the order is sought. If leave to make the application for judicial review is granted it is made to the Queen's Bench Division of the High Court.

5.64 In the case of *R v Comrs C & E, ex p Leonard Howarth* QBD 17 July 1985 it was ruled that Customs and Excise had not exercised their discretion properly. A yacht, which had been involved in drug smuggling, was owned (but not sailed) by a person. Customs and Excise had seized the vessel which was liable to forfeiture under CEMA 1979, s 141. However, under CEMA 1979, s 152, Customs and Excise could have mitigated this effect but did not do so, claiming that it was their policy to exercise mitigation in favour of an owner only where it had been clearly established that such a person was free of any prior knowledge or complicity in the criminal act (ie drug smuggling). Although the owner had been interrogated he had not been charged. The Court ruled that the power of mitigation should be exercised in accordance with the ordinary rules of fairness and directed Customs and Excise to reconsider the exercise of their discretionary power.

Professional privilege

5.65 By virtue of FA 1985, Sch 7, para 3, Customs and Excise's information seeking powers were extended to provide that any person concerned in the supply of goods and services in the course or furtherance of a business must, on demand by Customs and Excise, furnish 'such information relating to the goods or services . . . as the Commissioners may reasonably specify' and also, if required, 'any document' relating to them. Prior to the FA 1985 alteration, the power in relation to services was limited to information relevant to the consideration for the services and it is apparent that the revised power could overcome the hurdle of professional privilege.

5.66 For example, if a solicitor had zero-rated certain services to an overseas client, but Customs and Excise wished to check that the services were properly zero-rated, rather than standard rated, they might require to look at the solicitor's file on the client, which in itself, might conflict with the concept of privileged information. Further, where Customs and Excise wish to see documents which would normally be in the taxable person's possession, but which are in the possession of his solicitor, the latter could be

5.66 Powers

compelled to disclose them to Customs and Excise. Any lien over the documents is, however, expressly preserved by FA 1985, Sch 7, para 3(3).

5.67 Solicitors and other practitioners should, however, be aware that during the Committee stage of the 1985 Finance Bill the Treasury Minister gave an assurance that 'until the Government reach a decision on the remaining privilege recommendations of the Keith Committee and any necessary legislation has been enacted, Customs and Excise will respect any reasonable claim to legal professional privilege in relation to the new power' (see Customs and Excise Press Notice No 1029 issued in August 1985). In these circumstances, it would appear that Customs and Excise will be the arbiters of what is 'reasonable' and until the necessary legislation clarifies the position practitioners should consider demands by Customs and Excise for information and their response with some caution.

5.68 By way of illustration of the problems which might arise, a case in 1983, *Comrs C & E v A E Hamlin and Co* [1983] STC 780, [1983] 3 All ER 654, considered the extent of Customs and Excise power to inspect and copy documents under VATA 1983, Sch 7, paras 8, 9 and 10. The respondents were a firm of solicitors who held documents belonging to two persons and which had been seized in Anton Piller (ie search and seize) raids. The solicitors had given an undertaking to the Court that the documents would be retained in safe custody. Customs and Excise, however, were investigating the VAT affairs of the two persons and sought to inspect and copy these documents. The Court held that notwithstanding Customs and Excise powers under VATA 1983, Sch 7, they could not inspect and copy documents without an order of the court. They also held, however, that it was proper in the case for the court to make such an order.

CONCLUSION

5.69 The foregoing paragraphs have covered certain of the important implications which might arise in considering the exercise of Customs and Excise powers in any given situation. It must be emphasised, however, that because the legislation and practice in this area is subject to frequent changes specialist professional advice on any particular set of circumstances should always be sought.

Appendix 1 Foreword to the Government paper entitled 'The Collection of VAT' (November 1984)

PROPOSALS TO IMPROVE THE COLLECTION OF VALUE ADDED TAX

Foreword by the Chancellor of the Exchequer

1. The first two volumes of the report of the Keith Committee were published in March 1983. The Committee's proposals were detailed and far-reaching, and I decided that the trade and professional bodies concerned, as well as individuals, should be given the fullest opportunity to comment on them before any conclusions were reached. On my instructions, the Revenue Departments carried out an extensive consultation exercise, and reported the outcome to me in March 1984. In reply to a Parliamentary Question on 18 May, I said that the Government hoped to announce conclusions on the Customs and Excise recommendations – mainly dealing with VAT – towards the end of 1984, in time for any necessary legislation to be included in the 1985 Finance Bill. My proposals, together with draft implementing clauses, are set out in this paper. Consultations on the Inland Revenue recommendations are continuing, and I hope to bring forward proposals on them in 1985, in time for legislation as necessary in the 1986 Finance Bill. Meanwhile, the proposals set out in this paper on VAT should not in any way be taken as prejudging the Government's likely conclusions in relation to the rather different taxes administered by the Inland Revenue.

2. The Government is grateful to Lord Keith and his colleagues for their careful and detailed analysis of the present administration of VAT, and to all those who have commented on their proposals. In considering the Committee's recommendations, I have been very much aware that a tax of such general application as VAT can be operated successfully only if it has a high degree of public acceptance. The tax should be seen to be evenly enforced; those traders who conscientiously comply with their legal obligations must not be put at a disadvantage compared with their competitors who do not; and the powers of enforcement needed for this purpose, while kept to the minimum, should be effective, certain in their application, and provide adequate safeguards for the taxpayer in his relations with Customs and Excise.

3. The Keith Committee were much concerned to balance the proposed strengthening of the powers of the Customs and Excise in certain respects with increased protection for the taxpayer. Almost all those who commented during the consultation exercise emphasized the importance of dealing with the recommendations as a package. I fully accept that approach, and in the very limited modifications which I propose to make to the original recommendations, I have sought to tilt the overall balance further in the taxpayer's favour. While I have decided that shifting the responsibility for the issue of VAT search warrants from magistrates to circuit judges would increase the burden on the higher judiciary without materially increasing the safeguards for the citizen, I have also decided that civil recovery actions for VAT debts should continue to be a matter for the High Court rather than the VAT Tribunals; that the names of those accepting civil penalties or compounded settlements in fraud cases should not automatically be published; and that in the third test for the proposed new civil default of

Appendix 1

" gross negligence " (to which I intend to give the more accurate and neutral title of " serious misdeclaration "), the reckonable defaults should be limited to those which equal or exceed 5% of the true amounts of tax due. In addition, the Customs and Excise should have much wider powers of general mitigation than the Committee envisaged.

4. Subject to these and the other modifications explained later in this paper, and to any further representations which may be made by interested parties, I now intend to bring forward the draft legislation set out in Appendix 5 as part of next year's Finance Bill. I believe that these proposals are an important and necessary stage in the evolution of value added tax, and will substantially improve both the fairness and the efficiency of its administration. On that basis, I commend them to all taxpayers and their professional advisers as a positive but measured response to the concern expressed over the years, not least by the Public Accounts Committee of the House of Commons, about the persistent non-compliance with VAT law to the detriment both of the Exchequer and of those taxpayers who are careful to observe their legal obligations.

NIGEL LAWSON

HM Treasury
November 1984

Appendix 2 Introduction by Customs and Excise to the Government paper entitled 'The Collection of VAT' (November 1984)

PROPOSALS TO IMPROVE THE COLLECTION OF VALUE ADDED TAX

Introduction

. . .

The Scale of the Compliance Problem

3. There are currently some 1·4 million traders registered for VAT providing an estimated net yield in 1984–85 of £18 billion. Whilst the Keith Committee generally approved of the way in which Customs and Excise use their existing powers to administer the tax, it expressed concern at the low level of compliance with the legal requirements for the furnishing of returns and the making of payments by the statutory due date. On more than one occasion this has been a matter for comment by the Committee of Public Accounts (PAC), most recently in their Thirty-Fourth Report of the 1983–84 Session (House of Commons Paper 430) in which they strongly supported the general approach of the Keith Committee.

4. In spite of the successful efforts made by the Department in recent years to improve compliance within the existing legal framework, over three quarters of those required to make quarterly returns and net payments of VAT do so late, with the result that on average during 1983–84, some £1·5 billion of tax due was outstanding at any one time. Although defaults of this kind technically constitute criminal offences it is practicable to prosecute in only a small proportion of the most serious cases. Most traders who submit their returns late, or who underdeclare their liability, run little risk of any financial penalty. The scope for interest-free use of tax collected from customers is the single most important cause of the present unacceptably low level of VAT compliance.

5. Against this background, the Government has accepted the case made by the Keith Committee for the introduction of an automatic, progressive, tax-geared surcharge for late payment or late submission of returns and the replacement of the present criminal code of regulatory offences by a new and more readily enforceable civil code providing for interest on underdeclarations and graduated tax-geared or frequency related penalties, determined according to objective criteria, but with greater scope for mitigation than envisaged by the Committee. Taken with the further safeguards recommended by the Committee, these arrangements would have important benefits for both taxpayers and the Exchequer. The taxpayer would know with certainty that particular consequences would follow particular defaults; the enforcement of VAT would become much more uniform; and the stigma of criminality would be removed from all but the most serious VAT offences. From the Exchequer's point of view, the incentive to prompt compliance should greatly improve the flow of revenue, and should enable considerable savings of staff engaged on enforcement work to be made.

Appendix 3 Specimen VAT return form (VAT 100)

Value Added Tax Return

For the period
to

Due to reach the VAT Central Unit by
These dates must not be altered.

H M Customs and Excise

For Official Use

Registration No   Period

Before you fill in this form please read the notes on the other side. You must complete all boxes — writing "none" where necessary. If you need to show an exact amount of pounds, please write "00" in the pence column. Don't put a dash or leave the column blank. Please write clearly in ink. You must ensure that the completed form and any VAT payable are received no later than the due date by the Controller, VAT Central Unit, H M Customs and Excise, 21 Victoria Avenue, SOUTHEND-ON-SEA X

An envelope is enclosed for your use.

| For Official Use | £ | p |

FOR OFFICIAL USE

VAT DUE in this period on OUTPUTS (sales, etc), certain postal imports and services received from abroad	1	
Underdeclarations of VAT made on previous returns (but not those notified in writing by Customs and Excise)	2	
TOTAL VAT DUE (box 1 + box 2)	3	
VAT DEDUCTIBLE in this period on INPUTS (purchases, etc)	4	
Overdeclarations of VAT made on previous returns (but not those notified in writing by Customs and Excise)	5	
TOTAL VAT DEDUCTIBLE (box 4 + box 5)	6	
NET VAT PAYABLE OR REPAYABLE (Difference between boxes 3 and 6)	7	

Please tick only ONE of these boxes:
- box 3 greater than box 6 — payment by credit transfer ☐ — payment enclosed ☐
- box 6 greater than box 3 — repayment due ☐

Value of Outputs (excluding any VAT) 8 [00]
Value of Inputs (excluding any VAT) 9 [00]

How to pay the VAT due
Cross all cheques and postal orders "A/C Payee only" and make them payable to "H M Customs and Excise". Make credit transfers through account 3078027 at National Girobank or 10-70-50 52055000 for Bank Giros and keep your payment slip. You can order pre-printed booklets of credit transfer slips from your local VAT office. In your own interest do not send notes, coins, or uncrossed postal orders through the post.
Please write your VAT registration number on the back of all cheques and credit transfer slips.

Please tick box(es) if the statement(s) apply:
- box 5 includes bad debt relief ☐
- box 8 includes exempt outputs ☐
- box 8 includes exports ☐

Retail schemes If you have used any of the schemes in the period covered by this return please tick the box(es) to show all the schemes used.

| A | B | C | D | E | F | G | H | J |

Remember, you could be liable to a financial penalty if your return and all the VAT payable are not received by the due date.
DECLARATION by the signatory to be completed by or on behalf of the person named above.

I, ... declare that the
(full name of signatory in BLOCK LETTERS)
information given above is true and complete.

Signed .... Date .... 19......
*(Proprietor, partner, director, secretary, responsible officer, committee member of club or association, duly authorised person)   *Delete as necessary

FOR OFFICIAL USE

VAT 100   F3790 (JULY 1986)

Appendix 3

NOTES

These notes and the pamphlet, *Filling in your VAT return*, will help you to fill in this form. You may also need to refer to other VAT notices and leaflets.

If you need help or advice, or any of the answers overleaf gives a negative figure, please contact your local VAT office quoting your VAT registration number.

Box 1 You must show the VAT due on all goods and services you supplied in this period. This is your *output* tax.

If you use a retail scheme the *How to work* pamphlet for your scheme will help you work out the output tax due.

Remember to include VAT due on:

- goods taken for private use
- gifts and loans of goods
- sales to staff
- sales of business assets
- imported services listed in *The VAT guide*, Appendix G
- postal imports — other than Datapost — with a value of £1300 or less.

Remember to subtract any VAT credited to your customers.

Box 2 If any of your previous returns showed too little VAT payable by you or too much VAT repayable to you, show the amount here — but leave out:

- adjustments notified in writing by Customs and Excise
- VAT declared on a previous return which you have not paid in full.

Box 4 You must show the amount of VAT deductible on any business purchases you have made, including imported goods and services and goods removed from bonded warehouse. This is your *input* tax.

If this is your first return include any VAT you can reclaim on goods and services received before registration (see *The VAT guide*, paragraph 33).

Exclude any VAT on:

- goods and services not supplied for the use of your business
- business entertainment (except of overseas customers)
- motor cars
- second-hand goods which have been sold to you under one of the VAT second-hand schemes.

If you are a builder see VAT Leaflet, *Construction industry*, about non-deductible input tax on fixtures and fittings.

Remember to subtract any VAT credited by your suppliers.

If you have exempt outputs this may affect the amount of input tax you can reclaim (see *The VAT guide*, paragraph 30).

Box 5 If any of your previous returns showed too much VAT payable by you or too little VAT repayable to you show the amount here.

Include:

- any VAT you are claiming back as bad debt relief under the conditions set out in the VAT Leaflet, *Relief from VAT on bad debts*, and tick the box on the front of this form.

Exclude:

- adjustments notified in writing by Customs and Excise
- repayments of VAT claimed on a previous return but not yet received from Customs and Excise
- assessments already paid in this or other periods.

DU 2113/2/86 (R)

Box 7 If the amount to be entered is under £1 you must still fill in this form and send it to the VAT Central Unit. You need not send any payment, nor will any repayment be made to you.

Boxes 8 and 9 Show your total outputs in box 8. Include zero-rated sales, exports, exempt income such as rents, and other business income. Leave out the VAT. If exports or exempt outputs are included please tick the appropriate box(es) on the front of this form.

Show your total inputs in box 9. Include imports and other business expenses. Leave out the VAT.

For both boxes 8 and 9 you should show net figures after deducting any credits. Do not deduct any cash discounts. If your accounts are net of cash discounts you should add back a reasonable amount for any discounts given or received.

Some income and expenses must be left out of boxes 8 and 9. There are two ways to work these boxes out — Basis A and Basis B. Use the same basis for both boxes. Whichever basis you use always leave out:

- VAT
- wages and salaries
- PAYE and National Insurance contributions
- money put into or taken out of the business
- loans, dividends, grants, gifts of money
- compensation payments or insurance claims
- Stock Exchange dealings.

If you use Basis A also leave out:

Box 8

- sales of cars on which you paid no VAT (see *The VAT guide*, Appendix B, paragraph 10)
- exempt outputs excluded from any partial exemption calculation.

Box 9

- exempt purchases
- MOT fees and vehicle licence duty
- local authority rates
- purchases on which you cannot reclaim input tax (see *The VAT guide*, paragraph 28).

If you decide to use Basis B check if either or both of your outputs or inputs are above £50,000 on average (or £20,000 if you make monthly returns). If they are you must tell Customs and Excise by attaching a letter to the first VAT return that you make using Basis B, quoting "reference 2B/Basis B".

If you later decide to change to Basis A, you must inform Customs and Excise in the same way.

Remember, you must tell your local VAT office about any changes in your business circumstances. You will find details in *The VAT guide*, Section XI.

115

Appendix 4 Extract from leaflet regarding the default surcharge system

VAT: Default surcharge
Information sheet

From 1 October 1986 failure to send in your VAT return or pay all the VAT due on time will not be a criminal offence. Instead, Customs and Excise will be able to impose a financial penalty—known as a "default surcharge".

How will the default surcharge work?

1. If your VAT return and all the VAT due for the period it covers are not received by the VAT Central Unit by the due date, you will be **in default**.

If you default twice in any 12 month period you will be sent a Surcharge Liability Notice. The Notice will warn you that if you default again in the following 12 months you will have to pay a surcharge on any VAT involved. Once a Notice has been issued, you will have to pay a surcharge each time you default until you have not been in default for 12 months.

Your VAT return and any VAT due **must reach** the VAT Central Unit by the due date shown on the return. Please remember to post it to arrive in good time.

> A surcharge will never be imposed without warning—a Surcharge Liability Notice will always be issued first.

How will the surcharge be calculated?

2. The surcharge will be calculated as a percentage of the VAT that is unpaid for the accounting period covered by the return. If you don't send in your return the amount of VAT you owe will be assessed and the surcharge will be calculated as a percentage of this amount.

How much will the surcharge be?

3. For the first default after a Surcharge Liability Notice has been issued the surcharge will be 5% of the VAT you owe. As long as a Notice is in force the surcharge will be increased by 5% each time you default—to a maximum of 30% of the VAT owed.

There will be an overriding minimum surcharge of £30.

Can I appeal against a surcharge?

4. If a surcharge has been imposed and you think that you have a reasonable excuse for the default you should ask your local VAT office to reconsider the matter. If you are still not satisfied you can appeal to an independent VAT tribunal. You will find more about the appeals procedure in "The VAT guide", Section XIII.

> Remember, it is not enough to claim that:
> - you can't afford to pay
> - your employee, agent, accountant or some other person failed to perform a task on your behalf.
>
> You can only appeal if you have a reasonable excuse.

Appendix 4

Further advice

5. Further guidance on this and other changes to be introduced on 1 October will be available later in the year. If, in the meantime, you need more help or advice, your local VAT office is always ready to help you. Addresses are in the phone book under "Customs and Excise".

> **Please remember**, if you account for VAT accurately and on time you will never have to pay a surcharge. Check now that your accounting system meets our requirements— don't wait until the surcharge is introduced.

1 February 1986

Appendix 5   Extract from leaflet regarding the repayment supplement scheme

VAT: Repayment supplement
Information sheet

From 1 October 1986 Customs and Excise will have to make a compensatory payment—known as a repayment supplement—if they fail to pay an acceptable claim within a reasonable period.

How will the repayment supplement work?

1. If your input tax exceeds your output tax in the period covered by a return you claim the difference when you send in your return. From 1 October the VAT Central Unit will have to pay you a supplement if they fail to pay an acceptable claim within a reasonable period—normally 30 days from the date it is received. But in cases where Customs have to check your claim or sort out errors it may be necessary for them to extend the 30 day period.

Are there any other conditions?

2. Yes. To qualify for a supplement—

(a) your VAT return must be received by the VAT Central Unit within one month of the due date shown on the form.
(b) you must have made returns and paid any VAT due for all earlier periods—a paid assessment doesn't count as a return.

> If, as a result of a mistake on your return, you have overclaimed by more than £100 you will not qualify for a supplement.

How much will the supplement be?

3. The supplement will be 5% of the payment due to you or £30—whichever is the greater. Any errors you have made will be corrected before the supplement is calculated.

How will the supplement be paid?

4. The supplement will be paid at the same time as your delayed claim. You won't need to make a separate claim or show it on a return for a later period.

Will the supplement apply to all kinds of claims?

5. No. Repayment supplements will be paid for most repayment claims made on a VAT return—the only exception is claims for bad debt relief. But it will not apply to other claims, such as—

(a) refunds paid to European Community traders;
(b) refunds to do-it-yourself housebuilders;
(c) claims relating to services received after deregistration.

Further advice

6. Further guidance on this and other changes to be introduced on 1 October will be available later in the year. If, in the meantime, you need more help or advice, your local VAT office is always ready to help you. Addresses are in the phone book under "Customs and Excise".

1 February 1986

Appendix 6   List of regulations and examples of Treasury orders

VAT (GENERAL) REGULATIONS 1985, SI 1985/886

No of reg   Brief Description

Registration

4(1)	Failure to notify liability to be registered on Form VAT 1.
4(1A)	Failure to sign Form VAT 1.
4(2)	Failure to notify details of each partner in a registration on Form VAT 2.
4(3)	Failure to notify change of registration details in writing.
4(4)	Failure to notify date of cessation in writing.

Discretionary registration (intending traders)

5(2)	Failure to repay payment or credit allowed.
5(3)	Failure to preserve tax invoices.
6(1)	Failure to keep and preserve records relating to building or site.
6(3)	Failure to repay payment or credit allowed in connection with building or site.
6(4)	
7(1)	Failure to keep and preserve records relating to housing association.
7(3)	Failure to repay payment or credit allowed to housing association.
7(4)	
8	Failure by intending traders to notify that they no longer intend to make taxable supplies.

Death, bankruptcy or incapacity

11(2)	Failure to notify death/incapacity of taxable person in writing.

Tax invoices

12(5)	Failure to supply a tax invoice within time limit.
13(1)	Failure to provide full particulars on a tax invoice.
13(3)	Failure to distinguish on tax invoice between standard rated, exempt and zero-rated supplies.
14	Failure to supply a credit note within time limit following a change of rate and to provide full information.
15(1)	Failure by a retailer to supply an invoice and to provide information.
15(2)	Failure to exclude zero-rated or exempt supplies from an invoice issued under 15(1).

Appendix 6

Partial exemption

34(1)	Failure to adjust provisional attribution of inputs on next return.
34(2)	Failure to adjust attribution on next return.
36	Failure to use special method for 2 years.
37(3)	Failure to comply with requirement under s 37(1).
37(4)	Failure to compile and preserve records as required to support claim under s 97(1).

Postal importations

41	Failure to show VAT registration number on the Customs declaration.

Temporary importations

42(2)	Failure to produce goods and make deposit at import.
42(3)	Failure to observe restrictions on use and supply of goods.
42(4)	Failure to produce goods.
42(5)	Failure to keep and produce records.
42(6)	Failure to export goods within the time limit.
42(7)	Failure to produce evidence of exportation.

Accounting and payment

58(4)	Failure to furnish a final VAT return by the appropriate date.
59	Failure by an auctioneer to furnish a statement of supplies deemed to be made on behalf of a registered person.
60(a)	Failure to account for all tax on a return.
61	Failure to adjust estimated output tax.
62(1)	Failure to provide evidence of input tax claimed.
62(2)	Failure to adjust estimated input tax.
63	Failure by personal representative to comply with requirements.
64	Failure to correct errors in return.

VAT TREASURY ORDERS

Examples

VAT (Cars) Order 1980	SI 1980/442
VAT (Special Provisions) Order 1981	SI 1981/1741
VAT (Horses and Ponies) Order 1981	SI 1983/1099
VAT (Imported Goods) Relief Order 1984	SI 1984/746
VAT (Place of Supply) Order 1984	SI 1984/1685

Appendix 7 Application for registration (VAT 1)

VALUE ADDED TAX — Application for Registration

For official use

Date of receipt

Local office code and registration number

Name

Trade name

Taxable turnover

Rept | Vol | Oversize name address | Computer user | Group Div | Intg | Overseas

Bn

You should read the notes opposite before you answer these questions. Please write clearly in ink.

Applicant and business

1 Full name

2 Trading name

3 Address

Phone no.

Postcode

4 Status of business

Limited company ☐ Company incorporation certificate no. _____ and date __/__/19__

Sole proprietor ☐ Partnership ☐ Other-specify _____

5 Business activity _____ Trade classification _____

6 Computer user ☐

7 Date of first taxable supply __/__/19__ Expected value of taxable supplies in the next 12 months £_____

Repayments of VAT

Bank sorting code and account no.

National Girobank account no.

8 ☐

VAT 1

please continue overleaf ⟶

121

Appendix 7

Compulsory registrations

9 Date from which you have to be registered — day / month / year 19☐

10 Exemption from compulsory registration ☐

expected value of zero-rated supplies in the next 12 months £☐

Other types of registration

11 Taxable supplies below registration limits ☐

value of taxable supplies in the last 12 months £☐

12 No taxable supplies made yet ☐

(a) expected annual value of taxable supplies £☐

(b) expected date of first taxable supply — day / month / year 19☐

Business changes and transfers

13 Business transferred as a going concern ☐

(a) date of transfer or change of legal status — day / month / year 19☐

(b) name of previous owner ☐

(c) previous VAT registration number (if known) ☐

14 Transfer of VAT registration number ☐

Related businesses

15 Other VAT registrations   Yes ☐   No ☐

Declaration You must complete this declaration.

16

I _____
(Full name in BLOCK LETTERS)

declare that all the entered details and information in any accompanying documents are correct and complete.

Signature _____ Date _____

Proprietor ☐   Partner ☐   Director ☐   Company Secretary ☐   Authorised Official ☐   Trustee ☐

For official use

Registration	Obligatory	Exemption	Voluntary	Intending	Transfer of Regn. no.
Approved –Initial/Date					
Refused – Initial/Date					
Form Issued – Initial/Date	VAT 9/ Other	VAT 8	VAT 7	Letter	Approval Letter

VAT1 F3733 (FEBRUARY 1986)

Appendix 7

9 You must answer this question even if you are applying for exemption under Question 10.

You should read paragraph 6 of the registration booklet before you answer this question.
If you decide that you have to register you must give the date from which you have to be registered.
If you wish to register from a date earlier than you have to, please enclose a letter explaining why and from what date.

10 You can apply for exemption from registration if you would not normally be liable to pay VAT to Customs and Excise because your taxable supplies are wholly or mainly zero-rated. If you want to apply for exemption from registration, you should:
- tick the box; and
- give the value of the zero-rated supplies you expect to make in the next 12 months.

Paragraph 7 of the registration booklet tells you more about this.

Please make sure that you have also answered Question 9.

11 Paragraph 8 of the registration booklet explains when you can apply for registration if the value of your taxable supplies is below the registration limits. If, having read this, you decide to apply, you should:
- tick the box;
- give the value of your taxable supplies in the last 12 months; and
- enclose a letter explaining why you need to be registered.

12 Paragraph 9 of the registration booklet explains when you can apply for registration if you are not yet making taxable supplies but intend to do so in the future. If, having read this, you decide to apply, you should:
- tick the box;
- give the annual value of taxable supplies you expect to make;
- give the date when you expect to make your first taxable supply; and
- enclose supporting evidence to show that you will be making taxable supplies by that date.

If you are answering Questions 13 and 14, you should read the leaflet *Selling or transferring a business as a going concern*, because of the special VAT rules which apply.

13 If you are taking over a business as a going concern, or changing the legal status of your existing business, for example from sole proprietor to partnership, you should:
- tick the box; and
- answer questions (a), (b) and (c).

14 Tick the box if you wish to retain the existing registration number of the business.

15 If, during the last twelve months, you have been (or now are) a director, sole proprietor or partner of any VAT registered business, you should:
- tick the YES box; and
- enclose a letter giving the name(s) of the business(es) and the VAT registration number(s).

If, during the last twelve months, you have not been a director, sole proprietor or partner of any VAT registered business, please tick the NO box.

16 Only the person specified below should sign the declaration and tick the appropriate box:
- for a sole proprietor – the sole proprietor
- for a partnership – a partner
- for a company incorporated under the UK Companies Acts – a director or the company secretary
- for a public corporation or nationalised body, or a local authority, or any other corporation – an authorised official
- for an unincorporated association – an authorised official
- for a trust – the trustee(s)
- for an overseas company, non-resident person or firm – see the leaflet *Overseas traders and United Kingdom VAT*.

Please remember, you must send the completed form(s), with any extra information requested, to the VAT office nearest your principal place of business.

Appendix 7

VALUE ADDED TAX

Application for Registration

The registration booklet *Should I be registered for VAT?* will help you decide whether you should register. If, having read this booklet, you decide that you have to register you must fill in this form.

Don't delay in returning this form. There are penalties for failing to notify promptly once you are liable to be registered. You may also have to account for VAT which you haven't collected and which you may not be able to recover from your customers.

If you will be importing goods you should ask your local VAT office to send you a Form C1416.

Remember, if you need more help or advice your local VAT office is always ready to help. You will find the address in the phone book under "Customs and Excise".

---

1 If the application is from a:
- sole proprietor – give your title (eg Mr) followed by your first name(s) and surname
- company – give the company name
- partnership – give the firm's name. If there is none, give the full names of all the partners. You must also fill in a Form VAT 2.

Please start at the beginning of each line, use block letters and leave a space between words. For example:

`M R   M A R K   J O H N   S M I T H`

Remember:
- it is the person not the business that is registered for VAT
- a person can be a sole proprietor, partnership, limited company, club or association or charity
- registration covers all the business activities of the registered person – no matter how varied these activities are

2 Show the trading name of your business if it is different from the name you gave at Question 1.

3 This should be the place where orders are received and dealt with and the day to day business activities carried on or managed. Don't forget to show the postcode and phone number where you can be contacted.

4 Tick the appropriate box. If the business is a limited company you should also give the number and date shown on the Certificate of Incorporation.

5 Give a brief description of your main business activity and put the trade classification code number which best fits it. A list of business activities and their codes is given in the booklet *VAT Trade Classifications* (VAT 41).

6 Tick the box if any part of your records or accounts will be prepared by computer.

7 Give the date on which you made, or expect to make, your first taxable supply. Then give the total value of taxable supplies – sales, etc – that you expect to make in the next 12 months.

You will find more about taxable supplies in paragraphs 2 and 3 of the registration booklet. Normally the value of your taxable supplies will be your total turnover. If you are unsure about whether or not to include some items – such as donations or grants – please check with your local VAT office.

8 If you expect regular repayments of VAT from Customs and Excise **because the VAT on your sales will normally be less than the VAT on your purchases** you should:
- tick the box; **and**
- give either your bank sorting code and account number **or** National Girobank account number.

Appendix 8 Compound settlement offer

NOTE 34

Example of a letter offering a compounded settlement in respect of VAT

12 June 1980

Dear Sir

The Commissioners of Customs and Excise have had under consideration a report from their officer on the failure of the partnership of X and Y to account for the full amount of value added tax.

The Commissioners consider that you have rendered yourself liable to prosecution under section 38 of the Finance Act 1972 and have contemplated ordering legal proceedings to be taken against you.

The Commissioners are prepared to compound proceedings and settle the arrears of value added tax which have been suppressed from the accounts of the partnership during the period 12 January 1976 to 31 October 1979 on payment of £18,000.00. Account has been taken of input tax to which you were entitled during the specified period and no further claims may be made in respect of it.

If you wish to accept this offer payment is to be made to:

The Accountant and Comptroller General
   Chief Cashier
   HM Customs and Excise
   Room 123
   King's Beam House
   39/41 Mark Lane
   LONDON
   EC3R 7HE

in the enclosed envelope. The reference ABC is to be quoted. Cheques are to be crossed and made payable to: "The Commissioners of Customs and Excise".

Appendix 8

This offer is without prejudice to the Commissioners' legal powers in respect of value added tax and if payment is not made by 30 June 1980 proceedings will be instituted without further notice.

Arrears of £606.44 in respect of which criminal proceedings are considered inappropriate are due in addition and are payable immediately but may be paid with the settlement if you wish.

The Commissioners must not be expected to exercise similar leniency in the event of any future irregularity on your part in relation to value added tax.

Yours faithfully

Appendix 9 Extra-statutory VAT concessions

Notice 748
(*January 1986*)

Extra-statutory concessions
1 January 1986

Her Majesty's Customs and Excise

Appendix 9

In certain circumstances where remission or repayment of VAT, customs duty or excise duty is not provided for by law, Customs and Excise may allow relief on an extra-statutory basis.

This notice lists Customs and Excise extra-statutory concessions in force at 1 January 1986. It includes the information about VAT concessions which was previously given in the VAT leaflet 'Extra-statutory concessions' (700/23/84) which is cancelled.

The concessions are set out in two lists:

    A: VAT concessions
    B: Other Customs and Excise concessions.

Where a concession involves more than one charge, such as VAT and customs duty, it is listed under its primary heading and the other reliefs are indicated in the text.

All of the concessions listed in this leaflet are for general use. Concessions for individual cases are not included.

You should remember that this notice does not give the detailed conditions for the concessions - but it will show you where to find them. You must always be able to meet all the conditions **before** you can use a concession. If you are in any doubt you should check with Customs and Excise. You will find addresses of local VAT offices and Collectors' Offices in the phone book under "Customs and Excise". But for more information about concessions 17(b), and 18-20 in List B you should contact Customs and Excise Headquarters at the address given below:

    RDA-2
    HM Customs and Excise
    Mark Lane
    London EC3R 7HE
    (Telephone: (01) 382-5058/5060).

In certain trades particular arrangements for applying VAT and other charges have been agreed with the appropriate trade associations. These are not extra-statutory concessions and are not listed in this Notice. You can get more information about these agreements from trade associations or from Customs and Excise.

Appendix 9

CONTENTS

Paragraph		Page

A: VAT CONCESSIONS

1.	Disposal of assets	4
2.	Bad debts	4
3.	Repossessed goods	4
4.	Misunderstanding	5
5.	Misdirection	5
6.	VAT charged by unregistered persons	5
7.	Business entertainment	6
8.	Charities etc	7
9.	Handicapped persons	7
10.	Insurance	8
11.	Linked goods schemes	8
12.	Dealer loader schemes	9
13.	Sailaway boats	9
14.	Goods supplied in duty-free shops	9
15.	Inland purchases by visiting forces	10

B: OTHER CUSTOMS AND EXCISE CONCESSIONS

1.	Containers and pallets	11
2.	Imported tobacco products	11
3.	Personal importations of private property	11
4.	Converted vehicles	12
5.	Demonstration cars	13
6.	Research and development cars	13
7.	Welfare vehicles for the handicapped	13
8.	Recycling of waste oil	13
9.	Hydrocarbon oil, duty-paid, for use in home waters	13
10.	Hydrocarbon oil for fairgrounds etc	14
11.	Hydrocarbon oil for aircraft of overseas airlines	14

Appendix 9

Paragraph		Page
12.	Hydrocarbon oil lost in transit	14
13.	Hydrocarbon oil delivered duty-paid to bonded distributors and bonded users	14
14.	Hydrocarbon oil delivered duty-paid for refinery boilers	15
15.	Third 'spare' gaming machines	15
16.	Sparkling wine	15
17.	Visiting forces	15
18.	International organisations	16
19.	UK products purchased by diplomats	16
20.	Foreign civil servants	16
21.	Excise duty on importations for examination or test	17

Appendix 9

A: VAT CONCESSIONS

Concession	Detailed information
1. Disposal of assets (a) The value of disposals of capital assets previously used in the business can be excluded from taxable turnover for the purpose of VAT registration or deregistration. (b) On deregistration, unless the business is being transferred as a going concern, VAT must be accounted for on the cost of goods forming part of the assets of a business. The cost of any used equipment can be taken as its price if bought in its used state. (c) If goods forming part of the assets of a business are disposed of for no consideration, so that they no longer form part of those assets, VAT must be accounted for on their cost. The cost of any used goods can be taken as their price if bought in their used state.	**Registration:** VAT Leaflet: 'Should I be registered for VAT?'. **Deregistration:** VAT Leaflet: 'Cancelling your registration'. VAT Leaflet: 'Cancelling your registration'. Ask your local VAT office.
2. Bad debts Relief from VAT on bad debts can be extended to goods supplied under a contract reserving the supplier's title to the goods until they have been paid for.	VAT Leaflet: 'Relief from VAT on bad debts'.
3. Repossessed goods When goods supplied under an agreement reserving the supplier's title to the goods until they have been paid for (hire-purchase, conditional sale etc) are subsequently repossessed, the supplier can, subject to certain conditions, reduce the value of the original supply by issuing a credit note to his customer.	Ask your local VAT office.

131

Appendix 9

Concession	Detailed information
This procedure cannot be used for goods dealt with under one of the VAT second-hand schemes.	
4. Misunderstanding In certain circumstances Customs and Excise may exceptionally waive VAT undercharged by a registered person as a result of a genuine misunderstanding which does not concern anything clearly covered in guidance published by Customs and Excise or in specific instructions given to that registered person.	Ask your local VAT office.
5. Misdirection If a Customs and Excise officer, with the full facts before him, has given a clear and unequivocal ruling on VAT in writing or, knowing the full facts, has misled a registered person to his detriment, any assessment of VAT due will be based on the correct ruling from the date the error was brought to the registered person's attention.	Ask your local VAT office.
6. VAT charged by unregistered persons Where an amount is shown or represented as VAT on an invoice issued by a person who is neither registered nor required to be registered for VAT at the time the invoice is issued, Customs and Excise require that person to pay an equivalent amount to them. In certain circumstances a person making such a payment may be permitted to deduct from it the amount of VAT incurred on supplies to him of goods and services that were directly attributable to the invoiced supplies. If the goods or services were supplied to a registered person Customs and Excise will, in certain circumstances, allow the recipient to treat the amount shown or represented as VAT as input tax.	Ask your local VAT office.

Appendix 9

Concession	Detailed information
7. Business entertainment The business entertainment provisions prevent input tax deduction on goods or services provided for business entertainment unless provided to employees or overseas customers. But: (a) Where capital goods are either purchased or taken on extended loan and used partly for business entertainment and partly for other business uses, a proportion of the input tax may be deductible.	'The VAT guide', Appendix D.
(b) Where goods or services are used for both business entertainment and other business purposes and these other business purposes are not incidental to the business entertainment, an apportionment may be applied to avoid the input tax being wholly blocked.	'The VAT guide', Appendix D.
(c) Where **subsistence** type meals and drinks are provided: — **by the organisers of agricultural shows, sporting and similar events,** to persons who may be regarded as temporary employees because they represent or act on behalf of the organiser during the course of the event, eg stewards, the input tax incurred may be deductible.	'The VAT guide', Appendix D.
— **by film production companies** to persons who, although essential to the production of the film, are not their employees, eg self-employed technicians and extras, the input tax incurred may be deductible.	Ask your local VAT office.

Appendix 9

Concession	Detailed information
(d) Where recognised representative sporting bodies necessarily provide accommodation and meals to amateur sport persons, the input tax incurred may be deductible.	Ask your local VAT office.

Concession	Detailed information
8. Charities etc (a) Where a charity or voluntary body, not carrying on a business, undertakes a construction project consisting of a new self-contained building to be used mainly for activities which: - benefit the aged, sick, disabled, needy or young people; **or** - are for social, cultural or artistic benefit of the community in general, Customs and Excise may allow a refund of the VAT incurred on purchases made for the project.	VAT Leaflet: 'Charities and other bodies engaged in new building projects on a self-build or self-help basis'.
(b) Goods exported by a charity may be treated as if they were exported in the course of a business carried on by the charity. This enables a VAT-registered charity to treat the VAT charged on these goods at the time of purchase as input tax.	Ask your local VAT office.

Concession	Detailed information
9. Handicapped persons (a) The supply of goods specially adapted for a particular handicapped person may be treated as two separate supplies: - a supply of standard-rated goods valued as in their original state; **and** - a supply of a zero-rated service of adaption.	VAT Leaflet: 'Aids for handicapped persons'.

134

Appendix 9

Concession	Detailed information
(b) From 1 June 1984 the supply to a handicapped person of the service of providing for the first time a bathroom, washroom or lavatory on the ground floor of that person's private residence is relieved from VAT under item 10 of Group 14 of the Zero Rate Schedule. The relief includes the supply of goods in connection with any of these services. This is extended from the same date to cover the supply to a handicapped person of the services of providing, extending or adapting any bathroom, washroom or lavatory in that person's private residence where this is necessary by reason of that person's condition.	VAT Leaflet: 'Aids for handicapped persons'.
10. Insurance Imported insurance services provided by overseas insurers may be treated as exempt from VAT if the services would have been exempt if supplied by a UK insurer permitted to carry on insurance business by the Department of Trade.	VAT Leaflet: 'Insurance'.
11. Linked goods schemes These are promotion schemes where a minor article is linked and sold with a main article at a single price - for example, a packet of soap powder sold with a washing machine. This is treated as a combined supply at a single price and if the articles are liable to VAT at different rates, the sale value must normally be apportioned. But provided the promotion is for a limited period and the minor article comes within certain limits it can be treated as taxable at the same rate as the main article.	VAT Leaflet: 'Business promotion schemes'.

Appendix 9

Concession	Detailed information
12. Dealer loader schemes These are promotion schemes in which additional goods are offered to trade customers in return for orders of a specified size as an inducement to purchase in greater quantities. The supplier can treat the cash price paid by the customer as applying to both the main goods ordered and the reward goods if: - he apportions the price between them on his tax invoice; **or** - where the goods are all of the same type, he invoices them under a single description.	VAT Leaflet: 'Business promotion schemes'.
13. Sailaway boats Where a boat is supplied to a UK resident who intends to export it under its own power within 7 days of delivery and keep the boat abroad for a continuous period of at least 12 months the supplier may zero-rate the supply of the boat after it has been exported.	VAT Leaflet: 'Sailaway boats supplied for export'.
14. Goods supplied at duty-free shops Where goods which are liable to VAT are supplied to intending passengers at duty-free shops approved by Customs and Excise, the supplier may be regarded as the exporter and zero-rate the supply of those goods which are exported.	

Appendix 9

Concession	Detailed information
15. Inland purchases by visiting forces In order to place inland purchases on the same footing as imported goods, VAT and car tax are waived on certain inland purchases by NATO military agencies, the US Government, SHAPE and its agents, and visiting forces and their personnel.	Ask Customs and Excise Headquarters.

Appendix 9

B: OTHER CUSTOMS AND EXCISE CONCESSIONS

Concession	Detailed information
1. Containers and pallets Duty and VAT may be waived on foreign owned containers and pallets which are temporarily imported for emptying or filling and subsequent re-exportation. This concession also extends to parts and accessories imported separately for the repair of, or for installation in, containers.	Notice 309 'Containers, pallets and packing'.
2. Imported tobacco products Imported tobacco products may be delivered on importation without payment of Tobacco Products Duty for deposit in premises registered under the Tobacco Products Regulations. The products are treated thereafter as if they had been manufactured in the UK.	Notice 476 'Tobacco Products Duty'.
3. Personal importations of private property Personal importations of private property (including motor vehicles) that meet the conditions described in Notice 3, "Bringing your Belongings to the United Kingdom" but:	
o are imported more than six months before or twelve months after a person takes up residence in the UK, or	Ask your Collector's office.
o were purchased duty and tax free before 1 January 1984, or	Ask your Collector's office.

Appendix 9

Concession	Detailed information
o were purchased duty and tax tax free by: diplomats, members of officially recognised international organisations and members and civilian staff of NATO and UK forces, or o the required period of use or possession and use of the goods is not met due to circumstances beyond the importer's control, may be relieved of customs duty, VAT, car tax and other excise duties.	Ask Customs and Excise Headquarters. Ask Customs and Excise Headquarters.
4. Converted vehicles (a) Car tax can be remitted when unused vehicles chargeable with car tax are converted into non-chargeable vehicles, eg estate cars into hearses. As convertors may not know at the time of purchase that a particular vehicle is to be converted, the car tax may be refunded on unused chargeable vehicles, including imported vehicles, which are converted into non-chargeable vehicles prior to being registered for road use in the UK. (b) When vehicles which are not chargeable with car tax are converted into vehicles which are, eg by fitting rear side windows into vans, car tax is payable. However, provided the conversion is notified to Customs and Excise car tax is not charged where the conversion is carried out more than six years after the vehicle was first registered for road use.	Notice 670 "Car Tax: General Guide". Notice 672 "Car Tax: Conversion of vehicles".

Appendix 9

Concession	Detailed information
5. Demonstration cars Subject to certain conditions VAT and car tax are not charged when British-made cars are demonstrated by manufacturers for sale purposes to visiting forces personnel or to bona-fide export customers.	Ask your local VAT office.
6. Research and development cars Relief from car tax may be allowed on cars either made or imported by a person registered for car tax provided Customs and Excise are satisfied that the cars are used for research and development purposes.	Notice 670 "Car Tax: General Guide".
7. Welfare vehicles for the handicapped Car tax may be remitted or repaid when a chargeable vehicle is supplied in accordance with the provisions of the VAT Act 1983, Schedule 5, Group 16, and is relieved from VAT under the VAT (Charities etc) Order 1984.	Notice 670 "Car Tax: General Guide".
8. Recycling of waste oil When hydrocarbon oil delivered from a refinery for home use on payment of duty has been produced wholly or in part from oil on which duty has previously been paid and not repaid, Customs and Excise may allow such credit of duty as they deem to have been previously paid.	Ask your Collector's office.
9. Hydrocarbon oil, duty paid, for use in home waters Provided Customs and Excise are satisfied that heavy oil has been delivered on board a vessel for use as fuel on a voyage in home waters they may repay any duty which they are satisfied has been paid and not repaid on the quantity of oil so	Ask your Collector's office.

Appendix 9

Concession	Detailed information
delivered, subject to the conditions which would apply if the oil concerned had been delivered from a refinery or warehouse without payment of duty.	
10. Hydrocarbon oil for fairgrounds etc Fairgrounds etc showmen may use rebated hydrocarbon oil in the engines of their vehicles to generate electricity provided the vehicle is immobilised by disconnection of the propeller shaft, and the fuel is supplied from a tank entirely separate from the vehicle.	Ask your Collector's office.
11. Hydrocarbon oil for aircraft of overseas airlines Excise duty need not be paid on hydrocarbon oil loaded in the UK by aircraft of overseas airlines and used to complete their inward international flights.	Notice 29 "Customs control of traffic by air".
12. Hydrocarbon oil lost in transit When hydrocarbon oil has been delivered in bulk from bonded storage for home use, Customs and Excise may allow a reduction of 0.07% on the excise duty payable to cover oil lost in transit. This concession does not apply to artificially heated oil or deliveries by road tanker.	Ask your Collector's office.
13. Hydrocarbon oil delivered duty-paid to bonded distributors and bonded users When duty paid oil is delivered to a bonded distributor or bonded user approved to receive that kind of oil duty free, Customs and Excise may repay the duty to the supplier, subject to the same conditions as apply to duty free deliveries.	Ask your Collector's office.

Appendix 9

Concession	Detailed information
14. Hydrocarbon oil delivered duty-paid for refinery boilers When unused duty-paid hydrocarbon oil has been delivered to an approved refinery for use as fuel to produce energy, Customs and Excise may repay to the supplier the duty paid, and not repaid, on the delivery.	Ask your Collector's office.
15. Third 'spare' gaming machines Subject to certain conditions laid down by Customs and Excise, gaming machine licence duty need not be paid on a third machine which is held for use only in the event of a breakdown of one of the two machines normally permitted under the Gaming Acts.	Notice 454 "Gaming machine licence duty".
16. Sparkling wine Wine and made-wine will not be regarded as having been 'rendered sparkling' provided their excess pressure is less than 1.5 bars at 20°C and they are not put up in a closed container with a mushroom stopper held in place by a tie or fastening.	Ask your Collector's office.
17. Visiting forces (a) **Imported goods.** In accordance with the NATO Status of Forces Agreement and the 1952 Exchange of Notes, relief from customs duty, excise duty and VAT is available on certain imported goods and hydrocarbon oil used by or on behalf of visiting forces.	Notice 431B: "USAF contracts for the conveyance of personnel and school children: repayment of Customs duty on Road Fuel". Notice 431: "Relief from Customs duty and/or value added tax on United States Government expenditure in the United Kingdom". Notice 316: "Contractors equipment temporarily imported for a NATO infrastructure contract

Appendix 9

Concession	Detailed information
	or in connection with the provision and maintenance of United States defence facilities in the United Kingdom; Customs duty and value added tax".
(b) **Gifts.** Duty and VAT are waived on gifts (other than tobacco goods or alcoholic liquor) sent from abroad for the personal use of visiting forces and on gifts made to charitable organisations by US forces.	Ask Customs and Excise Headquarters.
18. **International organisations** Privileges are allowed to certain international organisations and their officials pending statutory relief under the appropriate Orders-in-Council.	Ask Customs and Excise Headquarters.
19. **UK products purchased by diplomats** So that home produced goods are not placed at a disadvantage, relief from excise duty and VAT is allowed on the same basis as imported goods on purchases by diplomats of UK produced alcoholic drink and tobacco goods.	Ask Customs and Excise Headquarters.
20. **Foreign civil servants** Where no statutory relief applies, Customs charges are waived on goods imported at the time of first arrival of Foreign and Commonwealth civil servants coming to the UK on an official tour of duty.	Ask Customs and Excise Headquarters.

Appendix 9

Concession	Detailed information
21. Excise duty on importations for examination or test The relief from Excise duty for trade samples provided by section 8 of the Customs and Excise Duties (General Reliefs) Act 1979 is extended to allow a relief similar to the relief from customs duty provided by Title XXI of Council Regulation (EEC) No 918/83. Such relief is to be limited to reasonable quantities of excise duty goods imported by producers and processors of such goods, manufacturers of tobacco machinery or research establishments for purposes of examination, analysis or test relevant to their operations, in which tasting and consumption form only a minor part.	Notice 374 'Goods for testing free of duty and tax'.

Appendix 10   List of public notices and leaflets

Value Added Tax

VAT Leaflet 700/13/86   1 January 1986

VAT Publications

Appendix 10

VAT LEAFLET 700/13/86 **1 JANUARY 1986**

VAT PUBLICATIONS

The following VAT notices and leaflets are freely available from any local VAT office.

There is a separate list of all other Customs and Excise publications, available from Collectors' offices.

For addresses of local VAT offices and Collectors' offices see local telephone directories under 'Customs and Excise'.

Notice No.	Leaflet No.	Title	Current Edition (and amendments if any)
700		The VAT guide	1/84 (Amdts 1 and 2)
	700/1/85	Should I be registered for VAT?	
	700/2/83	Registration for VAT - Group treatment	
	700/3/84	Registration for VAT - Corporate bodies organised in divisions	
	700/4/83	Overseas traders and United Kingdom VAT	(Amdt)
	700/5/85	Hire-purchase and conditional sale: repossessions and transfers of agreements	

Appendix 10

Notice No.	Leaflet No.	Title	Current Edition (and amendments if any)
	700/6/80	Management services	
	700/7/81	Business promotion schemes	
	700/8/84	Returnable containers	
	700/9/85	Selling or transferring a business as a going concern	
	700/10/84	Processing and repair of goods and exchange units	
	700/11/85	Cancelling your registration	
	700/12/85	Filling in your VAT return	
	700/13/86	VAT publications	
	700/14/82	Supplies of video cassettes: rental and part-exchange	
	700/15/84	The Ins and Outs of VAT	
	700/16/82	"Party plan" selling and "direct" selling	
	700/17/83	Funded pension schemes	
	700/18/83	Relief from VAT on bad debts	
	700/19/83	Guide to the Value Added Tax Act 1983	
	700/20/83	Transactions in gold bullion, gold coin and gold scrap	
	700/21/86	Keeping records and accounts	
	700/22/84	Admissions	
	700/24/84	Delivery charges	
	700/25/84	Taxis and hire-cars	
	700/26/85	Visits by VAT officers	
	700/27/85	Guide to the Value Added Tax (General) Regulations 1985	
	700/28/85	Services supplied by estate agents	
	1/77/VMG	Barristers and advocates: tax point on ceasing to practise	
	10/74/VMF	Indemnities under property lease agreements	

Appendix 10

Notice No.	Leaflet No.	Title	Current Edition (and amendments if any)
	701/1/84	Charities	
	701/5/84	Clubs and associations	
	701/6/85	Donated medical and scientific equipment etc	
	701/7/84	Aids for handicapped persons	(Amdt)
	701/8/85	Postage stamps and philatelic supplies	
	701/9/85	Terminal markets: dealings with commodities	
	701/10/85	Printed and similar matter	
	701/12/84	Sales of antiques, works of art etc from stately homes	
	701/13/84	Amusement and gaming machine takings	
	701/14/84	Food	
	701/15/84	Animal feeding stuffs	
	701/16/85	Sewerage services and water	
	701/18/84	News services	
	701/19/85	Fuel and power	
	701/20/84	Caravans and houseboats	
	701/21/84	Gold and gold coin	
	701/22/84	Tools for the manufacture of goods for export	
	701/23/84	Protective boots and helmets	
	701/24/84	Parking facilities	
	701/25/84	Pet food	
	701/26/84	Betting and gaming	
	701/27/84	Bingo	
	701/28/84	Lotteries	
	701/29/85	Finance	
	701/30/84	Education	
	701/31/85	Health	(Amdt)

Appendix 10

Notice No.	Leaflet No.	Title	Current Edition (and amendments if any)
	701/32/85	Burial and cremation	
	701/33/84	Trade unions and professional bodies	
	701/34/84	Competitions in sport and physical recreation	
	701/35/84	Youth clubs	
	701/36/85	Insurance	(Erratum)
	701/37/84	Live animals	
	701/38/84	Seeds and plants	
	701/39A/84	VAT Liability law	(Erratum and Amdt)
	701/40/84	Abattoirs	
702		Imports	2/79 (Amdts 1 and 2)
	702/1/85	VAT on imports and warehoused goods	
	702/2/85	Horses temporarily imported before 1 January 1986	
703		Exports	5/83 (Amdt 1)
	703/1/83	Freight containers supplied for export	
	703/2/83	Sailaway boats supplied for export	
704		Retail exports	3/85 (Amdt 1)
	704/1/85	VAT refunds for visitors to the United Kingdom	(Amdt)
	704/2/85	VAT refunds for UK residents going abroad and crews of ships and aircraft	(Amdt)

Appendix 10

Notice No.	Leaflet No.	Title	Current Edition (and amendments if any)
705		Personal exports of new motor vehicles	1/86
706		Partial exemption	4/84
	706/1/83	Self-supply of stationery	
	708/1/85	Protected buildings (listed buildings and scheduled monuments)	
	708/2/85	Construction industry	
	708/3/85	Civil engineering	
	SHP/10	Charities and other bodies engaged in new building projects on a self-build or self-help basis	
	709/1/82	Industrial catering, including catering in hospitals, schools etc	
	709/2/85	Catering and take-away food	
	709/3/85	Hotels and holiday accommodation	
	709/4/85	Package holidays and other holiday services	
	710/1/83	Theatrical agents and Nett Acts	
	710/2/83	Agencies providing nurses and nursing auxiliaries	
	710/3/83	Private investigators: Expenses charged to clients	
711		Second-hand cars (issued with 711/1/84: VAT and the Second-hand Car Scheme)	7/84 (Amdt 1)

150

Appendix 10

Notice No.	Leaflet No.	Title	Current Edition (and amendments if any)
712		Second-hand works of art, antiques and collectors' pieces	1/85
		(issued with 712/2/85: VAT and second-hand works of art, antiques and collectors' pieces)	(Amdt 1)
713		Second-hand motor cycles	9/85
714		Young children's clothing and footwear	2/76 (Amdts 1 and 2)
717		Second-hand caravans and motor caravans	9/85
719		Refund of VAT to "do-it-yourself" housebuilders	11/81 (Amdt 1)
720		Second-hand boats and outboard motors	12/85
721		Second-hand aircraft	12/85
722		Second-hand electronic organs	12/85
723		Refunds of VAT to European Community traders	12/80 (Amdts 1, 2 and 3)
724		Second-hand firearms	4/85 (Amdt 1)
726		Second-hand horses and ponies	1/85 (Amdt 1)
727		Retail schemes	4/83
	727/1/83	Retail Florists - Accounting for VAT on Teleflorist transactions	
	727/2/83	Retail Florists - Accounting for VAT on Interflora transactions	
	727/6/83	Choosing your retail scheme	

Appendix 10

Notice No.	Leaflet No.	Title	Current Edition (and amendments if any)
	727/7/83 to 727/15/83*	How to work Scheme A-J	
741		International services	1/84 (Amdt 1)
742		Land and property	1/84 (Amdt 2)
744		Passenger transport, international freight, ships and aircraft	1/84 (Amdt 1)
748		Extra-statutory concessions	1/86

Explanatory leaflet: Appeals to Value Added Tax Tribunals (Also available from any VAT Tribunal Centre)

---
* separate leaflets describing each retail scheme

Appendix 11 VAT tribunal forms

Trib 1

Value Added Tax
Tribunals

Notice of Appeal

Trib 1 (October 1984)   F 3886 (October 1984)   Dd 8340372 9/84 (11037)

Appendix 11

A. Notes to Notice of Appeal

A.1 How to appeal to a Value Added Tax Tribunal is explained in a booklet **Appeals and Applications to Value Added Tax Tribunals** obtainable at any tribunal centre or Customs and Excise VAT office. This also contains the address of the appropriate tribunal centre to which the completed Notice of Appeal should be delivered or sent.

A.2 An acknowledgement of receipt of a Notice of Appeal at the appropriate tribunal centre will be sent by post.

A.3 In this Notice of Appeal,

Paragraph 1

(a) Partners may appeal in the name of their firm.

Paragraph 2

(b) Insert the date of the assessment or letter containing the disputed decision from the Commissioners.

(c) Insert the address of the office of the Commissioners from which the disputed decision was sent.

(d) Insert the address to which the disputed decision was sent if that address was different from the address inserted in paragraph 1.

(e) State the decision against which you are appealing.

Paragraph 3

(f) State why the decision is disputed.

Paragraph 4

(g) Insert the name and address of any representative appointed to deal with the appeal on behalf of the appellant.

Signature

(h) The Notice must be signed by the person appealing or his representative.

(i) If the Notice is signed by a representative, insert his status (e.g. solicitor, accountant, friend etc.).

A.4 An appeal to a tribunal should be received at the appropriate tribunal centre within 30 days of the date of the disputed decision. If the Commissioners have extended your time for appealing, please attach a copy of their letter doing so to your Notice of Appeal. If the time for your appeal, including any extension given by the Commissioners has expired, you may apply to a tribunal for an extension or further extension of time. If you wish to do so please complete the Notice of Application at the bottom of page 4 stating your grounds for seeking such an extension from the tribunal.

A.5 A form of Notice of Application for an appeal to be entertained without payment or deposit of tax is printed on the back of the Notice of Appeal.

B. Note to Notice of Application for an Appeal to be Entertained without Payment or Deposit of Tax

B.1 If the appeal is against an assessment or the amount of an assessment for output tax or concerns the tax chargeable on the supply of any goods and services or on the importation of any goods, the disputed tax has to be paid or deposited with the Commissioners unless the appellant satisfies the Commissioners or a tribunal that such payment would cause him hardship. Accordingly you may ask the Commissioners to waive the requirement as to payment or deposit of that tax or, alternatively you may apply to a tribunal for a direction that your appeal be entertained without payment or deposit of the tax. If you wish to make such an application please complete the Notice of Application which is printed on the back of the Notice of Appeal.

If you need any help with the completion of the Notices you may apply either in writing or by telephone to one of the Tribunal Offices whose addresses are given in Section 5 of the Explanatory Booklet.

Appendix 11

Value Added Tax Tribunals

Form Trib 1

Please read the notes on page 2 carefully before completing this Notice or the Notices overleaf.

For completion by the Tribunal Centre
Ref. number: ....
Date of service: ....
Ack : ....
Notified: ....

Notice of Appeal

by

....
(Insert the name of the person appealing – see Note A.3(a))

1. The appellant whose address is ....
   (Insert the address of the person appealing)

   ....

   and whose VAT Registration Number (if any) is ⎕⎕⎕⎕⎕⎕⎕⎕⎕

   appeals against the decision of the Commissioners of Customs and Excise mentioned below.

2. The disputed decision of the Commissioners is contained in a letter dated ....
   (See Note A.3(b))

   and was sent from their office at ....
   (See Note A.3(c))

   to ....
   (See Note A.3(d))

   and is ....
   (See Note A.3(e))

   ....

3. The decision of the Commissioners is disputed on the grounds that ....
   (See Note A.3(f))

   ....

4. The name and address of the person (if any) instructed to deal with this appeal on behalf of the appellant are

   ....
   (See Note A.3(g))
   ....

5. There is attached to this Notice of Appeal a copy of any letter extending the time for this appeal as indicated in notes.

   Signed ....
   (See Note A.3(h))

   Dated ....

   Status of signatory ....
   (See Note A.3(i))

   Telephone number (if any) ....

Before sending this form please detach the notes.

Form Trib 1 (October 1984)

Appendix 11

Notice of Application for an Appeal to be Entertained Without Payment or Deposit of Tax

For completion by the Tribunal Centre
Ref. number: ....
Date of service: ....
Ack: ....
Notified ....

by

1. ....
   (Insert the name of the person applying)

   for a direction that he may appeal without payment or deposit of the tax disputed in his appeal notified

   overleaf (or notified on .... 19 ....)

2. The grounds for this application are that payment or deposit of the disputed tax would cause hardship *(See Note B on page 2)*.

3. Signed ....
   (See Note A.3(h) on page 2)

   Dated .... 19 ....

   Status of signatory ....
   (See Note A.3(i) on page 2)

Notice of Application for an Extension of Time

For the completion by the Tribunal Centre
Ref. number: ....
Date of service: ....
Ack: ....
Notified: ....

by

1. ....

   for a direction that time to serve a Notice of Appeal and if applicable a Notice of Application for an appeal to be entertained without payment or deposit of tax may be extended.

2. The grounds for this application are ....
   (See Note A.4 on page 2)
   ....
   ....

3. Signed ....
   (See Note A.3(h) on page 2)

   Dated .... 19 ....

   Status of signatory ....
   (See Note A.3(i) on page 2)

Appendix 11

Form Trib 2

VALUE ADDED TAX TRIBUNALS

Tribunal Centre:

Reference number:

....
(Insert name of person appealing)

and

The Commissioners of Customs and Excise

LIST OF DOCUMENTS

1. The documents in *my/our possession, custody and power relating to the matter of this appeal which *I/we intend to produce at the hearing of this appeal are:—

....
....
....
....
....
....

(If necessary, the list may be continued on a separate sheet, which should be attached to this form.)

157

Appendix 11

2. The foregoing documents may be inspected and copies thereof taken during the period

from .... to ....
   (Insert first and last dates of period)

at ....
   (Insert address at which the documents may be inspected)

*I/we am/are willing to supply copies of the documents to the other party on written request.

Signed ....

Dated ....

†Status of signatory ....

*Delete as necessary

†If this document is signed by an agent of the person appealing, insert the status of the agent (e.g., solicitor, accountant, friend, etc.)

For completion by the tribunal centre

Date of service: ....

Ack: ....

Notified: ....

Form Trib 2

Appendix 11

Form Trib 3

VALUE ADDED TAX TRIBUNALS

Tribunal Centre:

Reference number:

....
(Insert name of person appealing)

and

The Commissioners of Customs and Excise

WITNESS STATEMENT

*State whether this statement is made for the person appealing or the Commissioners.

on behalf of*..

1. My name is..
   (Insert full name of witness)

2. My address is..
   (Insert full address of witness)
   ....

3. My occupation is..
   (Insert description of occupation)

Appendix 11

4. I propose at the hearing of this appeal to say (if required to do so) as follows:—

....
....
....
....
....
....
....

(If necessary, the statement may be continued on a separate sheet Form Trib 3a (continuation) which should also be signed and attached hereto.)

| This statement must be signed by the witness and dated. | Signed .... |
| | Dated .... |

For completion by the tribunal centre

Date of service: .... Notified: ....

Ack: .... Objection received: ....

Form Trib 3

Appendix 11

Form Trib 4

VALUE ADDED TAX TRIBUNALS

Tribunal Centre:

Reference number:

....

(Insert name of person appealing)

and

The Commissioners of Customs and Excise

NOTICE OF OBJECTION

*Delete as necessary   *I/we object to the witness statement signed by

....

(Insert full name of witness)

Appendix 11

on the .... day of .... 197......
   (Insert date)   *(Insert month and year)*

Signed ....

Dated ....

†Status of signatory ....

†If this document is signed by an agent of the person appealing, insert the status of the agent (e.g., solicitor, accountant, friend, etc.).

For completion by the tribunal centre

Date of service: ....

Ack: ....

Notified: ....

Form Trib 4

Appendix 11

Form Trib 5

VALUE ADDED TAX TRIBUNALS

Tribunal Centre:

Reference number:

....
(Insert name of person appealing)

and

The Commissioners of Customs and Excise

NOTICE OF APPLICATION

*Delete as necessary

1. *My/our name and address are..
....

2. *I/we apply for a direction that..
....
....

Appendix 11

3. The grounds for this application are..
   ....
   ....
   ....
   ....
   ....

†If this document is Signed ....
signed by an agent of
the person appealing, Dated ....
insert the status of
the agent (e.g., soli- †Status of signatory..............
citor, accountant,
friend, etc.)

For completion by the tribunal centre

Date of service: ....

Ack: ....

Notified: ....

Form Trib 5

Appendix 12   The Value Added Tax Tribunal Rules 1986

1986 No 590   ★

The Value Added Tax Tribunals Rules 1986

Made . . . . *26th March 1986*
Laid before the House of Commons . . . . . *9th April 1986*
Coming into Operation . . . . *1st May 1986*

ARRANGEMENT OF RULES
1. Citation, commencement, revocation and savings.
2. Interpretation.
3. Method of appealing.
4. Time for appealing.
5. Acknowledgment and notification of an appeal.
6. Notice that an appeal does not lie or cannot be entertained.
7. Statement of case, defence and reply in a section 13 penalty appeal.
8. Statement of case in an appeal, other than a section 13 penalty appeal and reasonable excuse and mitigation appeals.
9. Further and better particulars.
10. Acknowledgment of and notification of formal documents served in an appeal.
11. Method of applying for a direction.
12. Partners.
13. Death or bankruptcy of an appellant or applicant.
14. Amendments.

Appendix 12

15. Transfers between tribunal centres.
16. Withdrawal of an appeal or application.
17. Appeal or application allowed by consent.
18. Power of a tribunal to strike out or dismiss an appeal.
19. Power of a tribunal to extend time and to give directions.
20. Disclosure, inspection and production of documents.
21. Witness statements.
22. Witness summonses and summonses to third parties.
23. Notices of hearings.
24. Hearings in public or in private.
25. Representation at a hearing.
26. Failure to appear at a hearing.
27. Procedure at a hearing.
28. Evidence at a hearing.
29. Awards and directions as to costs.
30. Decisions and directions.
31. Service at a tribunal centre.
32. Sending of documents to the parties.
33. Delegation of powers to the Registrar.

The Commissioners of Customs and Excise, in exercise of the powers conferred upon them by paragraph 9 of Schedule 8 to the Value Added Tax Act 1983 and after consultation with the Council on Tribunals, in accordance with section 10 of the Tribunals and Inquiries Act 1971, hereby make the following Rules—

Citation, commencement, revocation and savings

1—(1) These rules may be cited as the Value Added Tax Tribunals Rules 1986 and shall come into operation on 1st May 1986.

(2) The Value Added Tax Tribunals Rules 1972, the Value Added Tax Tribunals (Amendment) Rules 1974, the Value Added Tax Tribunals (Amendment) Rules 1977, and the Value Added Tax Tribunals (Amendment) (No 2) Rules 1977 are hereby revoked.

(3) Anything begun under or for the purpose of any rules revoked by these rules may be continued under or, as the case may be, for the purpose of the corresponding provision of these rules.

(4) Where any document in any appeal to, or other proceedings before, a tribunal refers to a provision of any rules revoked by these rules, such reference shall, unless a contrary intention appears, be construed as referring to the corresponding provision of these rules.

Interpretation

2 In these rules, unless the context otherwise requires,—

"the Act" means the Value Added Tax Act 1983;
"appellant" means a person who brings an appeal under section 40 of the Act;
"the appropriate tribunal centre" means the tribunal centre for the time being appointed by the President for the area in which is situated the address to which the disputed decision was sent by the Commissioners or the tribunal centre to which the appeal against the disputed decision may be transferred under these rules;
"chairman" has the same meaning as in Schedule 8 to the Act, and includes the President and any Vice-President;
"the Commissioners" means the Commissioners of Customs and Excise;
"costs" includes fees, charges, disbursements, expenses and remuneration;

Appendix 12

"disputed decision" means the decision of the Commissioners against which an appellant or intending appellant appeals or desires to appeal to a tribunal;

"mitigation appeal" means an appeal which, according to the notice of appeal or other document received from the appellant at the appropriate tribunal centre, is against a decision of the Commissioners with respect to the amount of a penalty on the grounds set out in section 13(4) of the Finance Act 1985;

"the President" means the President of Value Added Tax Tribunals or the person nominated by the Lord Chancellor to discharge for the time being the functions of the President;

"proper officer" means a member of the administrative staff of the value added tax tribunals appointed by a chairman to perform the duties of a proper officer under these rules;

"reasonable excuse appeal" means an appeal which, according to the notice of appeal or other document received from the appellant at the appropriate tribunal centre, is against a decision of the Commissioners with respect to the amount of a penalty or surcharge on grounds confined to those set out in sections 14(6), 15(4), 16(4), 17(9) and 19(6) of the Finance Act 1985;

"the Registrar" means the Registrar of the value added tax tribunals or any member of the administrative staff of the value added tax tribunals authorised by the Lord Chancellor to perform for the time being all or any of the duties of a Registrar under these rules;

"section 13 penalty appeal" means an appeal against an assessment to a penalty under section 13 of the Finance Act 1985 which is not solely a mitigation appeal and any accompanying appeal by the appellant against an assessment for the amount of tax alleged to have been evaded by the same conduct;

"tribunal centre" means an administrative office of the value added tax tribunals;

"Vice-President" means a Vice-President of value added tax tribunals.

Method of appealing

3—(1) An appeal to a tribunal shall be brought by a notice of appeal served at the appropriate tribunal centre.

(2) A notice of appeal shall be signed by or on behalf of the appellant and shall—

(a) state the name and address of the appellant;
(b) state the address of the office of the Commissioners from which the disputed decision was sent;
(c) state the date of the document containing the disputed decision and the address to which it was sent;
(d) set out, or have attached thereto a copy of the document containing the disputed decision; and
(e) set out, or have attached thereto a document containing, the grounds of the appeal, including in a reasonable excuse appeal, particulars of the excuse relied upon.

(3) A notice of appeal shall have attached thereto a copy of any letter from the Commissioners extending the appellant's time to appeal against the disputed decision and of any further letter from the Commissioners notifying him of a date from which his time to appeal against the disputed decision shall run.

(4) Subject to any direction made under rule 13, the parties to an appeal shall be the appellant and the Commissioners.

Time for appealing

4—(1) Subject to paragraph (2) of this rule and any direction made under rule 19, a notice of appeal shall be served at the appropriate tribunal centre before the expiration of 30 days after the date of the document containing the disputed decision of the Commissioners.

Appendix 12

(2) If, during the period of 30 days after the date of the document containing the disputed decision, the Commissioners shall have notified the appellant by letter that his time to appeal against the disputed decision is extended until the expiration of 21 days after a date set out in such letter, or to be set out in a further letter to him, a notice of appeal against that disputed decision may be served at the appropriate tribunal centre at any time before the expiration of the period of 21 days set out in such letter or further letter.

Acknowledgment and notification of an appeal

5   A proper officer shall send—

(a) an acknowledgment of the service of a notice of appeal at the appropriate tribunal centre to the appellant; and
(b) a copy of the notice of appeal and of any accompanying document or documents to the Commissioners;

and the acknowledgment and such copy of the notice of appeal shall state the date of service of the notice of appeal.

Notice that an appeal does not lie or cannot be entertained

6—(1) Where the Commissioners contend that an appeal does not lie to, or cannot be entertained by, a tribunal they shall serve a notice to that effect at the appropriate tribunal centre containing the grounds for such contention and applying for the appeal to be struck out or dismissed, as the case may be, as soon as practicable after the receipt by them of the notice of appeal.

(2) Any notice served by the Commissioners under this rule shall be accompanied by a copy of the disputed decision unless a copy thereof has been served previously at the appropriate tribunal centre by either party to the appeal.

(3) In a reasonable excuse or a mitigation appeal the hearing of any application made by the Commissioners under the provisions of this rule may immediately precede the hearing of the substantive appeal.

(4) A proper office shall send a copy of any notice or certificate served under this rule and of any document or documents accompanying the same to the appellant.

Statement of case, defence and reply in a section 13 penalty appeal

7—(1) Unless a tribunal shall otherwise direct, in a section 13 penalty appeal—

(a) the Commissioners shall within 42 days of the date of the service of the notice of appeal or the withdrawal or dismissal of any application made by them under rule 6 hereof (whichever shall be the later) serve at the appropriate tribunal centre a statement of case in the appeal setting out the matters and facts on which they rely for the making of the penalty assessment and (where also disputed) the making of the assessment for the tax alleged to have been evaded by the same conduct;
(b) the appellant shall within 42 days of the date of the service of such statement of case serve at the appropriate tribunal centre a defence thereto setting out the matters and facts on which he relies for his defence; and
(c) the Commissioners may within 21 days of the date of the service of such defence serve at the appropriate tribunal centre a reply to a defence and shall do so if it is necessary thereby to set out specifically any matter or any fact showing illegality, or

(i) which they allege makes the defence not maintainable; or
(ii) which, if not specifically set out, might take the appellant by surprise; or
(iii) which raises any issue of fact not arising out of the statement of case.

(2) At any hearing of a section 13 penalty appeal the Commissioners shall not be

Appendix 12

required to prove, or to bring evidence relating to, any matter or fact which is admitted by the appellant in his defence.

(3) Every statement of case, defence and reply hereunder shall be divided into paragraphs numbered consecutively, each allegation being so far as convenient contained in a separate paragraph.

(4) Each such document shall contain in summary form a brief statement of the matters and facts on which the party relies but not the evidence by which those facts are to be proved.

(5) A party may raise a point of law in such documents.

Statement of case in an appeal other than a section 13 penalty appeal and reasonable excuse and mitigation appeals

8   Unless a tribunal otherwise directs, in appeals other than reasonable excuse and mitigation appeals and section 13 penalty appeals the Commissioners shall within 30 days of the date of the service of the notice of appeal or the withdrawal or dismissal of any application in the appeal under rule 6 hereof (whichever shall be the later) serve at the appropriate tribunal centre a statement of case in the appeal setting out the matters and facts on which they rely to support the disputed decision.

Further and better particulars

9—(1) A tribunal may at any time direct a party to an appeal to serve further particulars of his case at the appropriate tribunal centre for the appeal within such period from the date of such direction (not being less than 14 days from the date thereof) as it may specify therein.

(2) Where on an appeal against a decision with respect to an assessment or the amount of an assessment the Commissioners wish to contend that an amount specified in the assessment is less than it ought to have been, they shall so state in their statement of case in that appeal, indicating the amount of the alleged deficiency and the manner in which it has been calculated.

Acknowledgment and notification of service of formal documents served in an appeal

10—(1) Any statement of case served by the Commissioners under rule 7 or rule 8 of these rules shall be accompanied by a copy of the disputed decision unless a copy of the disputed decision has been served previously at the appropriate tribunal centre by either party to the appeal.

(2) In a reasonable excuse or a mitigation appeal the Commissioners shall serve a copy of the disputed decision at the appropriate tribunal centre as soon as practicable after the receipt by them of the copy of the notice of appeal unless a copy of the disputed decision has been so served previously by the appellant.

(3) A proper officer shall send—

(a) an acknowledgment of the service at the appropriate tribunal centre of any statement of case, defence, reply or particulars in any appeal to the party serving the same; and

(b) a copy of such document or particulars and any other document accompanying the same to the other party to the appeal.

Method of applying for a direction

11—(1) An application to a tribunal, made otherwise than at a hearing, for a direction (including a direction that an appeal or intended appeal may be entertained notwithstanding that an amount of tax has not been paid or deposited with the Commissioners of for the issue or the setting aside of a witness summons) shall be made by notice served at the appropriate tribunal centre.

Appendix 12

(2) A notice under this rule shall—

(a) state the name and address of the applicant;
(b) state the direction sought or details of the witness summons sought to be issued or set aside; and
(c) set out, or have attached thereto a document containing, the grounds of the application.

(3) In addition to the requirement of paragraph (2) hereof, any notice of application by an intending appellant shall—

(a) state the address of the office of the Commissioners from which the disputed decision was sent;
(b) state the date of the disputed decision and the address to which it was sent;
(c) set out shortly the disputed decision or have attached thereto a copy of the document containing the same; and
(d) have attached thereto a copy of any letter from the Commissioners extending the applicant's time to appeal against the disputed decision and of any letter from the Commissioners notifying him of a date from which his time of appeal against the disputed decision shall run.

(4) A notice of application for an appeal to be entertained without payment or deposit of the disputed tax shall be served at the appropriate tribunal centre within the period for the service of a notice of appeal.

(5) Except as provided by rule 22, the parties to an application shall be the parties to the appeal or intended appeal.

(6) Except as provided by rule 22, a proper officer shall send—

(a) an acknowledgment of the service of a notice of application at the appropriate tribunal centre to the applicant; and
(b) a copy of such notice of application and of accompanying document or documents to the other party to the application (if any);

and the acknowledgment and copy of the notice of application shall state the date of service of the notice of application.

(7) Within 14 days of the date of service of a notice of application the other party to the application (if any) shall indicate whether or not he consents thereto and, if he does not consent thereto, the reason therefor.

Partners

12 Partners in a firm which is not a legal person distinct from the partners of whom it is composed may appeal against a decision of the Commissioners relating to the firm or its business, or apply to a tribunal in an appeal or intended appeal, in the name of the frim and, unless a tribunal shall otherwise direct, the proceedings shall be carried on in the name of the firm, but with the same consequences as would have ensued if the appeal or application had been brought in the names of the partners.

Death or bankruptcy of an appellant or applicant

13 Where, at any stage in the proceedings in an appeal or application, the liability or interest of the appellant or applicant, by reason of his death or bankruptcy or for any other reason whatsoever, is assigned or transmitted to or devolves upon some other person, the appeal or application shall not abate or determine, but a tribunal, on the application of the Commissioners or of such other person, may direct that such other person if he so consents in writing be made a party to the appeal or application, and the appeal or application be carried on by such other person as if he had been substituted for the appellant or applicant.

Appendix 12

Amendments

14—(1) For the purposes of determining the issues in dispute or of correcting an error or defect in an appeal or application or intended appeal, a tribunal may at any time, either of its own motion or on the application of any party to the appeal or application, or any other person interested, direct that a notice of appeal, notice of application, statement of case, defence, reply, particulars or other document in the proceedings be amended in such manner as may be specified in such direction on such terms as it may think fit.

(2) This rule shall not apply to a decision or direction of a tribunal.

Transfers between tribunal centres

15 A tribunal on the application of a party to an appeal may direct that the appeal and all proceedings in the appeal be transferred to such tribunal centre as may be specified in such direction whereupon, for the purposes of these rules, the tribunal centre specified in such direction shall become the appropriate tribunal centre for such appeal and all proceedings therein, without prejudice to the power of a tribunal to give a further direction relating thereto under this rule.

Withdrawal of an appeal or application

16—(1) An appellant may at any time withdraw his appeal or application by serving at the appropriate tribunal centre a notice of withdrawal signed by him or on his behalf, and a proper officer shall send a copy thereof to the Commissioners.

(2) The withdrawal of an appeal or application under this rule shall not prevent a party to such appeal or application from applying under rule 29 for an award or direction as to his or their costs or under section 40(4) of the Act for a direction for the payment or repayment of a sum of money with interest or prevent a tribunal from making such an award or direction if it thinks fit so to do.

Appeal or application allowed by consent

17 Where the parties to an appeal or application have agreed upon the terms of any decision or direction to be given by a tribunal, a tribunal may give a decision or make a direction in accordance with those terms without a hearing.

Power of a tribunal to strike out or dismiss an appeal

18—(1) A tribunal shall—

(a) strike out an appeal where no appeal against the disputed decision lies to a tribunal; and
(b) dismiss an appeal where the appeal cannot be entertained by a tribunal.

(2) A tribunal may dismiss an appeal for want of prosecution where the appellant or the person to whom the interest or liability of the appellant has been assigned or transmitted, or upon whom such interest or liability has devolved, has been guilty of inordinate and inexcusable delay.

(3) Except in accordance with rule 17, no appeal shall be struck out or dismissed under this rule without a hearing.

Power of a tribunal to extend time and to give directions

19.—(1) A tribunal may of its own motion or on the application of any party to an appeal or application extend the time within which a party to the appeal or application or any other person is required or authorised by these rules or any decision or direction of a tribunal to do anything in relation to the appeal or application (including the time for service for a notice of appeal or notice of application) upon such terms as it may think fit.

Appendix 12

(2) A tribunal may make a direction under paragraph (1) of this rule of its own motion without prior notice or reference to any party or other person and without a hearing.

(3) Without prejudice to the preceding provisions of this rule a tribunal may on the application of a party to an appeal or application or other person interested give or make any direction as to the conduct of or as to any matter or thing in connection with the appeal or application which it may think necessary or expedient to ensure the speedy and just determination of the appeal.

(4) If any party to an appeal or application or other person fails to comply with any direction of a tribunal, a tribunal may allow or dismiss the appeal or may summarily award a penalty not exceeding £1,000, or both.

(5) A tribunal may, of its own motion or on the application of any party to an appeal or application, waive any breach or non-observance of any provision of these rules or of any decision or direction of a tribunal upon such terms as it may think just.

Disclosure, inspection and production of documents

20.—(1) The parties to an appeal other than a reasonable excuse or a mitigation appeal and the parties to an application for a direction that an appeal be entertained without payment or deposit of the tax in dispute shall, before the expiration of the time set out in paragraph (2) of this rule, serve at the appropriate tribunal centre a list of the documents in his possession, custody or power which he proposes to produce at the hearing of the appeal or application.

(2) The time within which a list of documents shall be served under paragraph (1) of this rule shall be—

(a) in a section 13 penalty appeal, a period of 15 days after the last day for the service by the Commissioners of any reply pursuant to rule 7(1)(c) hereof;

(b) in any other appeal except a reasonable excuse or a mitigation appeal, a period of 30 days after the service of the notice of appeal or application.

(3) In addition, and without prejudice to the foregoing provisions of this rule, a tribunal may, where it appears necessary for disposing fairly of the proceedings, on the application of a party to an appeal direct that the other party to the appeal shall serve at the appropriate tribunal centre for the appeal within such period as it may specify a list of the documents or any class of documents which are or have been in his possession, custody or power relating to any question in issue in the appeal, and may at the same time or subsequently order him to make and serve an affidavit verifying such list.

(4) If a party desires to claim that any document included in a list of documents served by him in pursuance of a direction made under paragraph (3) of this rule is privileged from production in the appeal, that claim must be made in the list of documents with a sufficient statement of the grounds of privilege.

(5) A proper officer shall send copy of any list of documents and affidavit served under paragraph (1) or paragraph (3) of this rule to the other party to the appeal or application and such other party shall be entitled to inspect and take copies of the documents set out in such list which are in the possession, custody or power of the party who made the list and are not privileged from production in the appeal at such time and place as he and the party who served such list of documents may agree or a tribunal may direct.

(6) At the hearing of an appeal or application a party shall produce any document included in a list of documents served by him in relation to such appeal or application under paragraph (1) or paragraph (3) of this rule which is in his possession, custody or power and is not privileged from production when called upon so to do by the other party to the appeal or application.

Appendix 12

Witness statements

21—(1) A party to an appeal may, within the time specified in paragraph (6) of this rule, serve at the appropriate tribunal centre a statement in writing (in these rules called "a witness statement") containing evidence proposed to be given by any person at the hearing of the appeal.

(2) A witness statement shall contain the name, address and description of the person proposing to give the evidence contained therein and shall be signed by him.

(3) A proper officer shall send a copy of a witness statement served at the appropriate tribunal centre to the other party to the appeal and such copy shall state the date of service and shall contain or be accompanied by a note to the effect that unless a notice of objection thereto is served in accordance with paragraph (4) of this rule, the witness statement may be read at the hearing of the appeal as evidence of the facts stated therein without the person who made the witness statement giving oral evidence thereat.

(4) If a party objects to a witness statement being read at the hearing of the appeal as evidence of any fact stated therein he shall serve a notice of objection to such witness statement at the appropriate tribunal centre not later than 14 days after the date of the service of such witness statement at the appropriate tribunal centre whereupon a proper officer shall send a copy of the notice of objection to the other party and the witness statement shall not be read or admitted in evidence at such hearing but the person who signed such witness statement may give evidence orally at the hearing.

(5) Subject to paragraph (4) of this rule, unless a tribunal shall otherwise direct, a witness statement signed by any person and duly served under this rule shall be admissible in evidence at the hearing of the appeal as evidence of any fact stated therein of which oral evidence by him at that hearing would be admissible.

(6) The time within which a witness statement may be served under this rule shall be—

(a) in the case of a section 13 penalty appeal, before the expiration of 21 days after the last day for the service by the Commissioners of a reply pursuant to paragraph (1)(c) of rule 7;
(b) in the case of a mitigation appeal or a reasonable excuse appeal, before the expiration of 21 days after the date of service of the Notice of Appeal; and
(c) in the case of any other appeal, before the expiration of 21 days after the date of the service of the statement of case by the Commissioners.

Witness summonses and summonses to third parties

22—(1) Where a witness is required by a party to an appeal or application to attend the hearing of an appeal or application to give oral evidence or to produce any document in his possession, custody or power necessary for the purpose of that hearing, a chairman or the Registrar shall, upon the application of such party, issue a summons requiring the attendance of such witness at such hearing or the production of the document, wherever such witness may be in the United Kingdom or the Isle of Man.

(2) Where a party to an appeal or application desires to inspect any document necessary for the purpose of the hearing thereof which is in the possession, custody or power of any other person in the United Kingdom or the Isle of Man (whether or not such other person is a party to that appeal or application) a chairman or the Registrar shall, upon the application of such party, issue a summons requiring either—

(a) the attendance of such other person at such date, time and place as the chairman or the Registrar may direct and then and there to produce such document for inspection by such party or his representative and to allow such

Appendix 12

party or his representative then and there to peruse such document and to take a copy thereof; or

(b) such other person to post the document by ordinary post to an address in the United Kingdom or Isle of Man by First Class Mail in an envelope duly prepaid and properly addressed to the party requiring to inspect the same.

(3) A chairman or the Registrar may issue a summons under this rule without prior notice or reference to the applicant or any other person and without a hearing and the only party to the application shall be the applicant.

(4) A summons issued under this rule shall be signed by a chairman or the Registrar and must be served personally upon the witness or third party by leaving a copy of the summons with him and showing him the original thereof not less than 4 days before the day on which the attendance of the witness or third party or the posting of the document is thereby required. A summons issued under this rule shall contain a statement, or be accompanied by a note, to the effect that the witness or third party may apply, by a notice served at the tribunal centre from which the summons was issued, for a direction that the summons be set aside.

(5) A witness summons issued under this rule for the purpose of a hearing and duly served shall have effect until the conclusion of the hearing at which the attendance of the witness is thereby required.

(6) No person shall be required to attend to give evidence or to produce any document at any hearing or otherwise under paragraph (2) of this rule which he could not be required to give or produce on the trial of an action in a court of law.

(7) No person shall be bound to attend any hearing or to produce or post any document for the purpose of a hearing or for inspection and perusal in accordance with a summons issued under this rule unless a reasonable and sufficient sum of money to defray the expenses of coming to, attending at and returning from such hearing or place of inspection and perusal was tendered to him at the time when the summons was served on him.

(8) A tribunal may, upon the application of any person served at the appropriate tribunal centre, set aside a summons served upon him under this rule.

(9) The parties to an application to set aside a summons issued under this rule shall be the applicant and the party who obained the issue of the summons.

Notice of hearings

23—(1) A proper officer shall send a notice stating the date and time when, and place where, an appeal will be heard to the parties to the appeal which, unless the parties otherwise agree, shall be not earlier than 14 days after the date on which the notice is sent.

(2) Unless a tribunal otherwise directs, an application made at a hearing shall be heard forthwith, and no notice thereof shall be sent to the parties thereto.

(3) Subject to paragraph (2) of this rule, a proper officer shall send a notice stating the date and time when, and the place where, an application will be heard which, unless the parties shall otherwise agree, shall be not earlier than 14 days after the date on which the notice is sent—

(a) in the case of an application for the issue of a witness summons, to the applicant;
(b) in the case of an applicant to set aside the issue of a witness summons, to the applicant and the party who obtained the issue of the witness summons;
(c) in the case of any other application, to the parties to the application.

Hearings in public or in private

24—(1) The hearing of an appeal shall be in public unless a tribunal, on the

Appendix 12

application of a party thereto, directs that the hearing or any part of the hearing shall take place in private.

(2) Unless a tribunal otherwise directs, the hearing of any application made otherwise than at or subsequent to the hearing of an appeal shall take place in private.

(3) Any member of the Council on Tribunals or the Scottish Committee of the Council on Tribunals in his capacity as such a member may attend the hearing of any appeal or application notwithstanding that the appeal or application takes place in private.

Representation at a hearing

25 At the hearing of an appeal or application—

(a) any party to the appeal or application (other than the Commissioners) may conduct his case himself or may be represented by any person whom he may appoint for the purpose; and
(b) the Commissioners may be represented at any hearing at which they are entitled to attend by any person whom they may appoint for the purpose.

Failure to appear at a hearing

26—(1) If, when an appeal or application is called on for hearing no party thereto appears in person or by his representative, a tribunal may dismiss or strike out the appeal or application, but a tribunal may, on the application of any such party or of any person interested served at the appropriate tribunal centre within 14 days after the date when the decision of the tribunal was released in accordance with rule 30, reinstate such appeal or application on such terms as it may think just.

(2) If, when an appeal or application is called on for hearing, a party does not appear in person or by his representative, the tribunal may proceed to consider the appeal or application in the absence of that party, but any decision or direction given in the absence of a party may, on the application of such party or of any other person interested served at the appropriate tribunal centre within 14 days after the date when the decision or direction of the tribunal was released as aforesaid, be set aside by a tribunal on such terms as it may think just.

Procedure at a hearing

27—(1) At the hearing of an appeal or application other than a section 13 penalty appeal the tribunal shall allow—

(a) the appellant or applicant or his representative to open his case;
(b) the appellant or applicant to give evidence in support of the appeal or application and to produce documentary evidence;
(c) the appellant or applicant or his representative to call other witnesses to give evidence in support of the appeal or to produce documentary evidence, and to re-examine any such witness following his cross-examination;
(d) the other party to the appeal or application or his representative to cross-examine any witness called to give evidence in support of the appeal or application (including the appellant or applicant if he gives evidence);
(e) the other party to the appeal or application or his representative to open his case;
(f) the other party to the appeal or application to give evidence in opposition to the appeal or application and to produce documentary evidence;
(g) the other party to the appeal or application or his representative to call other witnesses to give evidence in opposition to the appeal or application or to produce documentary evidence and to re-examine any such witness following his cross-examination;
(h) the appellant or applicant or his representative to cross-examine any witness

Appendix 12

called to give evidence in opposition to the appeal or application (including the other party to the appeal or application if he gives evidence);

(i) the other party to the appeal or application or his representative to make a second address closing his case; and

(j) the appellant or applicant or his representative to make a final address closing his case.

(2) At the hearing of a section 13 penalty appeal the tribunal shall follow the same procedure as is set out in paragraph (1) of this rule for the hearing of an appeal or application as if the same were herein repeated with the substitution of the words "the Commissioners" for "the appellant or applicant" and the words "in opposition to" should be substituted for the words "in support of" in rule 27(1)(b), (c) and (d) and the words "in support of" should be substituted for the words "in opposition to" in rule 27(1)(f), (g) and (h).

(3) At the hearing of an appeal or application the chairman and any other member of the tribunal may put any question to any witness called to give evidence thereat (including a party to the appeal or application if he gives evidence).

(4) Subject to the foregoing provisions of this rule, a tribunal may regulate its own procedure as it may think fit.

(5) A chairman or the Registrar may postpone the hearing of any appeal or application.

(6) A tribunal may adjourn the hearing of any appeal or application on such terms as it may think just.

Evidence at a hearing

28—(1) Subject to paragraph (4) and (5) of rule 21 a tribunal may direct or allow evidence of any fact to be given in any manner it may think fit and shall not refuse evidence tendered to it on the grounds only that such evidence would be inadmissible in a court of law.

(2) A tribunal may require oral evidence of a witness (including a party to an appeal or application) to be given on oath or affirmation and for that purpose a chairman and any member of the administrative staff of the tribunals on the direction of a chairman shall have power to administer oaths or take affirmations.

(3) At the hearing of an appeal or application the tribunal shall allow a party to produce any document set out in his list of documents served under rule 20 and unless a tribunal otherwise directs—

(a) any document contained in such a list of documents which appears to be an original document shall be deemed to be an original document printed, written, signed or executed as it respectively appears to have been; and

(b) any document contained in such list of documents which appears to be a copy shall be deemed to be a true copy.

Award and direction as to costs

29—(1) A tribunal may direct that a party or applicant shall pay to the other party to the appeal or application—

(a) within such period as it may specify such sum as it may determine on account of the costs of such other party of and incidental to and consequent upon the appeal or application; or

(b) the costs of such other party of and incidental to and consequent upon the appeal or application to be taxed by a Taxing Master or District Registrar of the Supreme Court of Judicature in England or by the Auditor of the Court of Session in Scotland or by the Taxing Master of the Supreme Court of Northern Ireland or by the Taxing Master of the High Court of Justice of the Isle of Man on such basis as it shall specify.

Appendix 12

(2) Where a tribunal gives a direction under paragraph 1(b) of this rule in proceedings in England and Wales the provisions of Order 62 of the Rules of the Supreme Court 1965 shall apply, with the necessary modifications, to the taxation of the costs as if the proceedings in the tribunal were a cause or matter in the Supreme Court of Judicature in England.

(3) Where a tribunal gives a direction under paragraph 1(b) of this rule in proceedings in Scotland the provisions of Rules 347 to 349 both inclusive of the Rules of Court enacted by the Act of Sederunt (Rules of Court) (Consolidation and Amendment) 1965 shall apply, with the necessary modifications, to the taxation of the costs as if those proceedings were a cause or matter in the Court of Session in Scotland.

(4) Where a tribunal gives a direction under paragraph 1(b) of this rule in proceedings in Northern Ireland the provision of Order 62 of the Rules of the Supreme Court (Northern Ireland) 1980 shall apply, with the necessary modifications, to the taxation of the costs as if those proceedings were a cause or matter in the High Court of Northern Ireland.

(5) Any costs awarded under this rule shall be recoverable as a civil debt.

Decisions and directions

30—(1) At the conclusion of the hearing of an appeal the chairman may give or announce the decision of the tribunal but in any event the decision shall be recorded in a written document containing the findings of fact by the tribunal and its reasons for the decision which shall be signed by a chairman; provided that if a party to the appeal shall so request by notice in writing served at the appropriate tribunal centre within one year of the date of a decision the outcome of the appeal and any award and direction as to costs or for the payment or repayment of any sum of money with or without interest given or made by the tribunal during or at the conclusion of the hearing of the appeal shall be recorded in a written direction which shall be signed by a chairman or the Registrar.

(2) At the conclusion of the hearing of an application the chairman may give or announce the decision of the tribunal but in any event the outcome of the application and any award or direction given or made by the tribunal during or at the conclusion of the hearing shall be recorded in a written direction which shall be signed by a chairman or the Registrar; provided that if a party to the application shall so request by notice in writing served at the appropriate tribunal centre within 14 days of the date of such direction the decision of the tribunal on the application shall be recorded in a written document containing the findings of fact by the tribunal and its reasons for the decision which shall be signed by a chairman.

(3) A proper officer shall send a copy of the decision and of any direction in an appeal to each party to the appeal and a duplicate of the direction and of any decision in an application to each party to the application.

(4) Every decision in an appeal shall bear the date when the copies thereof are released to be sent to the parties and such copies and any direction, and all copies of any direction, recording the outcome of the appeal shall state that date.

(5) Every direction on an application shall bear the date when the copies thereof are released to be sent to the parties and such copies and any decision on that application given or made under the proviso to paragraph (2) of this rule and all copies thereof shall state that date.

(6) A chairman or the Registrar may correct any clerical mistake or other error in expressing his manifest intention in a decision or direction signed by him but if a chairman or the Registrar corrects any such document after a copy thereof has been sent to a party, a proper officer shall as soon as practicable thereafter send a copy of the corrected document, or the page or pages which have been corrected, to that party.

Appendix 12

(7) Where a copy of a decision or a direction dismissing an appeal or application or containing a decision or direction given or made in the absence of a party is sent to a party or other person entitled to apply under rule 26 to apply to have the appeal or application reinstated, the copy shall contain or be accompanied by a note to that effect.

Service at a tribunal centre

31—(1) Service of a notice of appeal, notice of application or other document shall be effected by the same being handed to a proper officer at the appropriate tribunal centre or by the same being received by post at the appropriate tribunal centre.

(2) Any notice of appeal, notice of application or other document handed in or received at a tribunal centre other than the appropriate tribunal centre may be sent by post in a letter addressed to a proper officer at the appropriate tribunal centre, or handed back to the person from whom it was received, or sent by post in a letter addressed to the person from whom it appears to have been received or by whom it appears to have been sent.

Sending of documents to the parties

32—(1) Any document authorised or required to be sent to the Commissioners may be sent to them by post in a letter addressed to them at the address of their office from which the disputed decision appears to have been sent, or handed or sent to them by post or in such manner and at such address as the Commissioners may from time to time request by a general notice served at the appropriate tribunal centre.

(2) Any document authorised or required to be sent to any party to an appeal or application other than the Commissioners may be sent by post in a letter addressed to him at his address stated in his notice of appeal or application, or sent by post in a letter addressed to any person named in his notice of appeal or application as having been instructed to act for him in connection therewith at the address therein stated, or sent by post in a letter addressed to such person and at such address as he may specify from time to time by notice served at the appropriate tribunal centre; provided that where partners appeal or apply to a tribunal in the name of their firm, any document sent by post in a letter addressed to the firm at the address of the firm stated in the notice of appeal or notice of application or to any person named in the notice of appeal or application as having been instructed to act for the firm at the address therein stated or to such other address as such partners may from time to time specify by notice served at the appropriate tribunal centre, shall be deemed to have been duly sent to all such partners.

(3) Subject to the foregoing provisions of this rule any document authorised or required to be sent to any party to an appeal or application or other person may be sent by post in a letter addressed to him at his usual or last known address or addressed to him or to such other person at such address as he may from time to time specify by notice served at the appropriate tribunal centre.

Delegation of powers to the Registrar

33—(1) All or any of the following powers of a tribunal or a chairman under these rules shall be exercisable by the Registrar, that is to say—

(a) power to give or make any direction by consent of the parties to the appeal or application;
(b) power to give or make any direction on the application of one party which is not opposed by the other party to the application;
(c) power to issue a witness summons;
(d) power to postpone any hearing; and
(e) power to extend the time for the service of any notice of appeal, notice of

Appendix 12

application or other document at the appropriate tribunal centre for a period not exceeding one month without prior notice or reference to any party or other person and without a hearing.

(2) The Registrar shall have power to sign a direction recording the outcome of an appeal and any award or direction given or made by the tribunal during or at the conclusion of the hearing of an appeal as provided by rule 30(1) and to sign any document recording any direction given or made by him under this rule.

Appendix 13 Letter and Notes regarding further appeals

LONDON TRIBUNAL CENTRE
VALUE ADDED TAX TRIBUNALS
15/17 Gt. Marlborough St, London. WIV 1AF.
Telephone 01-437-7495/8244

Your reference

Our reference

Date

Dear

Appellant ....

I enclose a copy of the Decision or Direction of the tribunal in relation to your Appeal/Application.

Your attention is draw to the Notes overleaf.

Any exhibits and copies of exhibits retained by the tribunal after the hearing may be collected from this tribunal centre by the party who produced them. Exhibits and copies of exhibits cannot, however, be stored indefinitely and the tribunal accepts no responsibility for any exhibit or copy exhibits not collected within six weeks after the date of this letter.

Yours faithfully

Trib 31   PROPER OFFICER

Appendix 13

NOTES

1. Section 13 of the Tribunal and Inquiries Act 1971 applies to a value added tax tribunal and, therefore, any party who is dissatisfied in point of law with a decision of a tribunal sitting in England or Wales may appeal to the High Court of Justice in England in accordance with the provisions of Order 94 Rule 8 of the Rules of the Supreme Court.

2. Under Order 55 of the Rules of the Supreme Court the persons to be served with notice of a motion by which an appeal from a value added tax tribunal to the High Court of Justice is brought are the chairman of the tribunal and every party to the proceedings in which the decision was given (other than the person appealing to the High Court).

3. Notice of such a motion must be served, and the appeal to the High Court of Justice must be entered, within 28 days after the date on which notice of the Decision was given by the tribunal centre to the person appealing.

4. Service on the chairman of a tribunal of notice of a motion by which an appeal to the High Court of Justice is brought may be affected by post. The address for service of the chairman is the address of the tribunal centre from which the decision was sent out. Any notice so served shall be sufficient although only addressed to the chairman by that designation without his name.

5. Service on the Commissioners of Customs and Excise of notice of a motion by which an appeal to the High Court of Justice is brought should be effected on "The Solicitor for Customs and Excise, King's Beam House, 39/41 Mark Lane, London EC3 7HE".

6. Legal aid is available in connection with proceedings in the High Court to any person (but not to a limited company) to whom a certificate has been issued under the Legal Aid (General) Regulations 1971 (as amended). Any person who wishes to make an application, or to enquire whether he is eligible, for the issue of such a certificate for the purpose of prosecuting or defending an appeal from a decision of a tribunal, or prosecuting proceedings against the Commissioners in relation to a matter outside the jurisdiction of a tribunal, should contact the Secretary of the Legal Aid Committee for his district, whose address and telephone number can be obtained from the telephone directory or the tribunal centre.

Appendix 14 Centrally issued VAT assessment

Notice of Assessment of Value Added Tax

Registration number	Period Ref.

Date   14 04 86

To the Registered Person named above.

It appears from our records that you have failed to make the return of Value Added Tax which by law you were required to make in respect of the period from

1 DECEMBER 1985   to   28 FEBRUARY 1986

TAKE NOTICE therefore that the Commissioners of Customs and Excise, by virtue of their statutory powers, assess the amount of tax payable by you in respect of the period as being

£7701.00

Immediate payment of the above sum is demanded.

VAT 151

For the Commissioners of Customs and Excise
Please see the notes overleaf ■▶

Appendix 14

	For Official Use
Remittance Slip **Notice of Assessment of Value Added Tax**	

Registration number   Period Ref.

Please tear off this slip and return it with your remittance to:–

For Official Use

HM Customs and Excise
Alexander House
21 Victoria Avenue
Southend-on-Sea X
SS99 1AB

Assessed amount   £7701.00

VAT 151   F3899 (March 1985) W07037

Appendix 14

NOTES

1. This assessment has been made because it appears you have not made a return for the tax period shown. (IF YOU HAVE SENT IN THE RETURN AND ANY TAX DUE PLEASE DISREGARD THIS NOTICE.)

2. Send your return IMMEDIATELY, with the full amount of tax due, to the Controller, VAT Central Unit, HM Customs and Excise, Alexander House, 21 Victoria Avenue, Southend-on-Sea X, SS99 1AB. Provided that the return and payment appear to be satisfactory, the Commissioners may adjust this assessment to the figure on the return.

3. If you cannot make the return, you should send the amount shown overleaf to the Controller at the above address. The remittance slip, which you should detach from this notice, must accompany your payment, except if you have arranged to pay by bank or Post Office Giro.

4. If you cannot make the return and do not pay this assessment the Commissioners may take action to recover the amount shown as tax due.

5. Failure to make a return is an offence for which you may be prosecuted. If you do make a return as in paragraph 2 above, it will not affect the fact that your return was late and that you were in breach of the Regulations.

6. The Commissioners are empowered to make an additional assessment if it is discovered that the amount of tax you have paid is less than the true amount due.

7. Cheques, postal orders etc. should be crossed and made payable to 'HM Customs and Excise'. In your own interests you should not send notes or coins through the post as credit cannot be given in respect of cash not received.

Appendix 15 Assessment issued on or following control visit

Value Added Tax

Tax Due

Notice of Assessment
Made At *(Official Address)*

LVO Number

Examination of your records has shown that the correct amounts of Value Added Tax have not been declared or, where appropriate, assessed for the periods shown.
The Commissioners of Customs and Excise, using their statutory powers, have made the following assessment(s) of tax for the period(s) shown. **The total amount due should be paid immediately. No reminder will be sent.**
Your attention is drawn to the notes overleaf about methods of payment and your right of appeal.
DO NOT ENTER ANY OF THE AMOUNTS SHOWN BELOW ON YOUR VAT RETURN.

*M	Reason Code (see over)	Dates From	Dates To	Period Reference	Assessments of Tax Due to Customs & Excise £	Type Code	Due from Customs & Excise £
					SUB TOTALS		
				TOTAL AMOUNT PAYABLE			

Assessing
Offs s Signature .... Name ....
(in BLOCK LETTERS)

VAT 191 (Trader's Copy) To be retained.

Appendix 15

*Please tear off this slip and
return it with your payment
To:–*

	For Official Use

The Controller,
H M Customs and Excise,
VAT Central Unit,
21 Victoria Avenue,
Southend-on-Sea X,
SS99 1 AT.

Registration Number

TOTAL AMOUNT PAYABLE

Signature ....

Date ....

For Official Use

VAT 191 (Trader's Copy)   F 4179 (June 1985)   Printed in the UK for HMSO D.3857546 400m 6/85.

Appendix 16 VAT leaflet: serious misdeclaration

HM Customs and Excise

VAT: Serious misdeclaration penalty

Information sheet

From 1 July 1988 if Customs and Excise find inaccuracies in your VAT records and accounts which mean that you have seriously underdeclared or overclaimed VAT they will be able to impose a financial penalty — known as a "serious misdeclaration penalty".

1. What is a misdeclaration?

    There is a misdeclaration if you:

    - underdeclare the amount of VAT due on a VAT return
    - claim a repayment to which you are not entitled
    - receive a centrally issued assessment which is too low and you fail to draw this to the attention of Customs and Excise within 30 days of the date of issue of the assessment.

2. What is a "serious" misdeclaration?

    A misdeclaration is serious and the penalty will apply where the amount of VAT involved equals or exceeds:

    - 30% of the true amount of tax; or
    - £10,000 or 5% of the true amount of tax, whichever is the greater; or
    - 15% of the true amount of tax if, in the last six years, there have been two other accounting periods with similar inaccuracies within a four year period.

    > The "true amount of tax" is the amount of tax due to Customs and Excise for an accounting period or the amount of the repayment due from them.

Appendix 16

3. **How will the penalty work?**

Where the "true amount of tax" is £33,333 or less the penalty will apply if there is a misdeclaration of 30% or more. Here are some examples:

True amount of tax	Penalty applies to misdeclarations which equal or exceed:	
£500	£150	(30% of the true amount of tax)
£7,500	£2,250	(" " ")
£25,000	£7,500	(" " ")
£33,333	£10,000	(" " ")

Where the "true amount of tax" is between £33,333 and £200,000 the penalty will apply if there is a misdeclaration of £10,000 or more. Here are some examples:

True amount of tax	Penalty applies to misdeclarations which equal or exceed:	
£50,000	£10,000	(more than 5% of the true amount of tax)
£100,000	£10,000	(" " ")
£150,000	£10,000	(" " ")

Where the "true amount of tax" is £200,000 or more the penalty will apply if there is a misdeclaration of 5% or more. Here are some examples:

True amount of tax	Penalty applies to misdeclarations which equal or exceed:	
£200,000	£10,000	(5% or the true amount of tax)
£225,000	£11,250	(" " ")

> Serious misdeclaration penalty will apply only to inaccuracies in accounting periods starting on or after 1 July 1988.

Appendix 16

4. **How much will the penalty be?**

   The penalty will be 30% of the amount of VAT misdeclared.

5. **Will I always have to pay the penalty?**

   You will not have to pay if:

   - you find the error and inform Customs and Excise before they begin an enquiry; **or**
   - you are able to show that you have a reasonable excuse.

   If you do incur a serious misdeclaration penalty but consider that it has been wrongly imposed or that you did have a **reasonable excuse** you should ask your local VAT office to reconsider the matter. If you are still not satisfied you can appeal to an independent VAT tribunal. You will find more about the appeals procedure in "The VAT guide", Section XIII.

   It is **not** a reasonable excuse to claim that:

   - you can't afford to pay
   - your employee, agent, accountant or some other person failed to perform a task on your behalf.
   ---

6. **Further advice**

   Further guidance on this and the other changes to be introduced in July 1988 will be available nearer to the time of the change. If, in the meantime, you need more help or advice, your local VAT office is always ready to help you. Addresses are in the phone book under "Customs and Excise".

   Please remember, if you account for VAT accurately and on time you will never have to pay a financial penalty.

Prepared by H M Customs and Excise   1 June 1986

Appendix 17 VAT leaflet: default interest

HM Customs and Excise

VAT: Default interest

Information sheet

From 1 July 1988, if Customs and Excise find inaccuracies in your VAT records and accounts you will be charged interest — known as "default interest" — on the VAT you owe.

How will default interest be charged?

1. If it is found that you have underdeclared or overclaimed VAT or if you have paid an assessment which later turns out to be too low, you will be issued with a Notice of Assessment, showing how much VAT you owe and the interest due.

When will interest apply?

2. Interest will apply only to inaccuracies in accounting periods starting on or after 1 July 1988.

It will be calculated from the date when you should first have paid the outstanding VAT until the date of issue of the Notice of Assessment. In the case of repayment claims, interest will run from 7 days after the date on which Customs and Excise authorised the payment to you.

How much will the interest be?

3. The interest will be a percentage of the VAT you owe. The rate will be set by the Treasury. It will be a simple — not a compound — rate and will be broadly in line with commercial rates of interest.

> You cannot offset any interest against your direct tax liability — the rate of interest set will reflect this.

When must the interest be paid?

4. You must pay the VAT and interest due as soon as you receive the assessment. You will be liable to a further interest charge if you don't pay the VAT within 15 days of the date of the assessment.

Appendix 17

Can I appeal against interest charges?

5. If you disagree with an interest charge that has been imposed you should ask your local VAT office to reconsider the matter. If you are still not satisfied you can appeal to an independent VAT tribunal. You will find more about the appeals procedure in "The VAT guide", Section XIII.

Further advice

6. Further guidance on this and the other changes to be introduced in July 1988 will be available nearer to the time of the change. If, in the meantime, you need more help or advice, your local VAT office is always ready to help you. Addresses are in the phone book under "Customs and Excise".

> **Please remember**, if you account for VAT accurately and on time you will never have to pay default interest.

Prepared by H M Customs and Excise   1 June 1986

Index

Note: references in this index are to paragraph numbers.

Accountant
  acquiring knowledge of offences and errors, 4.26
  role of, at control visit, 3.36
Accounts
  annual—
    comparison of VAT returns with, 3.46
    production of, at control visit, 3.37
  errors in, 4.04, 4.05
  false accounting, criminal offence of, 2.38
Administration
  burdens as to, 1.03–1.06
  record keeping, 1.04
Administration Directorate, VAT, 3.06, 307, 4.11
Agents
  Customs and Excise powers as to, 5.22–5.23
Antiques
  relief as to, 5.11, 5.30
Appeal. *See also* VAT TRIBUNALS
  appealable decision, considerations as to whether, 4.19
  civil fraud, against, 1.39, 4.67
  Court of Appeal, to, 4.67, 5.04
  Court of Session, to, 4.66
  default surcharge, as to, 1.79
  discretionary powers, against, rights as to, 5.05, 5.59–5.61
  FA 1985, changes brought about by, 4.67–4.68
  further, 4.66
  giving notice of, 4.42
  grounds for, 4.41, 4.67
  High Court, to, 4.66, 5.62, 5.63
  judicial review, application for, 5.62–5.64
  pre-appeal conditions, 4.43
  protective, 3.39, 4.21–4.22, 4.37, 4.38
  provision of security, as to, 2.28–2.31
  settlement of, without recourse to VAT Tribunal 4.67, 4.68
  statistics as to, 4.37–4.39
  tax evasion, as to, right of, 1.39
  VAT Tribunal, to. *See* VAT TRIBUNALS
Arrest
  Customs and Excise powers of, 5.04, 5.48
Assessments. *See also* DEFAULT SURCHARGE; PENALTIES
  action prior to issue of, 4.09–4.12

Assessments—*continued*
  appeal as to. *See* APPEAL; VAT TRIBUNALS
  appealable, consideration as to whether, 4.19–4.22
  arithmetical errors, to correct, 5.04, 5.47
  'best judgement' of Customs and Excise, must be made to, 5.42
  changes in, powers as to, 5.04
  circumstances for making, 5.41–5.42
  civil fraud, time limit as to, 1.38, 5.04
  disputes. *See* DISPUTES
  failure to notify liability for registration, where, 1.70
  further, power to make, 5.04, 5.47
  interest charged on, 1.29, 1.93, 1.94, 1.95, 5.04. *See also* INTEREST
  mark-ups and, 3.66–3.69
  misdirection, following, 4.15
  output tax, understatement of, and, 3.61–3.62
  powers to make, 5.04, 5.41–5.47
  time limits, 1.38, 5.04, 5.43
  underdeclarations, in cases of, 3.48
  VAT Tribunal decisions as to, 3.47
Attachment of earnings orders
  powers to make use of, 5.49

Bad debt relief, 2.09, 5.15
Bankruptcy
  VAT preferential debt in, 5.49
Breaches of regulations
  cessation of taxable supplies, failure to notify, 1.28, 1.31, 1.98, 2.41
  documents, failure to produce, 1.28, 1.31, 1.98, 2.39, 2.40, 2.44
  implementation of provisions, 1.31, 1.96, 1.99
  information, failure to furnish, 1.28, 1.31, 1.98, 2.39, 2.40, 2.44
  make VAT return or pay tax by due date, failure to. *See* VAT
  penalties for—
    alternative to default charge, as, 1.80
    amount of, 1.97
    application of, 1.99
    breach of walking possession agreements, for, 1.100
    interaction with other penalties, 1.40, 1.50, 1.99, 1.105, 1.107

193

Index

Breaches of regulations—*continued*
  penalties for—*continued*
    introduction of new, 1.96, 5.04
    'reasonable excuse', where, 1.101
    regulations to which penalties apply, 1.103
    replaced criminal penalties, 1.96
    table of, 1.98
  provisions as to, 1.28
  records, failure to keep and preserve, 1.28, 1.31, 1.98, 2.39, 2.43
  regulations or rules made under VATA 1983, failure to comply with, 1.28, 1.31, 2.45
  walking possession agreements, breaches of, 1.28, 1.31, 1.100, 5.04, 5.46
  written warnings, 1.102

Bribery
  Commissioners, etc, of, criminal offence of, 2.36, 2.37

Businesses. *See also* COMPANIES; SMALL BUSINESS
  burdens on—
    administration of VAT as, 1.03–1.04
    analysis of, 1.05–1.06
    overseas, 5.16
    transfer of going concern, 5.24

Cheating
  revenue, the, criminal offence of, 2.38

Civil fraud. *See also* DISHONEST CONDUCT; EVASION OF TAX
  appeal against, 1.39, 4.67
  burden of proof, 1.39
  commentary on offence of, 1.41–1.43
  conduct involving dishonesty as, 1.33
  'evading tax', meaning of, 1.34
  evasion of tax as, 1.33
  induced evidence, 1.37
  interaction with criminal code, 1.35
  interaction with other civil penalties, 1.40, 1.50, 1.66, 1.99, 1.105, 1.107
  meaning of, 1.33
  mitigation, 1.36
  new offence of, 1.33, 5.04
  penalties for, 1.36. *See also* interaction with other civil penalties, *above*
  time limit for assessment, 1.38

Civil penalty provisions
  background to—
    reasons for change, 1.18–1.26
    'The Collection of VAT', 1.15–1.17, 1.23–1.26
    See also KEITH COMMITTEE
  breaches of regulations, penalties for, 1.28, 1.29. *See also* BREACHES OF REGULATIONS
  checklist of considerations, 1.108
  default surcharge. *See* DEFAULT SURCHARGE
  dishonest conduct, for. *See* CIVIL FRAUD; DISHONEST CONDUCT
  evading tax, for. *See* CIVIL FRAUD; EVASION OF TAX

Civil penalty provisions—*continued*
  former criminal penalties replaced by, 1.28, 2.39 et seq
  implementation of—
    generally, 1.27
    timetable for, 1.31–1.32
  interaction of penalties, 1.40, 1.50, 1.66, 1.99, 1.105, 1.107
  interest on assessments. *See* INTEREST
  introduction of, 1.27–1.30, 5.54
  list of acts or omissions giving rise to, 1.28–1.30
  registration, failure to notify liability for. *See* REGISTRATION
  repayment supplement. *See* REPAYMENT SUPPLEMENT
  serious misdeclaration, for. *See* SERIOUS MISDECLARATION
  table of, under FA 1985 . . . 1.28. *See also* BREACHES OF REGULATIONS
  tax recovered or recoverable by assessment, interest on. *See* INTEREST
  unauthorised issue of invoices. *See* INVOICES

'Collection of VAT'
  paper entitled, 1.15–1.17, 1.24–1.26

Companies. *See also* BUSINESSES; SMALL BUSINESS
  group registration of, 1.71, 5.19
  large, VAT control of—
    areas of error in particular trade sectors, 3.43
    centralisation as to, 3.41
    need for, 3.40
    questionnaires, issue of, 3.41–3.42
    reporting systems of large organisations, 3.44–3.45
  VAT registration of. *See* REGISTRATION

Compounding criminal offences
  acceptance of, and review of assessment, 2.64
  considerations in relation to practice of, 2.52–2.55
  example, 2.51, 2.52
  offer as to, 2.60
  powers as to, 2.50–2.51, 5.53
  prosecute, decision whether to, 2.58–2.59
  publicity, 2.63–2.64
  regulatory matters and, 2.56
  settlement—
    level of, 2.61–2.62
    table of, 2.57

Computer
  records—
    access to, 5.04, 5.34
    failure to produce, 2.03
  systems, power to inspect, 5.04, 5.34

Control of VAT. *See* VAT CONTROL

Control visits
  accountant, role of, at, 3.36
  action following—
    control officer, by, 3.38
    registered person, by, 3.39

Index

Control visits—*continued*
  advice given by control officer, 3.33
  annual accounts, 3.37
  appointments, 3.23
  conduct of, 3.27–3.29
  credibility checks on, 3.46
  disputes emanating from, 3.31, 4.03–4.07. *See also* DISPUTES
  duration of, 3.24
  duties of VAT officer on, 3.29
  errors, discovery of, 3.30, 4.03–4.04
  frequency of, 3.21
  information available to the officer before, 3.22
  meaning of, 3.17
  overdeclaration of VAT discovered on, 3.01–3.02, 3.29
  professional adviser, role of, at control visit, 3.36
  purpose of, 3.20
  questions from control officer, dealing with, 3.34–3.35
  records, place of production of, 3.26, 5.32
  reliance on, 3.32
  underdeclaration of VAT discovered on, 1.22, 3.01–3.04, 3.29, 3.38
  visiting officer, 3.25
Convicted person
  penalties in case of, 1.66, 1.99, 1.105
Corporation tax
  interest and, 1.94
  repayment supplement and, 1.90
Costs
  administering VAT, of, 1.03
  VAT Tribunals, as to, 4.62–4.64
Court of Appeal
  appeals to, 4.67, 5.04
Court of Session
  appeal to, 4.66
Credit transfer
  payment by, 1.82
Criminal offences. *See also* CRIMINAL PROCEEDINGS
  bribing a Commissioner, etc—
    penalty for, 2.37
    provision as to, 2.36
  cheating the revenue, 2.38
  compounding. *See* COMPOUNDING CRIMINAL OFFENCES
  conduct involving commission of certain offences, 2.03, 2.19–2.23, 2.39
  decriminalised—
    implications as to, 2.40 et seq
    tables of, 1.28, 2.39
    See also CIVIL PENALTY PROVISIONS
  documents, failure to produce, prior to 25.7.86 . . . 2.39, 2.40, 2.44. *See also* DOCUMENTS
  failure to furnish VAT return or pay tax by due date, 2.03, 2.32–2.34, 2.39. *See also* VAT
  false accounting, 2.38

Criminal offences—*continued*
  false documents. *See* DOCUMENTS
  fraudulent evasion of VAT. *See* EVASION OF TAX
  generally, 2.01, 2.02
  goods or services—
    receiving, where supplier evades tax, 2.03, 2.24–2.25, 2.39
    supplying without providing security, 2.03, 2.39
  information, failure to furnish, prior to 25.7.85 . . . 2.39, 2.40, 2.44. *See also* INFORMATION
  input tax fraud, 2.04, 2.09
  invoices, unauthorised issue of, prior to 25.7.85 . . . 2.39, 2.40, 2.42. *See also* INVOICES
  legislation arising under, 2.02
  obstructing an officer performing various duties—
    penalty for, 2.03, 2.37
    provision as to, 2.36
  obtaining a pecuniary advantage by deception, 2.38
  penalties for—
    interaction of, with civil penalties, 1.107
    table, 2.03, 2.39
  perjury, 2.38
  position from 25 July 1985—
    criminal law, offences arising under, 2.38
    Customs and Excise legislation, offences under, 2.35–2.37
    generally, 2.02
    VAT legislation, offences under, 2.03–2.34
  position prior to 25 July 1985 . . . 2.39–2.49
  procedural matters, 2.65–2.71. *See also* CRIMINAL PROCEEDINGS
  records, failure to keep or preserve, prior to 25.7.85 . . . 2.39, 2.40, 2.43. *See also* RECORDS
  register, failure to, prior to 25.7.85 . . . 2.39–2.40, 2.41. *See also* REGISTRATION
  regulations or rules made under VATA, failure to comply with, prior to 25.7.85 . . . 1.28, 1.31, 2.45
  services. *See* goods or services, *above*
  statements which are false in a material particular, making. *See* STATEMENT
  untrue declarations, making—
    penalty for, 2.37
    provision as to, 2.36
Criminal proceedings
  evidence, 2.70–2.71
  institution of, 2.68
  onus and standard of proof, 2.69
  service of summons, 2.67
  time limit, 2.66
Customs and Excise
  appeal against decisions of. *See* APPEAL
  comments on proposed changes, 1.06, 1.23, 1.26

195

Index

Customs and Excise—*continued*
control methods of. *See* VAT CONTROL
disputes with. *See* DISPUTES
Keith Committee, evidence to, 1.12, 1.19–1.20, 2.58, 2.61, 3.38
legislation, offences under, 2.35–2.37
local visits, 3.16–3.17
organisation of—
  Board of Commissioners, 3.06
  Directorates—
    specialist units within other, 3.09
    VAT Administration, 3.07
    VAT Control, 3.08
  local VAT offices—
    functions of, 3.11
    structure of, 3.10–3.11
  VAT officers, role of, 3.10
  VAT sub-offices, 3.12
powers of—
  administration of VAT, as to, 5.29
  agents, as to, 5.22–5.23
  arrest, as to, 5.48
  assess tax due, to, 5.04, 5.41–5.47
  attachment of earnings order, as to, 5.49
  bad debts, as to, 5.15
  bankruptcy, in cases of, 5.49
  business overseas, repayment of tax to those in, 5.16
  collection of VAT, as to, 5.29
  commentary on, 5.55–5.69
  compound proceedings, as to, 2.50–2.51, 5.53. *See also* COMPOUNDING CRIMINAL OFFENCES
  computer systems, to inspect, 5.04, 5.34
  discretionary, 5.05, 5.59
    right of appeal against, 5.05, 5.60–5.61
  distrain for payment, as to, 5.39–5.40, 5.49
  divisional registration, as to, 5.20
  Do-It-Yourself Housebuilders, refunds to, 5.14
  dutiable goods in a warehouse, as to supplies of, 5.25
  EEC Governments, as to recovery of tax due to, 5.52
  EEC member states, as to disclosure of information to, 5.51
  enforcement, as to, 5.29
  entry, as to, 3.23, 5.37, 5.40
  evidence, as to productions of, 5.38
  exceeding, what to do, 5.55, 5.56–5.58
  exports, as to, 5.10
  further assessments, to make, 5.04, 5.47
  gaming machines, to open, 5.04, 5.36
  garnishee proceedings, as to, 5.49
  goods imported for private purposes, as to, 5.17
  Government departments, other refunds to, 5.18
  group registration, as to, 5.19
  history of, 5.01–5.02
  imports, as to, 5.12

Customs and Excise—*continued*
powers of—*continued*
  information for statistical purposes, as to disclosure of, 5.27
  Inland Revenue, as to exchange of information with, 3.38, 5.50
  input tax, as to, 5.08, 5.09
  interlocutory injunctions, as to, 5.49
  new civil penalty provisions, as to. *See* CIVIL PENALTY PROVISIONS
  partial exemption, as to, 5.09
  personal representatives, as to, 5.21
  professional privilege and, 5.65–5.68
  recovery proceedings, as to, 5.49
  refunds of tax, as to, 5.13, 5.14, 5.18
  registration, as to, 5.06. *See also* REGISTRATION
  retail schemes, 5.05, 5.30
  samples, to take, 5.35
  search, as to, 5.37
  second-hand goods relief, 5.11
  security, to require, 2.26, 5.38
  strengthening of, 5.03, 5.04
  time of supply, as to, 5.07
  trading stamp schemes, as to, 5.26
  transfer of going concerns, as to, 5.24
  unincorporated bodies, as to, 5.21
  valuation, as to, 5.28
  VAT legislation, under 5.05 et seq
  VAT records, as to, 5.04, 5.31–5.33. *See also* RECORDS
  zero-rated goods, as to, 5.10, 5.35
Public Notices and leaflets, relevance of, 4.30

Deception
obtaining a pecuniary advantage by, criminal offence of, 2.38

Declarations
making untrue, criminal offence of, 2.36, 2.37
misdeclaration, serious. *See* SERIOUS MISDECLARATION
overdeclarations, 3.01–3.02, 3.29
underdeclarations. *See* UNDERDECLARATION OF VAT

Decriminalisation. *See also* CIVIL PENALTY PROVISIONS; CRIMINAL OFFENCES
implications of, 2.40 et seq
tables as to, 1.28, 2.39

Default surcharge
amount of, 1.73
appeal to VAT Tribunal, 1.79
breach of regulatory matters, penalty under as an alternative to, 1.80
commentary on, 1.81–1.86
default in respect of prescribed accounting period, when in, 1.74, 1.75
further surcharge liability notice, issue of, 1.77, 1.78
implementation of provision, 1.31, 1.73, 1.81

Index

Default surcharge—*continued*
  interest in case of, 5.46
  introduction of, 1.29, 5.04
  liability for, 1.73–1.79
  payment on account, 1.82
  penalties where also subject to, 1.99
  phased increase in amount of, table of, 1.76
  powers as to, 5.04, 5.44
  procedure, 1.86
  small businesses, effect on, 1.85
  surcharge liability notice, 1.75
  will not arise, circumstances when, 1.79
Direction
  issued by VAT Tribunal, non-compliance with, 4.48
Dishonest conduct. *See also* CIVIL FRAUD
  'civil fraud' as offence of, 1.33
  implementation of provision, 1.31
  interest in case of, 5.46
  provision as to, 1.28
Disputes
  appealable decisions, consideration of, 4.19–4.22
  control visit, emanating from, 3.31, 4.03–4.07
  Customs and Excise Public Notices and leaflets, consideration of, 4.30
  dealing with—
    assessment, action prior to issue of, 4.09–4.12
    completion of VAT returns pending resolution, 4.13–4.14
    discussions with Customs and Excise, 4.12
    mark-ups, as to, 4.10
    policy as to, 4.08
    zero-rated goods or services, as to, 4.11
  departmental review, 4.20
  equity or letter of the law, reliance on, 4.32
  errors in returns—
    accountants acquiring knowledge of, 4.26
    accounting errors, 4.04, 4.05
    notification of, 4.25
    reasons for, 4.04
    technical errors, 4.04, 4.06–4.07
    types of error, 4.03
  extra-statutory concessions, 4.18
  generally, 4.01–4.02
  how disputes arise, 4.03–4.07
  misdirection, due to. *See* MISDIRECTION
  offences, acquiring knowledge of, 4.26
  prevention of—
    acquiring knowledge of offences and errors, 4.26
    checklist as to, 4.24 et seq
    decision-making personnel, by, 4.28
    entering into transactions, VAT considerations when, 4.31
    generally, 4.23
    interaction of VAT and direct taxes, consideration of, 4.29
    notification of errors, 4.25
    time to pay, 4.27

Disputes—*continued*
  protective appeals, 3.39, 4.21–4.22, 4.37, 4.38
  waiver of tax, 4.17
Distrain for payment
  Customs and Excise powers to, 5.39–5.40, 5.49
  distraint visit, 3.17
Do-It-Yourself Housebuilder's Scheme
  refund of tax under—
    Customs and Excise powers as to, 5.14
    fraudulent evasion as to, 2.09
Documents
  copy of, admissible as evidence, 2.71
  criminal proceedings, in, 2.70
  Customs and Excise powers to remove, 5.04
  failure to produce—
    implementation of provision, 1.31
    penalty for, 1.98, 2.39
    provisions as to, 1.28, 2.40, 2.44
  false—
    penalty for use of, 2.03, 2.15, 2.39
    use of—
      changes introduced by FA 1985 . . . 2.15
      conduct involving commission of offence as to, 2.03, 2.19–2.23, 2.39
      criminal offence, remains a, 2.04
      liability for offence of, 2.12–2.15
    'with intent to deceive', meaning of, 2.13
  falsifying, criminal offence of, 2.36, 2.37
  photograph of, admissible as evidence, 2.71
  VAT Tribunal hearing, to be referred to, at, 4.45

Educational/registration visit
  purpose of, 3.17
Entry
  Customs and Excise powers as to, 3.23, 5.37, 5.40
  forcible, warrant for, to levy distress, 5.40
Errors
  accountants acquiring knowledge of, 4.26
  accounting, 4.04, 4.05
  arithmetical, power to increase assessment to correct, 5.04, 5.47
  assessment, leading to, 4.09
  discovery of, on control visit, 3.30, 4.03–4.04
  honest mistake, 1.54, 1.55
  innocent, 1.54
  major, within particular trade sectors, 3.43
  notification of, 4.25
  returns, in, types of, 4.03
  technical, 4.04, 4.06–4.07
European Economic Community
  Directives—
    effect of, on VAT Tribunal decisions, 4.60
    Eighth Directive Refund Scheme, claims for repayment of tax under, 2.09
    valuation, as to, 5.28
  disclosure of information to, Customs and Excise powers as to, 5.51

197

Index

European Economic Community—*continued*
  Governments, power to recover tax due to, 5.52
  recovery proceedings in member states on behalf of UK courts, 5.49

Evasion of tax. *See also* CIVIL FRAUD
  appeal, right of, 1.39
  'civil fraud' as offence of, 1.33
  conduct involving dishonesty, as, 1.28, 1.31, 1.33–1.43
  fraudulent—
    act knowingly, must, 2.05, 2.06
    conduct involving commission of offence as to, 2.03, 2.19–2.23, 2.39
    criminal offence, remains a, 2.04
    failing to register for VAT, 2.08
    liability for offence of, 2.05–2.09
    overclaimed amounts as, 2.09
    penalties for, 2.03, 2.04, 2.39
    prosecutions for, 2.46
    understating payment due, 2.07
  implementation of provision, 1.31
  interest in case of, 5.46
  meaning of 'evading tax', 1.34
  provision as to, 1.28
  receiving goods or services where supplier evades tax, penalty for, 2.03, 2.39

Evidence
  criminal proceedings, in, 2.70–2.71
  Customs and Excise powers as to production of, 5.38
  induced, 1.37
  VAT Tribunal, at, 4.52

Exports
  Customs and Excise powers as to, 5.10

Fraud
  cases concluded in 1981/82, table of, 3.48
  civil. *See* CIVIL FRAUD
  classification of offences of, 2.46
  'gold frauds', 2.48–2.49
  input tax, 2.04, 2.09
  power to arrest in respect of, 5.04, 5.48
  suspected, disclosure of information to Inland Revenue, 3.38, 5.50

Gaming machines
  Customs and Excise powers to open, 5.04, 5.36

Garnishee proceedings
  powers make use of, 5.49

Gold frauds, 2.48–2.49

Goods
  assumed sales, 3.51
  consumption of trading stock in the business, 3.57
  dutiable, in a warehouse, 5.25
  exports, 5.10
  imports, 5.12, 5.17
  mark-up. *See* MARK-UP EXERCISES
  pilferage of, 3.55
  purchase for re-sale, cost of, 3.52–3.53

Goods—*continued*
  receiving, where supplier evades tax—
    liability for offence of, 2.24–2.25
    penalty for, 2.03, 2.39
  samples of, Customs and Excise powers to take, 5.35
  second-hand, 5.11, 5.30
  security—
    failure to provide—
      appeals to VAT Tribunal, 2.28–2.31, 5.38
      liability for offence of, 2.26–2.27
      penalty for, 2.03, 2.39
    power to require, 2.26, 5.38
  status of customer and VAT liability, 4.18
  stock losses, 3.54
  supply of, via an agent, 5.23
  time of supply of, 5.07
  wastage of, 3.56
  zero-rated, 4.11, 5.10, 5.35

Government departments
  refunds to, 5.18

Hearing
  VAT Tribunal—
    date of, 4.49
    postponement of, 4.50
    preliminary, of opposed matters, 4.46

High Court
  appeal to, 4.66, 5.62, 5.63

Imports
  Customs and Excise powers as to, 5.12
  goods imported for private purposes, 5.17

Income tax. *See also* INLAND REVENUE
  interest and, 1.94, 1.107
  repayment supplement and, 1.90

Inflation
  allowance for, 3.64

Information
  Customs and Excise powers to obtain, 5.04
  disclosure of for statistical purposes by Customs and Excise, 5.27
  EEC member states, disclosure to, 5.51
  failure to furnish—
    implementation of provision, 1.31
    penalty for, 1.98, 2.39
    provisions as to, 1.28, 2.40, 2.44
  false, prosecutions for, 2.46
  Inland Revenue and Customs and Excise, exchange with, 3.38, 5.50
  professional privilege as to, 5.65–5.68
  requirement to furnish, 5.32

Inland Revenue *See also* INCOME TAX
  exchange of information with Customs and Excise, 3.38, 5.50

Input tax
  Customs and Excise powers as to, 5.08, 5.09
  failure to make provisional partial exemption restriction of, 2.45
  fraud, 2.04, 2.09

Index

Interest
circumstances when charged, 1.93
commentary on, 1.95
dishonest conduct, in case of, 5.46
evasion of tax, in case of, 5.46
examples, 1.94
implementation of provision, 1.31, 1.93
income tax and, 1.94
introduction of powers to charge, 1.29, 5.04
powers as to, 5.04, 5.44, 5.45, 5.46
'reckonable date', 1.94
serious misdeclaration, in case of, 5.46
tax repaid or unpaid, following VAT Tribunal appeals, 4.65

Interlocutory injunctions
powers to make use of, 5.49

Investigation techniques. *See also* DOCUMENTS; INFORMATION
credibility checks, 3.46
underdeclarations, treatment of, 3.48
VAT Tribunal decisions, 3.47

Investigation visits
purpose of, 3.17, 3.46

Invoices
checking, on control or investigation visits, 3.46
details required, failure to include all, 2.45
issue when requested, failure to, 2.45
persons authorised to issue, 2.42
unauthorised issue of—
implementation of, 1.31, 1.104
meaning of unauthorised person, 1.106
penalties for, 1.104–1.105, 2.39, 5.46
prosecutions for, 2.46
provisions as to, 1.28, 2.40, 2.42

Judicial review
application for, 5.62–5.64

Keith Committee
conduct involving commission of certain criminal offences, consideration of, 2.20–2.21
considerations of, 1.12–1.13, 1.19
Customs and Excise, evidence of, 1.12, 1.19–1.20, 2.58, 2.61, 3.38
fraud cases, table of, 3.48
principles of, 1.11
proposals and recommendations of, 1.14
proposed implementation of recommendations of, 1.15–1.17
setting up of, 1.08
terms of reference of, 1.09, 1.10

Liquidation
VAT preferential debt in, 5.49

Local authorities
refunds to, 5.13

Local visits
types of, 3.16–3.17

Mareva injunction
powers to make use of, 5.49

Mark-up exercises
assumed sales, 3.51
calculations of mark-up inappropriate, 3.68
consumption of trading stock in the business, 3.57
credibility checks as part of, 3.46
inflation, effect of, 3.64
information, need for care, 4.10
pilferage, 3.55
purchases, cost of, 3.52–3.53
retail businesses' mark-up policy, 3.50
stock losses, 3.54
tax rate, changes in, 3.63
understated output tax, calculation of, 3.61–3.62
variations in mark-up, 3.65–3.67
VAT Tribunals, views of, 3.69
wastage, 3.56
weighted mark-up, 3.58–3.60

Misdeclaration, serious. *See* SERIOUS MISDECLARATION

Misdirection
concession, circumstances when applicable, 1.59, 4.15–4.16
considerations as to, 4.16
details of, 4.18
previous visit, during, 4.07, 4.15
serious misdeclaration through 1.59

Obstruction
officer, of, 2.03, 2.36, 2.37

Output tax
understated, calculation of, 3.61–3.62

Overdeclarations of VAT
control visits, discovered on, 3.01–3.02, 3.29
serious misdeclaration, as, 1.48

Overseas
repayment of tax to those in business, 5.16
traders, VAT agents of, 5.22

Payment
assessment for. *See* ASSESSMENTS
credit transfer, by, 1.82
Customs and Excise power to distrain for, 5.39–5.40, 5.49
VAT returns. *See under* VAT

Penalties. *See also* PROSECUTIONS
civil offences—
breaches of regulations, for, 1.50, 1.96–1.103, 1.107. *See also* BREACHES OF REGULATIONS
civil fraud, for, 1.36, 1.40, 1.50, 1.66, 1.99, 1.107
default surcharge, where also subject to, 1.99
failure to notify liability for registration, for, 1.40, 1.63, 1.66–1.69, 5.46
furnish VAT return or pay tax by due date, failure to, 1.28

199

Index

Penalties—*continued*
civil offences—*continued*
interaction of, 1.40, 1.50, 1.66, 1.99, 1.105, 1.107
serious misdeclaration, for, 1.40, 1.45, 1.50, 1.53, 1.99, 1.107
unauthorised issue of invoices, for, 1.104–1.105, 5.46
criminal offences, for—
computer records, for failure to produce, 2.03
computing 'amount of tax' for purposes of, 2.10
conduct involving commission of certain criminal offences, for, 2.03
Customs and Excise legislation, under, 2.37
false documents, for use of, 2.03, 2.15, 2.39
false statements, for making, 2.03
fraudulent evasion of VAT, for, 2.03
furnish VAT return or pay tax by due date, failure to, 2.03, 2.34
goods or services—
receiving, where supplier evades tax, 2.03
supplying without providing security, 2.03
interaction with civil penalties, 1.107
maximum, 2.03, 5.04
services. *See* goods or services, *above*
settlement penalty, 2.61
VAT legislation, under, table of maximum penalties, 2.03
decisions of VAT Tribunal, for failing to comply with, 4.67
year ended 31.3.85, during, 2.47, 2.49
Perjury
criminal offence of, 2.38
Personal representatives
Customs and Excise powers as to, 5.21
Photograph
document, of, admissible in criminal proceedings, 2.71
Pilferage
losses from, 3.55
Postal services
postal delay causing late notification of liability, 1.72
postal strike, Customs and Excise powers in event of, 1.84
postmark date, record of, 1.81
receipt by Post Office, whether regarded as receipt by Customs and Excise, 1.83
Professional adviser
role of, at control visit, 3.36
Professional privilege, 5.65–5.68
Prosecutions. *See also* PENALTIES
classification by offence of, 2.46
compounding criminal offences and, 2.57–2.59
convictions and, 2.47

Prosecutions—*continued*
Keith Committee, evidence to, on, 1.19–1.20
Protective appeals, 3.39, 4.21–4.22, 4.37, 4.38
Purchases
re-sale, for, cost of, 3.52–3.53

Reasonable excuse
claims of, 1.58–1.61, 1.79, 1.101
dilatoriness of person relied upon not a, 1.58, 1.79
inaccuracy on part of person relied upon not a, 1.58, 1.79
insufficiency of funds not a, 1.58, 1.79
reliance on another person not a, 1.58, 1.79
unauthorised issue of invoices, for, 1.105
Records
computer—
access to, 5.04, 5.34
failure to produce, 2.03
copy, power to, 5.33
keep—
failure to—
implementation of provision, 1.31
penalty for, 1.98, 2.39
provisions as to, 1.28, 2.43
requirement to, 5.05, 5.30–5.31
place of production of, 3.26, 5.32
preserve, failure to—
implementation of provision, 1.31
penalty for, 1.98
provisions as to, 1.28, 2.40, 2.43
production of, power to require, 5.32
remove, power to, 5.33
retention, of, 5.04, 5.31
Recovery proceedings
Customs and Excise powers as to, 5.49
Refunds
Do-It-Yourself House builders, to, 2.09, 5.14
tax, of, 5.13
Registration
administration of, 3.13
administrative burden on those obliged to register, 1.03–1.04
cancellation of, 5.06
cessation of taxable supplies, failure to notify, 1.28, 1.31, 1.98, 2.41
changes in circumstances, failure to notify—
implementation of provision, 1.31
provisions as to, 1.28, 2.41
Customs and Excise powers as to, 5.06, 5.19
details, failure to notify change of, 2.45
divisional, 5.20
exemption from, 5.06
failure to notify liability for—
fraudulent evasion of tax, where, 2.08, 2.11
implementation of provision, 1.31
late notification, 1.72
offence of—
commentary on, 1.70–1.72

Index

Registration—*continued*
  failure to notify liability for—*continued*
    offence of—*continued*
      examples, 1.67
      generally, 1.62
      penalties for—
        amount of, 1.63, 1.67, 2.39
        application, date of, 1.67
        assessment of, 1.70
        defence against, 1.68
        interaction with other civil penalties, 1.40, 1.66
        material change not notified, where, 1.69
        prosecutions for, 2.46
        provision as to, 1.28, 2.41
        reasonable excuse, defence of, 1.68
        VAT group registration, inadvertently not included in, 1.71
  group—
    company inadvertently not included in, 1.71
    Customs and Excise powers as to, 5.19
  liability for—
    exemption as to, 1.64, 1.69
    late notification, 1.72
    requirements as to, 1.64, 1.65
  notification of, 5.06
  taxable turnover does not exceed compulsory limits, where, 5.06

Regulations
  breaches of. *See* BREACHES OF REGULATIONS

Repayment supplement
  amount of, 1.87
  commentary on, 1.91
  conditions when payable, 1.87–1.88
  disregarded for income and corporation tax purposes, 1.90
  industrial action at VAT Central Unit, provision for, 1.89
  introduction of, 1.29, 1.87
  procedure, 1.92

Returns
  VAT. *See under* VAT

Revenue
  collected from VAT, 1.02

Sales. *See also* GOODS
  assumed, 3.51
  mark-up. *See* MARK-UP EXERCISES

Search
  Customs and Excise powers as to, 5.37

Search warrants
  increased safeguards on issue of, 5.04

Second-hand goods
  relief as to, 5.11, 5.30

Security
  goods, as to. *See* GOODS
  services, as to. *See* SERVICES

Serious misdeclaration
  application of, concern over potential, 1.51–1.57

Serious misdeclaration—*continued*
  exceptions, 1.49
  honest mistake, through, 1.54, 1.55
  ignorance, through, 1.54
  implementation of provision, 1.31
  innocent error, through, 1.54
  insufficiency of funds not a reasonable excuse, 1.58
  interaction with other penalties, 1.50
  interest in case of, 5.46
  limits in relation to, 1.47
  misdirection by Customs and Excise, through, 1.59
  offence of—
    commentary on, 1.51–1.57
    generally, 1.44, 3.04
  overdeclaration, 1.48
  penalty for, 1.45, 1.53, 5.04
    interaction of penalties, 1.40, 1.50, 1.99, 1.107
  persistent misdeclarations, 1.46
  provision as to, 1.28
  reasonable excuse, claims of, 1.58–1.61
  reliance on another person not a reasonable excuse, 1.58
  small businesses and, 1.53
  underdeclarations, 1.48

Services
  receiving, where supplier evades tax—
    liability for offence of, 2.24–2.25
    penalty for, 2.03, 2.39
  security—
    failure to provide—
      appeals to VAT Tribunal, 2.28–2.31
      liability for offence of, 2.26–2.27
      penalty for, 2.03, 2.39
    power to require, 2.26, 5.38
  status of customer, VAT liability and, 4.18
  supply of, via an agent, 5.23
  time of supply of, 5.07
  zero-rated, 4.11

Small business. *See also* BUSINESSES; COMPANIES
  burden of VAT, 1.05
  credibility checks at, 3.46
  default surcharge, effect of, on, 1.85
  serious misdeclaration penalties and, 1.53
  VAT officer visiting, 3.18, 3.25

Statement
  case, of, produced by Customs and Excise, 4.44
  criminal proceedings, in, 2.70
  false, making—
    conduct involving commission of an offence as to, 2.03, 2.19–2.23, 2.39
    criminal offence, remains a, 2.04
    liability for offence of, 2.16–2.18
    penalty for, 2.03, 2.39
  witness, at VAT Tribunal, 4.47

Stock losses, 3.54

Index

Summons
  issued by VAT Tribunal, non-compliance with, 4.48
  service of, in criminal proceedings, 2.67
Supplies
  exempt, 5.09
  taxable—
    cessation of, failure to notify, 1.28, 1.31, 1.98, 2.41
    Customs and Excise powers as to, 5.09
    material changes in, failure to notify, 2.41

Tax evasion. *See* EVASION OF TAX
Taxable supplies. *See under* SUPPLIES
Trading stamp schemes
  Customs and Excise powers as to, 5.26
Transfer
  going concerns, of, Customs and Excise powers as to, 5.24

Underdeclaration of VAT
  control visits, discovered on, 1.22, 3.01–3.04, 3.29, 3.38
  interest on. *See* INTEREST
  serious misdeclaration, as, 1.48
  treatment of, 3.48
Unincorporated bodies
  Customs and Excise powers as to, 5.21

Valuation
  Customs and Excise powers as to, 5.28
VAT
  administration—
    Administration Directorate, 3.07, 4.11, 4.20
    burdens of, 1.03–1.06
    powers of, 5.29
    See also CUSTOMS AND EXCISE
  agents, 5.22
  Central Unit, role of, 3.15
  changes in tax rate, 3.63
  collection of, 3.01, 5.29
    paper entitled 'Collection of VAT', 1.15–1.17, 1.24–1.26
  control. *See* VAT CONTROL
  direct taxes and, interaction of, 4.29
  enforcement, 5.29
  evasion of. *See* EVASION OF TAX
  failure to pay by due date—
    civil offence of, 1.28, 1.31, 1.98
    criminal offence of, 2.03, 2.04
    default surcharge to replace existing legislation, 2.04, 2.32–2.33. *See also* DEFAULT SURCHARGE
    penalties for, 2.03, 2.34, 2.39
  fraud. *See* FRAUD
  fraudulent evasion of. *See* EVASION OF TAX
  increased protection for taxpayer, 5.03, 5.04
  introduction of, 1.01
  invoices. *See* INVOICES

VAT—*continued*
  legislation—
    criminal offences under, 2.03–2.04
    interpretation of, by VAT Tribunal, 4.59
  local VAT offices, 3.10–3.11
  officer—
    action by, following control visit, 3.38
    advice given by, 3.33
    dealing with questions from, 3.34–3.35
    duties of, on routine control visit, 3.29.
      See also CONTROL VISITS
    grade of, 3.18
    misdirection by. *See* MISDIRECTION
    obstruction of, 2.03, 2.36, 2.37
    role of, 3.10
    senior officer, grade of, 3.18
    surveyor, grade of, 3.18
    visiting, 3.25
    See also CONTROL VISITS
  preferential debt in bankruptcy, 5.49
  records. *See* RECORDS
  recovery proceedings, 5.49
  refunds, 5.13, 5.14, 5.18
  registering for. *See* REGISTRATION
  returns—
    completion of, pending resolution of a dispute, 4.13–4.14
    credibility checks, 3.46
    default surcharge to replace existing legislation, 2.04, 2.32–2.33. *See also* DEFAULT SURCHARGE
    errors in, 4.03
    failure to make by due date—
      civil offence of, 1.28, 1.31, 1.98
      criminal offence of, 2.03, 2.04
      penalties for, 2.03, 2.34, 2.39
    false, prosecutions for, 2.46
  revenue from, 1.02
  staff—
    grades of, 3.18
    training, 3.19
    See also officer, *above*; CONTROL VISITS
  sub-offices, 3.12
  Tribunal. *See* VAT TRIBUNALS
  waiver of, 4.17
  zero-rated goods or services, 4.11, 5.10
  1985 legislation—
    announcement of, 1.06, 1.27
    background to—
      reasons for change, 1.18–1.26
      'The Collection of VAT', 1.15–1.17, 1.23–1.26
      See also KEITH COMMITTEE
    civil penalty provisions. *See* CIVIL PENALTY PROVISIONS
    criminal penalties remaining under, 2.01, 2.04 et seq. *See also* CRIMINAL OFFENCES
    generally, 1.27
VAT control
  control visits. *See* CONTROL VISITS
  credibility checks, 3.46

Index

VAT control—*continued*
  Customs and Excise, organisation and structure of, 3.06–3.12. *See also* CUSTOMS AND EXCISE
  Directorate, 3.08
  large payers, of. *See* COMPANIES
  local visits, types of, 3.16–3.17
  mark-up exercises. *See* MARK-UP EXERCISES
  objectives, 3.14
  registrations, administration of, 3.13
  staff. *See under* VAT
  techniques, 3.13 et seq
  underdeclarations, treatment of, 3.48. *See also* UNDERDECLARATION OF VAT
  VAT Central Unit, role of, 3.15
  VAT Tribunal decisions and, 3.47. *See also* VAT TRIBUNALS
  verification of tax liability, need for, 3.01–3.05

VAT Tribunals
  access to, 4.40
  administrative responsibility for, 4.34
  appeals to, 1.60, 1.61, 1.79, 2.28–2.29, 2.64, 5.04
  assessments appealable to, consideration of, 4.19–4.22
  centres, 4.35
  composition of, 4.36
  constitution of, 4.34
  costs, 4.62–4.64
  decision appealable to, consideration of, 4.19–4.22
  decisions by, 3.47, 4.58, 4.61
  direction issued by, non-compliance with, 4.48
  documents to be referred to at hearing, 4.45
  EEC Directives, effect of, 4.60
  environment, 4.51–4.52
  evidence at, 4.52
  FA 1985, changes brought about by, 4.67–4.68
  findings of, 4.37, 4.39
  giving notice of appeal, 4.42
  grounds for appeal to, 4.41, 4.67
  hearing—
    date of, 4.49
    postponement of, 4.50

VAT Tribunals—*continued*
  hearing—*continued*
    preliminary, of opposed matters, 4.46
    interest on tax repaid or unpaid, 4.65
    interpretation of VAT legislation, 4.59
    order of events at, 4.53–4.58
    penalties for failing to comply with decisions of, 4.67
    powers of, 1.61
    pre-appeal conditions, 4.43
    preliminary hearings of opposed matters, 4.46
    procedure at, 4.53–4.58
    protective appeal, lodging a, 3.39, 4.21–4.22
    role of, 4.34–4.35
    room, arrangement of, 4.51
    statement of case, 4.44
    statistics of appeals to, 4.37–4.39
    summons issued by, non-compliance with, 4.48
    views of, as to mark-up calculations, 3.69
    witness—
      examination of, 4.52
      order of events as to, 4.53, 4.55, 4.56
      statements, 4.47

Visits
  control. *See* CONTROL VISITS
  distraint, 3.17
  educational/registration, 3.17
  investigation, 3.17, 3.46
  local, types of, 3.16–3.17
  miscellaneous, 3.17

Walking possession agreements
  breaches of, 1.28, 1.31, 1.100, 5.04, 5.46

Warrant
  forcible entry to levy distress, for, 5.40
  search, 5.04

Witnesses
  VAT Tribunal, at—
    examination of, 4.52
    order of events as to, 4.53, 4.55, 4.56
    witness statements, 4.47

Zero-rated goods
  Customs and Excise powers as to, 5.10, 5.35
  disputes in relation to, 4.11